AF361571

PAKISTAN'S ISI

PAKISTAN'S ISI

A CONCISE HISTORY OF THE INTER-SERVICES INTELLIGENCE DIRECTORATE

JULIAN RICHARDS

Georgetown University Press / Washington, DC

The publisher is not responsible for third-party websites or their content. URL links were active at time of publication.

Library of Congress Cataloging-in-Publication Data

Names: Richards, Julian (Julian James), author.
Title: Pakistan's ISI : a concise history of the Inter-Services Intelligence Directorate / Julian Richards.
Description: Washington, DC : Georgetown University Press, 2024. | Series: Concise histories of intelligence series | Includes bibliographical references and index.
Identifiers: LCCN 2023042314 (print) | LCCN 2023042315 (ebook) | ISBN 9781647124663 (hardcover) | ISBN 9781647124670 (paperback) | ISBN 9781647124687 (ebook)
Subjects: LCSH: Pakistan. Inter Services Intelligence—History. | Military intelligence—Pakistan—History. | Intelligence service—Pakistan—History. | Terrorism—Pakistan.
Classification: LCC UB251.P35 R53 2024 (print) | LCC UB251.P35 (ebook) | DDC 327.125491—dc23/eng/20230908
LC record available at https://lccn.loc.gov/2023042314
LC ebook record available at https://lccn.loc.gov/2023042315
∞ This paper meets the requirements of ANSI/NISO Z39.48-1992 (Permanence of Paper).

25 24   9 8 7 6 5 4 3 2 First printing

Printed in the United States of America

Cover design by Jeremy John Parker

Interior design by Paul Hotvedt

Contents

Acknowledgments

Researching and writing a book on a secretive organization such as the ISI is no easy endeavor. It relies on the help and assistance of a wide range of people, past and present, for whom I would like to register my enormous thanks. First, I must express my gratitude again to the wide range of friends and supporters in Pakistan who helped me to assemble my PhD many years ago, some of whom are sadly no longer with us. You opened my eyes to the extraordinary country of Pakistan and ensured its special place in my heart. More recently, colleagues and associates, including the very notable case of my good friend Dr. Muhammad Tahir Mahmood, have helped enormously, not only with specific points of detail but with a general feel for life in Pakistan and its daily challenges. (You also helped with the supply of the most wonderful food!) My wife, Lynne, has been unfailingly patient and understanding when I have worked away for hours on the project. Thanks also go to my sanity checker and proofreader in chief, my father; and, of course, to my mother, who patiently allowed him to disappear for hours while he read through the drafts. I must express my gratitude to Don Jacobs and the whole team in and around Georgetown University Press, who have always displayed the utmost professionalism and made the process very smooth. My thanks also go to my friend and colleague, Professor Mark Phythian, who suggested the whole idea in the first place. Last, but certainly not least, I feel it is entirely necessary and appropriate to register my appreciation of all those nameless people who have laid down their lives in Pakistan in the generational fight against terrorism and extremism. I can only write about the situation, but you have done so much more.

Abbreviations

BJP	Bharatiya Janata Party (Indian People's Party)
CIA	Central Intelligence Agency
COAS	chief of army staff
DG	director general
FIA	Federal Investigation Agency, Pakistan
GHQ	general headquarters
HIG	Hezb-e-Islami Gulbuddin (Gulbuddin Islamic Group)
humint	human intelligence
IB	Intelligence Bureau, Pakistan
IJI	Islami Jamhoori Ittehad (Islamic Democratic Alliance)
ISI	Inter-Services Intelligence Directorate, Pakistan
ISPR	Inter-Services Public Relations, Pakistan
LeT	Lashkar-e-Taiba (Army of the Pure)
MI	Military Intelligence, Pakistan
MI5	Security Service, UK
MI6	Secret Intelligence Service, UK
MKM	Makhtab-ul Khidmat-ul Mujahideen (Mujahideen Services Bureau)
MQM	Mohajir Qaumi Movement (Mohajir National Movement)
NACTA	National Counter Terrorism Authority, Pakistan
NATO	North Atlantic Treaty Organization
NWFP	North-West Frontier Province

PEMRA   Pakistan Electronic Media Regulatory Authority
PIC   Pakistan intelligence community
PM   prime minister
PML   Pakistan Muslim League
PPP   Pakistan People's Party
PTI   Pakistan Tehrik-e Insaf (Pakistan Movement for Justice)
RAW   Research and Analysis Wing, India
sigint   signals intelligence
TTP   Tehrik-e Taliban Pakistan (Pakistan Taliban Movement)

Chronology

1947   The two new states of India and Pakistan come into being at midnight on August 15, with the Partition of India.

1948   An initial Pakistani attempt to seize Jammu and Kashmir by coordinating with local militias ends in failure, following accession to India and the arrival of the Indian army in the province.

        October: Brig. Syed Shahid Hamid is directed by Joint Services Commanders Committee Secretary Maj. Gen. Bill Cawthorn to stand up a new coordinating military intelligence service, which becomes known as the Inter-Services Intelligence Directorate.

1958   October: The first civilian government collapses, and Gen. Muhammad Ayub Khan imposes martial law. Intelligence agencies become increasingly drawn into domestic as well as overseas and military affairs. Brig. Riaz Hussain becomes one of the longest-serving directors of the ISI.

1962   October/November: Sino-Indian conflict flares around a border dispute in the far north of India. Indian troops are pushed back in all areas, following which a Line of Actual Control is agreed.

1965   January: Pakistani forces achieve a successful strike and annexation of territory against Indian forces in the Rann of Kutch region bordering both countries. The success fuels an attempt in August to try again to seize Kashmir by infiltrating militants, under the notorious Operation Gibraltar. This spirals into a wider conflict with India. Despite some tactical military successes, the result is a strategic failure for Pakistan as no territory is recovered.

1969   March: General Ayub Khan hands over power to Gen. Yahya Khan following mounting civil protests, especially in East Pakistan.

1971   Following a brutal crackdown in East Pakistan against liberationist militants, in which the ISI is instrumental, a wider conflict with India develops, leading to the formal surrender of Pakistani forces at Dhaka racecourse on December 16 and the birth of the nation of Bangladesh. In September Lt. Gen. Ghulam Jilani Khan is appointed as the new director general of ISI, later becoming the first three-star general in post.

Zulfikar Ali Bhutto of the Pakistan People's Party is appointed as the new president of Pakistan, becoming prime minister in 1973.

1973   Jilani establishes the Special Operations Bureau, often referred to as the Afghan Bureau, to coordinate with proxy Islamist militants in the Afghanistan region and launch a new era of unrestricted warfare.

1974   May: India tests its first nuclear weapon in the Rajasthan desert, much to the surprise of intelligence services around the world.

1977   July: Bhutto is arrested and deposed in a military coup led by Gen. Muhammad Zia-ul-Haq on grounds of corruption and disorder, ending the second civilian administration in Pakistan since independence.

1979   Bhutto is executed at Rawalpindi Central Jail on April 4.

December: The Soviet Union commences a comprehensive invasion and occupation of Afghanistan. ISI operations begin to coordinate military resistance by a loose coalition of seven Islamist militias forming the core of the Mujahideen.

1984   Islamist militant Abdullah Azzam forms the Makhtab al-Khidmat bureau to coordinate funding and military supplies to the Mujahideen. Osama bin Laden becomes a key figure working for the bureau on the ground, establishing the basis of what later becomes the Al-Qaeda organization.

1988   September: General Zia and many of his top officials (including a former but not the serving ISI director general, Hamid Gul) are killed in an as-yet-unexplained plane crash in Pakistan. Zulfikar

Ali Bhutto's daughter, Benazir, returns to Pakistan to widespread acclaim. Her Pakistan People's Party becomes the largest party in the December elections, and she is subsequently appointed as prime minister.

1989   February: The last Soviet troops cross the Amu Darya River and leave Afghanistan. A tumultuous period ensues in which various factions and warlords vie for control of the war-torn state.

1990   October: Elections follow the dismissal of Benazir Bhutto's government on charges of corruption and maladministration—elections in which the ISI is believed to have played a major role in manipulation against Bhutto's Pakistan People's Party. Nawaz Sharif's Pakistan Muslim League party wins, and he forms the next government.

1993   October: After the Pakistan Muslim League is dismissed in government by President Ghulam Ishaq Khan on the same grounds as Bhutto in 1990, fresh elections see the Pakistan People's Party fall just short of an overall majority but score enough to eventually head the next government. Bhutto is reinstalled for her second term as prime minister.

1996   September: The Taliban movement seizes control of Kabul, completing a gradual takeover of most of the country and forming the de facto government of Afghanistan.

October: Bhutto's government is again mired in charges of widespread corruption, and her government is dismissed. Fresh elections see Nawaz Sharif's return to power as prime minister.

1998   May: Pakistan conducts its first tests of nuclear weapons in a mountainous region in Baluchistan Province, shortly after a second set of tests by India.

1999   March: Pakistan infiltrates troops into the lofty Siachen Glacier area on the border between India and Pakistan, triggering a brief military skirmish called the Kargil conflict. International pressure forces a swift ceasefire amid tension about the two nuclear-armed states going to war.

September: Following mounting tension between the chief of army staff, Gen. Pervez Musharraf, and the civilian prime minister, Nawaz Sharif, the army seizes power in a coup when Sharif attempts to have Musharraf detained; thus commences the third major period of military rule in Pakistan.

2001   September: Al-Qaeda conducts the 9/11 terrorist attacks in the United States. Strenuous demands from the United States to the Taliban government in Afghanistan to hand over bin Laden and other Al-Qaeda militants are rebuffed.

December: A NATO force headed by the United States invades Afghanistan, largely driving Al-Qaeda out of the country and causing the Taliban government to collapse. The International Security Assistance Force begin the process of fighting the Taliban and attempting to establish a new civilian administration in Afghanistan.

2002   October: Elections under the presidency of General Musharraf, in which the ability of the mainstream parties to run are severely restricted, install a pro-Musharraf Pakistan Muslim League–Quaid administration.

2005   September: Presidential elections in Afghanistan confirm Hamid Karzai in post, following his interim installation by the United States in December 2001. These and subsequent elections are dogged by charges of corruption and controversy.

2007   December: Returning to Pakistan to campaign for the forthcoming elections, Benazir Bhutto is assassinated in Rawalpindi by a suicide bomber. Although never proven, US intelligence suggested Al-Qaeda, or a sympathetic proxy, was behind the attack.

2008   August: Elections in Pakistan see a return to civilian democracy as a Pakistan People's Party–led coalition defeats Musharraf's party and Yusuf Raza Gilani becomes prime minister. Musharraf later goes into exile in Saudi Arabia.

November: The militant Lashkar-e-Taiba organization launches a major terrorist attack in Mumbai, India. Despite fierce denials, evidence appears to point toward coordination from Pakistan by elements of the ISI.

2011   May: Osama bin Laden is killed in a covert raid by US Special Forces at his compound in Abbottabad, northern Pakistan. In a subsequent inquiry, ISI director general Ahmad Shuja Pasha fiercely denies that his agency had any knowledge of bin Laden's presence in Pakistan.

2014   April: Presidential elections in Afghanistan eventually replace the incumbent Hamid Karzai with Ashraf Ghani.

2018   July: Imran Khan's new Pakistan Tehrik-e Insaf party surprisingly wins the general election, beating the two traditional mainstream parties, and he becomes prime minister.

2021   August: Following the signing of a withdrawal agreement in February 2020, the International Security Assistance Force precipitately withdraws from Afghanistan early in the Biden administration. The Taliban very quickly reestablish control and form the de facto new government within two weeks.

Introduction

Pakistan's Inter-Services Intelligence Directorate (ISI) is probably one of the better-known intelligence agencies in the Global South. Its role became particularly significant on the world stage after the Soviet invasion of Afghanistan in 1979, which ushered in a new period of violent strategic politics in the region once at the heart of the Great Game between colonial Britain and Russia. During that period of international tension and conflict, which eventually led to the end of the Cold War, the ISI suddenly found itself driving the mobilization of resistance against the Soviet incursion. As far as the history books can tell us, the agency was hugely successful in this endeavor, through a strategy of standing up and coordinating the Mujahideen organization.

Since this time, whether by design or accident, the ISI has cloaked itself in an almost mythical status of brutal effectiveness. This extends not only to operations abroad (and notably those directed at India) but also to internal repression in such regions as Baluchistan Province and the general repression of dissent against the country's military leadership. Like all covert agencies, there is perhaps merit in developing an opaque aura of greatness that may well belie more modest capabilities in reality. At the same time, in the West especially, the agency has also taken on a reputation of duplicity and raw Machiavellianism, in which the usefulness of its effectiveness as an intelligence partner has to be balanced with a sometimes distinct lack of trust.

In this book, I look at the development of the ISI from the birth of Pakistan in August 1947 to the reinstatement of the Taliban in Afghanistan in 2021. As far as possible, I attempt to scratch below the surface of myth and hyperbole to establish as true a picture of this particular intelligence agency as can be found. This, of course, is a complex challenge, perhaps especially so in the South Asian information environment, in which myth and conspiracy theories are virulent elements of daily discourse. This factor means that some of the assessments necessarily must be presented as hypotheses and possibilities rather than certainties. Probably the most pivotal recent event in which such a consideration applies is the question of whether the ISI was fully aware that Osama bin Laden had been living in Pakistan, and indeed under the nose of an army base in the north of the country, before the United States undertook a unilateral operation to neutralize him in May 2011. In this analysis, I suggest that some in the ISI's hierarchy must have known—it is inconceivable they did not—but this does not necessarily mean the top leaders were fully cognizant of developments. In this can be found a key structural consideration in the composition and internal workings of the ISI, which is, perhaps, both a flaw in its character and a useful device for disavowing some of its darker activities. I suggest that establishing the full truth, however, is probably impossible.

The second key factor making the writing of this book a complex endeavor is the persistent culture of extreme secrecy around the ISI's internal workings and structure. Assessments must be made on the chinks of light that appear in a combination of memoirs, media reports, and the very occasional government inquiries (most of which, as we will see, have been furiously suppressed by the military hierarchy). The chronology of the ISI will show a few tenuous attempts in Pakistan's short history to place the intelligence services under some sort of statutory footing. All of these have resolutely failed because the civilian administration in Pakistan remains structurally feeble in the face of a very dominant and army-led powerbase at the center of the country's administration.

In this observation lies one of the key purposes of this book. While some excellent and comprehensive analyses of the ISI have been produced, with the list most appropriately headed by the books of Owen Sirrs (2017) and Hein Kiessling (2016), this publication attempts to contextualize the story of the ISI in a somewhat wider set of consider-ations. First, I show that the ISI is not just a fascinating case study of an intelligence service but has been part and parcel of the development of the fifth most populous state in the world. As with many states in the Global South, the continuing dominance of the army as the single most capable institution at the state's birth has been a key factor in the story of Pakistan and continues to be so despite some very encouraging moves toward the entrenchment of civilian democracy. The story of the ISI is, in many ways, the story of Pakistan.

Second, when placing the history of the ISI within the wider context of academic disciplines such as international relations, intelligence stud-ies, and security sector reform, this analysis attempts a degree of com-parative analysis with case studies of other states in the Global South, both within Pakistan's neighborhood and further afield, to consider how this particular state and intelligence service have progressed when com-pared to others on similar trajectories. In this way, it is envisaged that this book can act as a useful case study for students and researchers working in these wider fields of study, alongside those with a general interest in this particular part of the world.

Finally, the normative approach taken to analyses of security institu-tions such as the ISI can best be described as highly critical. It should be stated straight away that this analysis does not necessarily deviate from that path. It is suggested that, if the ISI is to deliver a long-term legacy that does not focus on internal repression and political manipulation, not to mention a very lamentable record on the intimidation of critical jour-nalism and dissent, then it has a great deal of work to do. The best way to make the changes, I suggest, is to return to the question of placing all the intelligence services in the state on a clearer and more robust statutory footing, which includes a realistic and workable process of oversight and accountability. In many ways, there is no avoiding this process in the longer term if the state is to flourish.

At the same time, some attempt is made here to frame the analysis in a rounded, objective, and pragmatic assessment of the challenges facing a state such as Pakistan, which finds itself in a region characterized by violent tumult for generations. Many of the choices the state of Paki-stan has to make around its national security approach, including such considerations as which strategic partners with whom to work, are not straightforward and are much more difficult than some of the challenges faced in more settled parts of the world. For all their faults, the armed forces of Pakistan, and the intelligence service that has become central to their operations, have been valiantly fighting against the most severe and difficult set of threats faced by almost any country in the world. Many officers have laid down their lives trying to do what they perceived to be the right things in the interests of Pakistan and its people. It is also the case that the army and ISI would not be able to arrogate themselves into positions of overlordship, as has happened frequently, if Pakistan's civilian administrations had shown a little more professionalism and effectiveness. This is absolutely not to excuse any acts of repression in any way, but merely to understand them and to place them in some sort of context.

The book is organized chronologically and thematically. The first chapter charts the beginnings of the ISI, which emerged shortly after Pakistan's independence in 1947, in an extraordinary environment of new state-building. In many ways, the agency's formation was as much reactive as proactive, precipitated as it was by an initial and largely unsuccessful conflict against India over the state of Kashmir Province and a related lacuna in intelligence capability.

In the second chapter, I explore the organization of the ISI over the years and into the contemporary era, and its army-dominated culture in which a praetorian "guardianship myth" has been developed. Here especially, the interplay between the failings of civilian government and the perceived need by the army to take the reins of power are particularly apparent.

The third chapter argues that a full chronology of the ISI is best understood through the lens of the various colorful and influential leaders at the helm of the agency through the years. Rising in importance through successive military and authoritarian regimes to eventually become a three-star general posting in the 1970s, the position of director general has sometimes been relatively unremarkable, but more frequently—and increasingly in the modern era—pivotal not only in intelligence management but in the very workings of the Pakistani state.

Chapter 4 focuses on the activities, operations, and analysis undertaken by the ISI over the years. A strategy of using proxy militant forces for regional strategic gain can be seen as the central theme in the agency's approach, accelerating particularly through the anti-Soviet Mujahideen operations in the 1980s and onward into the eras of the Lashkar-e-Taiba (LeT) and the Taliban in Afghanistan.

Chapter 5 examines the ISI and Pakistan within the context of the range of international partnerships and interactions that characterize the operations of every major intelligence agency. In the ISI's case, the picture is a complex and fluid one in which the difficulties of working within a complicated neighborhood flanked by India, Afghanistan, and Iran sit alongside the imperatives of a fluctuating East–West orientation between America and China. In the case of the former, while the United States has been the most materially significant partner for the ISI over the years, the relationship has sunk to arguably its lowest ebb in the most recent era.

The penultimate chapter of the book revisits the question of the ISI's ideology and worldview by taking a look at how this has been projected in the realm of popular culture. This includes not only the pervading environment of the movie-house in South Asia, in which the Indian movie industry remains very dominant, but also in terms of the ISI's own, arguably quite professional forays into the world of public relations and outreach. Set against this development, however, chapter 7 ends the book with an assessment of the legacy the ISI will leave to Pakistan and the wider world. The assessment is a critical one, shining a light on the essentially repressive and authoritarian nature of this large and powerful intelligence case study. I reiterate the suggestion that there is an imperative and, indeed, a tremendous opportunity for the ISI and its cloaking army hierarchy to take tangible and substantive steps in the modern era toward a more accountable and defined role within the state of Pakistan. This includes making good on a promise already made by the chief of army staff that the ISI will no longer interfere in domestic politics. The comparative analyses show that similar states have managed to make tentative progress in these directions. The ISI can show the professionalism it professes to embody by realizing the democratic and accountable transformation so sorely needed for Pakistan's development.

1

Foundation

The broader history of intelligence in Pakistan sensibly begins with the particular circumstances of the foundation of the state in 1947. From this flows a number of important observations. First, the state of Pakistan was somewhat hastily constituted, having been carved from the boundaries of British India in the early part of the twentieth century in an atmosphere of mounting crisis. While it is true that many postcolonial states were drawn on the map on the basis of colonial considerations rather than of local community dispositions on the ground—or, indeed, of a coherent history of national identity—Pakistan's case can perhaps be described as particularly complex and challenging. It is also the case that, unlike some other postcolonial states in which the military forces were broadly constituted by the time of independence, and which, in many cases, were instrumental in the national liberation movement, Pakistan did not have a coherent military or intelligence structure of its own at independence. These institutions had to be rather swiftly assembled from within the broken-up British Indian Army (BIA).

This, in turn, meant that a number of senior British officers were retained in the early stages of the establishment of the Pakistan armed forces, particularly in the army, for some years after independence. At one level, this was a perhaps surprisingly uncontroversial arrangement, since many of the British and Pakistani officers had trained together at the Sandhurst Military Academy in the UK and shared a particular military culture. This included the need to uphold fierce discipline and loyalty in the ranks of the officer class: a role that the contemporary Military Intelligence (MI) organization in Pakistan has enthusiastically embraced over the years. It is also the case that some of the British and Pakistani officers at the time of the Partition had served together in World War II, which ended barely two years before Pakistan's independence. With that said, however, we can see the emergence of political machinations in and around the army right from independence.

On the intelligence front, Maj. Gen. Walter (Bill) Cawthorn,[1] a former Australian army officer who was commissioned into the BIA after serving as the director of Military Intelligence in Delhi from 1941, played a pivotal role in establishing the ISI. In 1948 he was appointed deputy chief of staff and secretary of the Joint Services Commanders Committee, under chief of staff of the Pakistan army Lt. Gen. Ross McKay. One of the first major tasks given to Cawthorn was to raise a new intelligence organization, initially called the Directorate of Forces Intelligence. It is not clear when the name of this organization changed to the ISI, but ISI seems to have become common parlance very shortly after foundation. (The position of director general of Military Intelligence, meanwhile, spanning the three armed forces, appears not to have been fully established as a separate post until the military coup of 1958.)

The generally accepted view is that a poor performance by the fledgling Pakistani armed forces in their confrontation with the Indian army in Kashmir in 1948, including an inability to coordinate disparate intelligence feeds on the ground, had strengthened the case for a new, coordinating intelligence organization across the three armed services. In this way, the ISI was formed in the white heat of military confrontation with India and—significantly—in a confrontation in which irregular warfare was part of the strategy: a point to which we will return many times.

The first appointed overarching director of Forces Intelligence, and the first director of the new ISI organization, was Brig. Syed Shahid Hamid, a two-star general in the Pakistan army who had fought on the Burmese front in World War II. Brigadier Hamid was tasked with raising the new ISI organization from scratch in October 1948 (Hamid 2021), which he did until he was relieved in August 1950 to become the defense attaché in London. Despite having faced considerable challenges, including a lack of experienced personnel and largely nonexistent records, Hamid was credited by Cawthorn with having established a "sound, working organisation" and achieving "far more than seemed possible" (Hamid 2021).

In addition to the imperative of improving the coordination of military intelligence in battlefield situations, the second, absolutely pivotal development in the early years of the ISI was the way a traditionally apolitical military organization and culture (under the British model) became inexorably drawn into involvement in domestic politics. The seeds of these developments began as early as a month after independence, when a faction of army officers began to conspire behind the scenes to develop a challenge to the civilian government. This effort became known as the Rawalpindi Conspiracy and was thwarted in 1951. Due to a shortage of senior officers in the new Pakistani state and a perceived imperative in London to forge the new administration cautiously, the commander in chief of the armed forces was still a British appointment at this time: Gen. Frank Messervy. However, it appears the Rawalpindi Conspiracy had been kept secret from Messervy, underlining the fact that the British and new Pakistani administration were not completely at one in the early months and years of the new state.

Thus began the tussle at the center of power between military and civilian power and a gradual recognition by the military that the intelligence services were not just about external confrontation with India but also about ensuring internal stability of the regime. It is also arguably the case that the military concluded early in Pakistan's existence that civilians were not up to the job of ensuring national security (Johnson 2009, 123). The civilian police-led intelligence agency, the Investigation Bureau, which had been similarly carved out of the British Indian administration, was ultimately eclipsed in power by the ISI. This was especially so after the first full military coup in October 1958, which installed General Ayub Khan in power. A long period of military rule that ended with the surrender to India at the end of the 1971 conflict effectively entrenched the ISI thereafter as the organization we know today and the preeminent intelligence agency in Pakistan on both external and internal fronts.

The Birth of Pakistan

While the founder of Pakistan, Muhammad Ali Jinnah, became the leader of the Muslim League in India in 1928, he did not explicitly champion a separatist agenda until the announcement of the Lahore Resolution of 1940, which brought the name Pakistan to wider public consciousness for the first time. By this time, political events leading to the disengagement of Britain from the subcontinent and the establishing of *swaraj* (home rule) were starting to move quickly. As the Indian National Congress, formed in 1885, was gaining political momentum, there is some evidence that the British colonial administration saw merit in supporting the Muslim League as a useful political counterbalance (Hardy 1972, 158). The Lahore Declaration of 1940 started to turn the tide after some fairly disastrous Legislative Assembly elections for the Muslim League in 1937, by polarizing the public vote and moving the independence movement toward partition rather than a unified India. At the next Legislative Assembly elections in 1945–46, the Muslim League strengthened its position greatly to win 75 percent of the vote in Muslim seats (Jalal 1990, 20). In May 1947 Lord Mountbatten became viceroy of India. After failing to convince Jinnah that India remain unified, Mountbatten set about putting together a Partition plan. On June 3, 1947, despite reservations, Jinnah formally announced the Muslim League's acceptance of the plan. At midnight on August 14, 1947, the new states of Indian and Pakistan were born.

Chaudhry Muhammad Ali, who is credited with coming up with the name Pakistan while studying at Cambridge University, put forward a theory that India's first prime minister, Jawaharlal Nehru, supported the Partition after having bitterly opposed it for years because he believed Pakistan would quickly fail after independence (Ali 1967, 122). Whatever the validity of this theory, it has persisted in elitist circles in Pakistan ever since independence. In 1966 Zulfikar Ali Bhutto, then foreign minister and later to become prime minister, repeated the narrative by claiming that "India cannot tolerate the existence of Pakistan" and that its destruction was a "sublime dream" in New Delhi (Pande 2011, 59). This could be said to be a critical foundational myth in political and military circles in Pakistan—despite the fact that, with the passing of time and entrenching of the reality of the new states, few in leadership positions in India would still be hoping or expecting Pakistan to disappear from the map in the foreseeable future, other than in the context of potential economic disintegration.

Independence for India and Pakistan eventually came very quickly: indeed, just seven years after the Lahore Declaration, in which many of the public in the subcontinent started to hear the name Pakistan for the first time. The process of Partition was chaotic and murderous, especially in the divided provinces of Punjab and Bengal. After the independence of the two new states came into effect at midnight on August 14–15, 1947, significant proportions of the population, especially across northern India, migrated in both directions between the two newly formed states, accompanied by scenes of appalling communal violence between Sikhs, Hindus, and Muslims. Reliable figures on the movements are hard to come by, but the 1951 censuses of Pakistan and India suggest that approximately 7.4 million people in Pakistan and 8.2 million people in India migrated across the borders after Partition (Census of Pakistan 1961; Census of India 1951). A. Tayyeb (1966, 169) quotes an International Labour Organisation study that suggested up to two million were killed in the communal violence. This may be a conservative estimate, although there have not been more reliable estimates since.

For Pakistan, based as it was, initially, in two wings in the northeast and northwest of the subcontinent, the spoils of Partition were mixed. The new national capital, Karachi, was chosen because it was the only viable port in the country, despite being a relatively small fishing port and only the twelfth-largest city in the subcontinent at the time of the 1941 Census of India. (Dacca, the provincial capital of East Pakistan, was the nineteenth largest: Davis 1951, 200.) It is also worth noting that the center of political power gravitated to West Pakistan, which proved pivotal in the run-up to the 1971 war, when a secessionist movement in East Pakistan eventually secured the independence of Bangladesh.

On the military and intelligence fronts, the northwest region of India that became West Pakistan had always been an important buffer zone against Russian and Persian influence further north and west, and this had led to the siting there of certain intelligence assets, such as signals intelligence (sigint) intercept stations around what became the North-West

Frontier Province (NWFP, later renamed Khyber Pakhtunkhwa). Partly for this reason, the BIA's Intelligence Corps training school was headquartered in Karachi (Ball 1996, 45), in reasonable proximity to the frontier. A sigint station also existed in Dacca in East Pakistan, and this became important for monitoring the secessionist Awami Party in the run-up to the 1971 war (Salik 1977, 43).

Lt. Gen. L. P. Sen, who led the Indian army for a period in the war against Pakistan in Kashmir in 1948, notes that an unnamed director of the Intelligence Bureau (IB) in British India promptly transferred to Pakistan on independence, taking with him a wealth of information and equipment (Sen 1994, 19). The IB was essentially the manifestation of the British state's internal security and secret police, whose main task had been to monitor potential insurgent threats such as those from communist revolutionaries and nationalists. In Sen's view, the hasty transfer of much of the office from Delhi meant that Pakistan was much better placed on its intelligence capability than was India immediately after Partition, though this capability's effectiveness in the war effort was probably not enormous given the general disruption to operations.

The military situation was particularly complicated in terms of post-Partition disentanglement. The BIA was split on a ratio of two-thirds to India and one-third to Pakistan, based not on territory but on the religious identity of personnel. This delivered a bias toward Pakistan in terms of numbers but was problematic in other ways at the unit level. Ayub Khan claimed the British had seen Muslim soldiers as a potential threat and had deliberately spread them around in such a way as to ensure there were not too many in any one unit (Khan 1967, 32). This was almost certainly a reaction to the trauma of the Sepoy Rebellion in 1857. The upshot was that there were no infantry battalions consisting wholly of Pakistan-enlisted personnel on the day of independence, for example, but whole battalions consisting of Indian-enlisted personnel, including some that were stationed in the NWFP. These subsequently needed to move to India, in a process that was slow and complex (Sen 1994, 25–26). These were the primary reasons British officers were retained for a period after Partition (348 were initially seconded to the Pakistan army), though their usefulness in the 1948 war was negated by an order from London that none of them should see active duty, presumably lest they end up fighting each other.

Early Tensions and Conflict

The peculiar and hasty conditions in which the state of Pakistan was born led to a variety of regional tensions, which, in many ways, have bedeviled the state's development ever since. At the time of Partition, two major regions were particularly problematic in this respect, namely, the new provinces of NWFP and Baluchistan.

In the northwest frontier region, the Pashtunistan issue (a notion of pan-Pashtun identity and determination) had been simmering since 1893, when the British struck a deal with the emir of Afghanistan, Abd al-Rahman, to establish a nominal boundary between the raj's and the emir's lands. This was demarcated as the Durand Line, named after the British civil servant who established where the line should go on the map. In practical terms, this split ethnic Pashtun tribes across two states, but the fluidity of the region was not seriously challenged until the creation of the state of Pakistan and the subsequent hardening of the Durand Line as a national border. (With that said, recent events in the region have highlighted the continued fluidity of the border in many areas.) For some in Afghanistan, and notably the family of King Zahid Shah, the Pashtunistan issue had been hot since the loss of Peshawar as the regional capital to the Sikh army of Ranjit Singh in 1834 (Bezhan 2014, 199). The fact that Peshawar became the regional capital of Pakistan's NWFP served only to entrench the discomfort for many in Afghanistan's political class.

On the Pakistan side of the border, a referendum shortly before the Partition showed overwhelming public support for joining the Dominion of Pakistan, despite fierce opposition from the chief minister of the region, Khan Abdul Jabbar Khan, and his activist brother, Abdul Ghaffar Khan, who had always opposed the Partition of India. (It should be noted that in this and other regional plebiscites, voters were offered only a binary choice between joining India or Pakistan.) In many ways, the notion of a Pashtunistan has never gained serious traction on either side of the border, but Pashtun nationalism has occasionally risen to the fore and always has the potential to develop further, both in Afghanistan and Pakistan. Indeed, the future military leader of Pakistan, General Ayub Khan, was himself posted to Waziristan in the frontier region around the time of Partition and had personally experienced firefights between

Pakistani troops and tribal militants on several occasions. Despite this, he later concluded that the problems in NWFP were "one of the minor problems facing the new state of Pakistan" (Khan 1967, 18, 19).

The situation in the expansive Baluchistan Province in the southwest corner of Pakistan has been much more troublesome in many ways. Since an 1876 treaty between the British and the Khan of Kalat, who governed a loose confederation of tribes in the region, there had been a nominal acceptance of semi-autonomy and freedom of governance. As Partition and a plebiscite on whether to accede to Pakistan approached, many of the regional tribal leaders wanted an option for complete independence rather than accession to the proposed new states. As Lawrence Lifschultz (1983, 736) describes, Baluchistan had always considered itself to have a special and separate relationship with the central administration of the British Empire, "equivalent to that of Nepal." A nine-month stalemate on the options following Partition led to forcible annexation of the province into the state of Pakistan by the Pakistani army. In subsequent years, a nationalist insurgency of waxing and waning seriousness has generally been met with violent repression by the Pakistani state and has been a major issue of intelligence interest for the ISI. As we will see in later chapters, allegations of serious human rights abuses by the military and intelligence services in Baluchistan have occasionally been brought to the public consciousness. There have also been continual allegations in Pakistan that the Indian security services are fomenting rebellion in the province in order to generally undermine Pakistan. (The iconic case of alleged Indian spy Kulbhushan Jadhav is examined in chapter 5.) As with all these allegations, there will probably be a mixture of occasional truth alongside frequent myth and embellishment, and each story will need to be taken with extreme caution.

At the same time as the tension in Baluchistan, a major confrontation with India unfolded in Jammu and Kashmir. Col. Akbar Khan, the director of weapons and military equipment at the Pakistani army headquarters, had formulated a plan largely unknown at the time to mobilize an incursion of Pashtun militants into Kashmir, who would precipitate a local revolt against the maharaja's rule and force the issue of accession to Pakistan. Indian accounts of the situation are that Operation Gulmarg, as it was known, was directly sponsored by the political leadership in Pakistan and particularly by the prime minister, Liaquat Ali (Ahmad et al. 2014, 41). Akbar Khan himself offered a slightly different view, in which Liaquat Ali and his colleagues discussed the plans with such informality that the military purpose was probably not fully understood. It also seems clear that Jinnah did not know about the plans, nor did the British (Schofield 2003, 50).

While the militants seized some land that became known in Pakistan as Azad (Free) Kashmir, the general verdict was that the operation was not a huge success, not least as it precipitated the maharaja's decision to formally accede to India in October 1947, allowing the Indian army's full deployment to the province. Perhaps more importantly, the eventual agreement between the Pakistani and Indian governments, brokered by the UN after the Pakistani military deployed to the region and which established a ceasefire in Kashmir on January 1, 1949, set in motion a sequence of events that led to the Rawalpindi Conspiracy of 1951. The case unfolded when a group of army officers led by Col. Akbar Khan attempted to mount a military coup against the civilian government, feeling that the political leadership had sold out to India. It was the first of many such attempts in Pakistan's subsequent history, with 1951 being unique only in its failure to seize power. A few months after the conspiracy was uncovered, Prime Minister Liaquat Ali was assassinated while delivering a speech in Rawalpindi, in a crime that has never been solved.

The 1948 conflict was highly significant as the first major direct confrontation between the two states, a situation that would be repeated in 1965 and 1971, not to mention a more limited skirmish in 1999. Excluding 1971 to some extent, all of these cases were precipitated over a flare-up of the Kashmir issue, and this remains the single most important area of tension between Islamabad and Delhi. The 1948 confrontation was also the first time intelligence and military capabilities could be tested out in earnest in the new states.

For Pakistan, the general verdict was rather poor in the sense that the supposedly deniable use of Pashtun insurgents did not deliver the desired effects of a broad uprising of popular support for Pakistan or subsequent major annexation of territory. This, in turn, reflected poor or lacking intelligence assessments of the situation on the ground in Kashmir. The Indian army's 161 Brigade spearheaded a defense of the region in very difficult circumstances and broadly achieved a successful rearguard action despite numerous setbacks. At the same time, the operation did show how the use of fanatical militants using guerrilla tactics could pose a stiff challenge for the Indian military, especially in the far-flung and difficult terrain of Jammu and Kashmir, where the proximity of supply lines from Pakistan was much more favorable than for Delhi.

For both armies, the very recent circumstances of post-Partition disentanglement, coupled with severely lacking equipment in many cases and a lack of decent communications infrastructure in the region, all contributed to a difficult operating environment for battlefield intelligence. At certain stages in the conflict, for example, it became apparent that both sides were using field radios on the same frequencies. This allowed the monitoring of each other's communications but also offered opportunities for deception (Nawaz 2008, 71).

Despite heroic tactical successes in the conflict, it was clear that a broader, strategic intelligence capability that could assess the geopolitical backdrop to the regional crisis was somewhat absent in the early days. This is not particularly surprising given the extreme lack of personnel, equipment, and resources available at the time. On the military intelligence front, Owen Sirrs (2017, 18) notes that the immediate capability of intelligence in Pakistan after Partition was limited, totaling 10 officers, 27 junior commissioned officers, and 102 noncommissioned officers. Departing British personnel had destroyed most of the records and materials at the training school in Karachi in accordance with protocols on sensitive information (Sirrs 2017).

The verdict on Col. Akbar Khan, who coordinated the rebel incursion into Kashmir, was that he might have been effective at spontaneous decision-making and creativity in the field but lacked a coherent plan and strategy (Sirrs 2017, 22). The need for more developed irregular warfare capabilities against India, which, it was recognized, were the best way to confront a much larger foe, was clearly understood by the end of the 1948 conflict.

By 1950 the fledgling ISI comprised thirty-nine personnel drawn from a mixture of the three armed services and civilians recruited through the Public Services Commission, mostly men but also a handful of women. Some of these had served in intelligence roles in Delhi but had moved to Pakistan after Partition to take up office in the initial headquarters in Karachi (Hamid 2021).

The initial structure of the ISI is thought to have comprised three units: the Joint Intelligence Bureau, the Joint Counter-Intelligence Bureau, and the Joint Signals Intelligence Bureau. Counterintelligence was a particular concern in the early days, and probably a considerable threat, since the armed forces of the two new states had been literally intertwined for years before, leading to a great deal of institutional knowledge about each other's capabilities. It was also an area of particular institutional challenge for the ISI, since both the IB and individual armed forces had been previously in charge of such investigations and were not entirely happy to give up all their records and sensitive information about personalities to the new agency. (This is not unusual in cases in which a new intelligence agency is inserted into an existing community.) It also appears to be the case that Cawthorn and his British colleagues were particularly worried about Pakistani information security in the immediate years after independence (Sirrs 2017, 20), probably not without cause.

On the strategic intelligence front, there is evidence that ISI Director Hamid undertook intelligence-gathering tours of key border zones with India, such as those adjacent to Jammu and Kashmir and further south in the sparsely populated and flat Rann of Kutch district, to consider the strategic threats and to develop cross-border contacts. Security arrangements were also made for the visits of important trade and political delegations from the Soviet Union and Iran (Hamid 2021). In 1948 an important intelligence assessment was produced on India's expanding arms production industry, a particular concern for Pakistan given that most of the arms manufacturing plants from the British era had ended up in India (Sirrs 2017, 22).

The key intelligence question at the end of the 1948 conflict in Kashmir was whether India intended to press home its advantage on the battlefield and directly threaten Pakistan: a threat taken seriously by many in the latter's military and political hierarchy given the aforementioned foundational myth surrounding India's strategic intentions toward its neighbor. Such fears reached fever pitch in 1950, when intelligence indicated that India was moving a major armored division from Meerut, near Delhi, toward the border with West Pakistan. This followed a rise in serious communal rioting in Calcutta, which spilled into East Pakistan and precipitated the flight of Hindu refugees across the border.

K. Sarwar Hasan (1951, 197) suggested that the sense in Pakistan was that there "was no doubt whatever that this time Nehru meant business." Pakistani prime minister Liaquat Ali famously delivered a rousing speech outside his house in Karachi in which he raised a clenched fist (*mukka*) and warned India that any military move against Pakistan would be met with a robust response. Liaquat Ali's confidence in delivering this gesture, which still resonates as a moment of triumphant Pakistani nationalism,[2] may have been backed up by good intelligence. In a moment that Syed Shahid Hamid (2021) describes as "probably the ISI's finest hour," a briefing he gave as ISI director to the PM on the urging of Defense Secretary Iskander Mirza revealed that the ISI had developed such a good network of human intelligence (humint) assets by this time that the intended movements of the Meerut battalion were very well known.

Of course, it would be easy and perhaps a mistake to view this situation as a simple story of good intelligence leading directly to a favorable strategic political outcome. In Pakistan Liaquat Ali is sometimes painted as heroically standing up to a belligerent Nehru, who was supposedly hell-bent on crushing Pakistan. As Pallavi Raghavan (2016, 1645) describes, analysis of the diplomatic correspondence at the time suggests a much more nuanced reading of history. Indeed, Indian commentators have often argued it was Nehru who was the peacemaker and Pakistan the recalcitrant warmonger (Burke 1972, 25). The No War Pact that Liaquat Ali and Nehru signed in late 1950 had been mooted by Nehru the previous year, and evidence suggests that both sides had been considering the idea favorably throughout the period after the 1948 conflict in Kashmir. Of course, military tensions were running high in 1950 following a range of contentious issues headed by large movements of refugees across the borders, but it is worth noting that an underlying diplomatic dialogue was continuing throughout.

Ayesha Jalal (1990, 112) notes that during the end of the Kashmir conflict, Pakistani intelligence services were "fabricating increasingly bizarre reports about the fledgling Communist party and its purported plans to destabilize the state." Contemporary US embassy cables suggested that ISI chief Hamid was "dreaming up phantoms" with a view to "seeking funds and authority to establish a large secret civilian intelligence agency" (113).

These developments suggest several important points. First, it was perhaps inevitable that the imperative for securing major US financial and political support in the early years of the state, not least to counterbalance India's leanings toward the Soviet Union, meant that alarmist reports of communist propaganda and infiltration were a good idea, even if they were based on flimsy evidence. In some ways, this established a continuation of Pakistan's strategic significance at the frontier with Soviet influence in central Asia: it also set the scene for subsequent alliances with the United States, both through the 1980s and in the later war on terror. The episode also illustrates how the ISI chief felt he had to use all means to establish the new agency as a strategic intelligence partner of worth in the region. Subsequent experience in Pakistan (at least in the western wing) is that communist parties and organizations have never achieved any sort of political momentum, unlike the situation in neighboring India, or indeed, in Bangladesh to a certain extent.

In 1950 ISI director Hamid was redeployed to the High Commission in London and shortly after established the record as the youngest ever officer to be promoted to general in Pakistan's army (Rashid 1993). In 1951 Cawthorn left Pakistan to become the director of the Joint Intelligence Bureau in Melbourne, returning later in the 1950s to act as Australia's high commissioner to Pakistan (Sirrs 2017, 33). On the question of ISI leadership during this period, the sources are somewhat conflicted. Elements of the media in Pakistan have suggested that Cawthorn was the DG of the ISI between 1950 and 1959, making him by far the longest-serving DG in the agency's history (Shah 2018). This seems unlikely given his assumption of other roles. Other sources suggest there was a succession of DGs or directors (the difference sometimes being ambiguous) through the 1950s, starting with Brig. Mirza Hamid Hussain (Kiessling 2016, 258), a Delhi-born veteran of the British army. What does seem clear is that ISI directorship was a generally short-lived experience, with few directors lasting more than three years in the post (Shah 2018).

Before his departure from the ISI, there is evidence that Syed Shahid Hamid was somewhat disgruntled with having to continually monitor the armed forces for potential dissidents and with the environment of distrust and suspicion this engendered across the intelligence community (Sirrs 2017, 33). The arrest of Col. Akbar Khan and uncovering of the Rawalpindi Conspiracy in 1951, ironically not at the behest of the

ISI but following police investigations, underlined the internal threat but also highlighted the ISI's initial failure to uncover it (31). The ignominy of the episode subsequently led the director of Military Intelligence, Maj. Muhammad Zaheeruddin, to commit suicide in disgrace (Hamid 2021). By 1958 Feroz Khan Noon's civilian government collapsed, and General Ayub Khan was installed as chief martial law administrator, marking the beginning of the first period of military rule in Pakistan's history.

Conclusions

Despite contentious accounts, a few key factors surrounding the ISI's foundation can be usefully considered. First, it does seem to be the case that, despite enormous challenges engendered by the peculiarly complex period of Partition, the Pakistani military and the new coordinating intelligence service, the ISI, started enthusiastically working on establishing operational effectiveness in a relatively short time. Considerable problems abounded, of course, and the 1950s were a period in which the agency's effectiveness likely remained severely limited. But progress was made toward standing up these essential institutions of state.

One of the drivers for progress was undoubtedly a nationalist zeal and determination to bring the idea of Pakistan into reality. Salman Rushdie's infamous description of Pakistan as a place "insufficiently imagined" (Oldenburg 1985, 711) certainly chimes with the speed at which the new state was established and the distinctly ambivalent attitude that some regional elements felt toward it at foundation. The immediate and ongoing challenges for the security state of Pakistan were to hold it together in the face of both internal and external forces that could easily have spelled its early demise.

Pitted against these fissiparous forces was a military class that was determined to bring the dream of the new state conceptualized by Jinnah and the Muslim League to fruition. Many from within this military class had physically migrated from other parts of India to join Pakistan amid scenes of appalling danger and violence. The first director of the ISI, Syed Shahid Hamid, and a future DG, Akhtar Abdul Rahman, were two among many migrants who experienced the horrors of migrating to Pakistan in 1947, passing terrible scenes of murder and mutilation. Rahman barely escaped with his life after being tied up by a mob of angry Hindu soldiers (Sirrs 2017, 14). The future military ruler of Pakistan, General Ayub Khan, also experienced such scenes on migrating to Pakistan, and wrote movingly about them in his 1967 autobiography, *Friends Not Masters*. It seems highly likely these experiences shaped the worldview.

One of the outcomes of such psychological disturbance has perhaps inevitably been a very particular bitterness about India and generally about the unhappy circumstances in which Pakistan was born. There may also be an inferiority complex, as the smaller country faced a much larger foe and had to work harder to establish its identity as a viable state. Ayub Khan (1967, 48) wrote, "India's attitude to Pakistan continued to be one of unmitigated hostility. Her aim was to cripple us at birth." In the long view, Shaun Gregory (2007b, 318) rather damningly summarizes the Pakistani military mindset as one beset by "complex ethno-religious-cultural elements of face-saving, fatalism, 'honour,' obduracy, over-confidence, risk-taking and victimhood."

As described, the foundational myth among Pakistan's military leaders (and many others besides) has been that India agreed to Partition on the understanding that Pakistan would fail and Delhi's supremacy across the entire subcontinent would eventually be reestablished. An initial conflict with India over Kashmir in 1948 scored some gains in the shape of a "liberated" zone, but the ultimate verdict was a frustrating one for Pakistan. Col. Akbar Khan, who spearheaded the militant incursion into Kashmir in 1948, believed that India's army was twice as large as Pakistan's, an assessment based on the proportional breakup of the BIA at Partition, which Nawaz (2008, 67) believes was a great underestimate in reality. Despite this, Khan felt it was not necessarily more effective and could be brought to heel by a clever use of irregular warfare techniques. This ultimately proved to be unsuccessful in 1948, but it set in place a paradigm that has been followed ever since by the Pakistani intelligence and the military, in which the use of strategic militant assets in a mode of irregular, asymmetric warfare is considered the best way to tackle a much larger foe such as India. The ISI has since shown its capability in this area, not only by mobilizing the Mujahideen against the Soviets in the 1980s but also by using the Taliban as a strategic asset in Afghanistan and mobilizing a set of militant jihadist groups in and around Kashmir, such as Lashkar-e-Taiba (Army of the Pure) and Jaish-e-Mohammed.

Immediately after Partition, however, the ISI's initial purpose was perhaps a more modest one: assembling from virtually nothing an analytical team that could coordinate intelligence across the armed services and take over some of the functions of the preexisting IB in such areas as counterintelligence. While the basic approaches followed the principles of intelligence agencies in other parts of the world, such as MI6 in the UK, the particular conditions of Pakistan were such that intelligence capability was being forged in an environment of particular insecurity at home and abroad.

On the domestic intelligence front, agencies such as the IB followed a model observed in many other postcolonial states, whereby intelligence and investigation were oriented more toward violent repression of dissent, and protection of the rulers, rather than toward an objective view of national security imperatives. In a study of policing in the Gold Coast (which became Ghana) and in Kenya, for example, Mathieu Deflem (1994, 46) found that contemporary policing models were significantly influenced by former colonial practices. Drawing on a wider set of cases in Africa and South Asia, Mike Brogden (2004, 635) similarly suggested that contemporary community-oriented policing models "simply assisted paramilitary policing agencies" in "reinforcing social inequalities." For Pakistan in the immediate years of independence, intelligence models likely followed many of the previous British practices. These included monitoring for seditious activity and playing a complicated game of mutual security cooperation with various tribes and communities, especially in such areas as the "Frontier" that had never been directly policed by the colonial state. As the ISI took on greater powers for itself through Pakistan's subsequent development, it could be argued that this essential notion of internal security and Machiavellian relationships with militant groups has substantially shaped the military and intelligence strategy—and the ISI has been very much at the heart of this process.

Notes

1. Often incorrectly rendered in internet sources as Cawthorne.

2. In Karachi, for example, there is a famous square adorned with a clenched fist sculpture, originally called Mukka Chowk (square) and renamed in 2016 as Liaquat Ali Khan Chowk.

2

Organization and Culture

From humble beginnings, the ISI gradually grew in size and remit over the years after independence, eventually becoming the most dominant element of the Pakistan intelligence community (PIC). By the time of the 9/11 terrorist attacks in the United States and subsequent invasion of Afghanistan, the agency was thought to number "about twenty-five thousand people" (Coll 2018, 25), including military and civilian personnel and ground-level "runners" or informants. This might seem like a large number, but it is worth noting that it is not unusual, especially outside of the most advanced intelligence powers, for intelligence work to be a fairly labor-intensive process. This is true both in terms of administering organizations and in a reliance on humint tradecraft to compensate for shortfalls in technical capability.

The ISI is one of three main intelligence agencies within the PIC; the others are the Intelligence Bureau (covering law enforcement and coordinating intelligence and investigations by regional special branches) and Military Intelligence (conducting primarily tactical battlefield intelligence from communications interception [sigint], imagery intelligence, and humint sources). Given its broadening role in both domestic and external intelligence functions, the ISI has an occasionally complex relationship with other investigatory and intelligence units in the wider PIC, such as the Federal Investigation Agency (FIA), which is tasked with investigating serious organized crime.

Researching the machinery of the PIC is not a straightforward task, as is the case with many countries, since there is little openly published about the governmental structures and processes in this area. As Robert Johnson (2009, 119) noted, the lack of relatively recent archival material open to investigation means that judgments about how the process works in Pakistan can only be speculative. Occasional reports about the activities of the intelligence services will emerge in the press in Pakistan, and the memoirs of former military officers and leaders such as General Ayub Khan can offer valuable insight into how intelligence performed at certain stages of history. The relationship between the ISI and the press in Pakistan could best be described as complex, tense, and occasionally violent, as will be explored later. Part of the problem is that the intelligence agencies in Pakistan do not sit under any sort of statutory footing as such. Formal oversight and accountability of their activities remains extremely thin, as does the ability to openly publish details of budget and resources.

Technically, the intelligence services of Pakistan have no specified powers and no defined extraordinary measures for derogating from normal constitutional rights and law. The only checks on their activities are from the Supreme Court, which can challenge and investigate a particular incident as being unconstitutional, or from applicable standard criminal law. Investigatory activities such as performing an arrest, entering a property, or monitoring private communications should technically be conducted only by mandated law enforcement bodies such as the police, and only then with an appropriate warrant signed by a magistrate. As Fréderic Grare (2015) describes, the reality is that agencies such as the ISI carry out such activities comprehensively, with impunity, and with no real oversight. Where the Supreme Court has held hearings on situations such as alleged abuses in Baluchistan, for example, no tangible outcomes that could be described as accountability have generally been achieved. In other cases, such as the highly controversial Hamoodur Rahman Commission report of 1974, which was critical of the Pakistani military's performance in the conflict with India in 1971, the details were made public by Gen. Pervez Musharraf only in 2000, after the report had been leaked to the media (Yadav and Barwa 2011, 98).

This creates an environment, established over many years of development, in which the ISI has become the chief lieutenant of the army in ensuring a military-dominated status quo is sustained. Until 2008, this facilitated repeated periods of lengthy military rule, with only minor interruptions by civilian governments. Since General Musharraf ceded to a civilian government in 2008, a new period has ensued, which could perhaps be described as military-compromised and overseen democracy, or more commonly a "hybrid" democracy (*Economist* 2021, 40).

This latter period is now the longest of civilian democracy in the country's history, with broadly free and fair elections in 2008, 2013, and 2018 and incorporating relatively peaceful handovers of power between administrations. At the same time, a culture of interference in democratic processes by the ISI and the military seems to have become an in-built part of the political process. This includes apparent facilitation by the ISI of destabilizing protest movements, such as that led by Imam Qadri in the run-up to the 2013 elections (which in the past have allowed a pretext for the military to suggest "restoring order") and the direct coordination of broad political alliances to stand against incumbent governments. Examples include the Islami Jamhoori Ittehad (Islamic Democratic Alliance, IJI), in whose formation the DG of the ISI at the time, Hamid Gul, was instrumental, and which successfully stood against Benazir Bhutto's Pakistan People's Party (PPP) in 1990. A more recent example is the alleged support for the foundation and eventual rise to power of Imran Khan's Pakistan Tehrik-e Insaf (Pakistan Movement for Justice, PTI; *Express Tribune* 2020) and then its unseating from power when the political tide turned against it.

It is also the case that attempts by democratic administrations to bring the ISI more under civilian government control have tended to run into the sand. The most recent serious attempt was in 2008, when the PPP attempted to reopen parliamentary dialogue about placing the intelligence services under a statutory footing. A subsequent move to resubordinate the ISI under the Interior Ministry was reversed within twenty-four hours, showing military rulers' influence even when they are not directly in power (Farooq 2011). It should also be noted that part of the proposals in this package of reform were concerned with making the budget of the PIC more open. The failure of the reforms meant that the budget for intelligence in Pakistan—as in many other countries—remains distinctly opaque.

The military culture—and, by extension, that of the ISI—has always included a lingering suspicion that the civilian leaders of the country are wholly ill equipped to build and lead the state competently and effectively. This in turn feeds into a notion that the military, with its relative professionalism, should be seen as a virtuous standard-bearer of national security and stability, even if this means occasionally sweeping the democratic administration aside in the interests of the nation. Such cultural factors are critical and have gradually fed into a propensity for domestic political interference by the ISI. This worldview is joined by an uncompromising and violent approach to regional insecurity, notably in East Pakistan during the 1971 crisis and ongoing in Baluchistan. On the foreign policy front, the strategy of irregular warfare using proxy militant groups that was initiated by the army in Kashmir in 1948 has become front and center in the ISI's approach to regional intelligence operations. In Kashmir, violent extremist movements such as LeT have taken the fight to India, including, most explosively, in the Mumbai attacks of 2008, which showed strong evidence of ISI patronage (Shams 2016). In the Afghanistan arena, the mobilization of the Mujahideen in the 1980s dovetailed with support for extremist groups such as the Haqqani Network, Hezb-e-Islami Gulbuddin, and later the Afghan Taliban (Mackenzie Institute 2015).

All of these approaches are essential elements of an ISI culture, very much hand-in-glove with that of the Pakistani military, which can be delineated around a number of key factors. First and most important is what Cohen (2002, 121) described as a "central operating principle" of "distrust of India." This, in many ways, absolutely defines the approaches taken by the ISI to promote Pakistani foreign policy, both in direct confrontations with India, mostly but not exclusively in Kashmir, and in wider regional considerations, particularly those concerning neighboring Afghanistan. It is also the case on domestic security issues, such as those concerning perceived Indian interference in East Pakistan up to 1971, and in promoting separatist violence in Baluchistan. In all of these cases, the ISI could be said to take as a starting point that India will need to be confronted at every turn.

The second key factor is a pervasive distrust in the competence of civilian government to properly defend the national security of Pakistan. Such distrust developed early in Pakistan's independent life and contributed to the first military takeover in October 1958, when President

Iskandar Mirza suspended the 1956 constitution and appointed General Ayub Khan as chief martial law administrator. Just over ten days later, Mirza was himself visited by a group of army generals and forced to resign. Ayub Khan later revealed that his "boys" had been "keeping tabs" on the deposed prime minister, Feroz Khan Noon, for some time prior to Ayub's appointment as chief martial law administrator (Kiessling 2016, 19–20). Such distrust has continued into the modern era and remains a constant shadow over civilian administrations.

A third defining factor in the ISI's culture, and one that is sometimes overlooked by observers outside the region, is the importance of religious ideology in a conception of national security, albeit to varying degrees of zealousness. As will be explored more fully later, the ISI's officer class, from the leader down through the ranks, has tended to contain a mixture of secular-minded, Western-educated military personnel and officers with a stronger and more outwardly devout approach to the significance of Islam to the central notion of Pakistan as a concept and as a state. In some ways, all of these factors are connected, in the sense that the central reason Pakistan split from what might have been a unified India in the first place was because of the imperative of Islamic identity as a separate identifier within a predominantly Hindu India. This is despite apparent paradoxes, such as the realization that Pakistan's founder, Jinnah, clearly felt that Pakistan should separate religion and state and be a broadly secular-minded state in its constitution (Jalal 1990, 279), and in the fact that approximately forty million Muslims remained in the state of India following Partition (Davis 1951, 198).

These issues notwithstanding, a deeper understanding of the importance of religion to the ISI's approach helps to explain the potentially perplexing relationship with such movements as the Taliban, a relationship that appeared to strengthen and deepen through the extremely troubled period of the post-2001 conflict in Afghanistan. In some ways, support for the Taliban in Afghanistan could be seen as a grimly pragmatic approach to ensuring some degree of stability and calm in an otherwise violent and restive country on Pakistan's western flank, but it should also be recognized that the orthodox and uncompromising interpretation of Islam that the Taliban espouses is shared by many not only in Pakistan generally but also within the ISI.

Organization

The ISI's staff is generally thought to comprise three components. At the level of senior leadership, the DG is now always a three-star general from the armed services, having been upgraded from a two-star during the government of Zulfikar Ali Bhutto in the 1970s (Kiessling 2016, 46). Below the military-dominated directorate of the organization, the bulk of the staff are military officers at the level of colonel or below, who are either immediately deployed into the ISI upon joining the military or are active soldiers who have failed to gain promotion up to the levels of general (Coll 2018, 46). It should also be noted that the vast majority of military personnel within the ISI are army officers, who sit alongside a much smaller number of colleagues from the Pakistan Navy and Air Force.

Complementing the military personnel is a civilian staff that falls into two categories. First are officials drafted into the agency via recruitment to the Pakistani civil service, who undertake a range of administrative and analytical tasks. More controversially, the ISI also uses a considerable number of temporary contract informants, "watchers," and other personnel, the precise number of which is difficult to quantify but probably accounts for more than half of the agency's total staff. These represent a key element of the ISI's day-to-day capability in the domestic realm in particular.

Some have suggested that the shady and less permanent nature of the latter category of employees offers the military leadership an opportunity to distance itself from some of the agency's more egregious activities where necessary (Coll 2018, 46). The structure might also contribute to what sometimes appears to be a less-than-perfect ability to manage all of the ISI's activities from the top, potentially allowing space for rogue and off-message operations to be undertaken. The most striking example of this in recent times might be that concerning knowledge of bin Laden's whereabouts and the fact that he was being harbored in Pakistan.

We have seen that the initial organization of the ISI broadly contained three divisions, namel,y those for coordinating intelligence, for counterintelligence, and for sigint collection (Sirrs 2017, 20). The late 1960s and early 1970s marked a watershed in the evolution of the ISI for a number of reasons. An ultimately poor set of outcomes from the ill-fated conflict with India in 1965 included problems with the coordination of battlefield and strategic intelligence. Some of these may have been attributable to an overemphasis on domestic political intelligence rather than military intelligence in the run-up to the conflict (Chengappa 2000, 1863). It seems to be the case that General Ayub Khan was still thinking primarily about Military Intelligence and the Intelligence Bureau as his primary organs of intelligence gathering rather than the fledgling ISI, as evidenced by the fact that the latter is barely mentioned in his 1967 autobiography, *Friends Not Masters*.

In the run-up to this period, serious internal challenges arose to supplement international tensions with India. Unrest in East Pakistan had already begun to develop in the 1950s, culminating, among other lamentable episodes, with the beating to death of the deputy speaker of the Dhaka Parliament, Shahed Ali Patwary, in September 1958. At the same time, riots against the oppressed religious minority the Ahmadiyyas had occasionally flared to the level of serious civil disorder, especially in cities in West Pakistan. In 1955 regional opposition to the One Unit Scheme that saw the dissolution of provincial administrations in West Pakistan led to major unrest in Baluchistan in particular, in which the Pakistani army eventually had to intercede in the face of fears of regional secession, arresting the Khan of Kalat for sedition and killing some of his associates (G. Khan et al. 2021, 78).

All of these situations in which the armed forces were used to restore domestic security ensured the ISI's growing importance as a coordinating intelligence body on both domestic and international fronts. When Zulfikar Ali Bhutto took over as civilian prime minister in 1972, the trend continued, perhaps surprisingly. Despite having founded the FIA and Federal Security Force as counterbalances to the ISI, Bhutto strengthened the ISI in the aftermath of the defeat by India, increasing its budget and establishing within it an internal security wing (Kiessling 2016, 45). He also elevated the status of the DG to a three-star general. Two things were certain during this period: Bhutto was paranoid about internal insurrections against his government, and he was far from unwilling to use the intelligence services to spy on potential competitors and foes. The end of his administration in 1977 culminated in the next major period of military rule, when Gen. Muhammad Zia-ul-Haq seized power and shortly thereafter (in an unconnected event) saw the invasion of Afghanistan by the Soviet Union. These developments further strengthened the central significance of the ISI at the helm of national security strategy and triggered a considerable growth in its size and capability.

By the contemporary era, the ISI is thought to be structured primarily around internal and external wings.[1] The internal mission, including what is often referred to as the ISI's "political wing," involves counterintelligence and counterespionage and domestic political activities. On the external front, a number of separate departments look at regional and thematic intelligence, from that relating to the Northern Areas and Jammu and Kashmir to that involving major organized crime activities (where they affect national security) and the activities of foreign intelligence services. Intelligence reports across these divisions are collated and prepared in a section called Joint Intelligence X.

A unit called Joint Intelligence Miscellaneous allegedly conducts espionage operations "in other countries," almost certainly primarily in India. On the technical front, the Joint Signal Intelligence Bureau remains a unit operating jointly with the army's Signal Corps and has, particularly since 2001, been closely connected with US surveillance operations and capabilities in the region, although this relationship has become strained in more recent years. Sigint activity comprises electronic intelligence and communications intelligence. A further division develops other technical capabilities for Pakistani intelligence, including capabilities to counter electronic warfare threats. This probably includes some degree of cyber capability, though how far this reaches is difficult to assess.

The last and perhaps most controversial element of the ISI is a shady division responsible for developing counterterrorism activities, including the development of contacts with militant groups used by Pakistan for strategic purposes. The Special Service Directorate became known by the CIA as Directorate S (Coll 2018, 47). It was absolutely central to the coordination of ISI activities in and around Afghanistan during the war on terror period and is the eponymous subject of Steve Coll's mammoth publication on this period of conflict in the region.

Intelligence Machinery

Like many intelligence machineries around the world, intelligence reporting in Pakistan likely makes its way directly to senior policymakers, mostly at the top of the military, without any particular coordination or collective assessment other than that performed within the ISI's own streams of intelligence collection. Part of the reason for this, as discussed further later, is a persistent distrust by the ISI of its sister intelligence agencies such as the IB.

Aside from the IB and MI, the other significant elements of the PIC include investigatory agencies primarily in the law enforcement space, under the governance of the Interior Ministry. These include the Federal Investigation Agency, which was established in 1974 to investigate serious and organized crime and offenses under the Official Secrets Act of India of 1923, which passed into Pakistani law on independence. It is not known whether or how the FIA cooperates with the ISI on intelligence issues. The ISI has been known to investigate the FIA, such as in a case reported in 2006 in which the ISI discovered some FIA officials at Pakistani airports taking bribes to allow suspected terrorists and others to transit into the country on fake passports (Azeem 2006). The DG of the ISI between 2008 and 2012, Ahmad Shuja Pasha, was also not afraid to blame the FIA (and other agencies) when giving evidence to the Abbottabad Commission hearings for failing to find and apprehend bin Laden in Pakistan (Scott-Clark and Levy 2017, 445). He could thus be said to have attempted to deflect criticism in a somewhat audacious way from the shortcomings of his own agency.

A more recent addition to the PIC is the National Counter Terrorism Authority (NACTA). Primarily tasked with formulating national counterterrorism strategy and communications, NACTA is also nominally tasked with cooperating with overseas intelligence agencies on international terrorism cases, including the exchange of intelligence. After a complicated initial period in which the parliamentary act launching the agency was delayed and its first chair resigned in frustration (*Dawn* 2011a), the NACTA Act was finally passed in 2013, allowing the agency to commence operation. Theoretically, NACTA poses a civilian-led challenge to the military ISI in the area of counterterrorism intelligence assessment, although the DGs of the three intelligence services including the ISI do sit on its governing board, which is chaired by the prime minister. In practical terms, NACTA is more in the space of policy formulation than operational intelligence, such as drafting the National Action Plan and compiling lists of proscribed individuals and organizations (Khan 2021). Time will tell whether friction occurs between this agency and the ISI.

In 2002, under some pressure from the United States and its allies in the immediate post-9/11 era, Pakistan's leader General Musharraf announced a reform of the Pakistani intelligence machinery. He explained that the role of the agencies was a broad, Sun Tzu–style remit to "preempt and forewarn . . . well ahead of any unfortunate incident" (cited in Janes 2002). There was evidence in Pakistan that earlier recommendations to establish an intelligence coordination body along the lines of the Joint Intelligence Committee in the UK, which were rejected in Pakistan during General Zia's rule in the 1980s, were being reconsidered (Janes 2002). There is no outward evidence that such a body has been established yet, and it seems unlikely that the ISI would tolerate the installation of a new organ between it and the upper echelons of power. Indeed, the Abbottabad Commission report in 2013 identified that, while there is a military-oriented Joint Intelligence Coordination Committee that meets regularly at the Joint Services Headquarters and which includes the three services plus the ISI, the situation across the wider PIC remains one of "sporadic and unstructured consultation and coordination" (Abbottabad Commission 2013, 309).

General Musharraf's other approaches toward reform included working to end the infiltration of militant groups over the border in Kashmir. He formally banned the two militant groups, LeT and Jaish-e-Mohammed: an announcement met with deep skepticism by India, and justifiably so in the light of subsequent events such as the LeT-authored terrorist attacks in Mumbai in 2008. Musharraf also made sweeping changes to the structure and personnel of the ISI in an attempt to bring it back under greater central control, including placing it formally under the scrutiny of the MI (Gregory 2007a, 1022). It was further reported that the "political wing" of the ISI was to be disbanded in favor of a shift of emphasis toward counterterrorism (*Dawn* 2011b). Again, more recent events such as the rise of Imran Khan's Pakistan Tehrik-e Insaf party and its subsequent fall from grace suggest that the ISI is far from finished with involvement in domestic political affairs.

Pakistan has made attempts to establish an overarching national security council (NSC) at various stages in its history, but the experience has usually been perfunctory. An NSC can act as a critical element of civil-military relations in democratic societies, delivering coordination, information, policy formation, and oversight functions (Bruneau et al. 2009). In this context, it is perhaps surprising to learn that the first NSC was established under the first military regime of General Ayub Khan, in 1968, following the ill-fated 1965 war. The general, as president at the time, was the chair, and the ministers of home and Kashmir affairs the vice chairs. While this was "a potentially useful forum for assessing intelligence and giving direction to the various intelligence agencies," Ayub's successor, Gen. Yahya Khan, was "generally allergic to this formal decision-making apparatus" and left its deliberations largely in the hands of his aide, Maj. Gen. Ghulam Umar (Nawaz 2008, 313). Yahya's style of leadership was such that he "only got news that he wanted to hear" (313), thus rendering the NSC somewhat constrained in its usefulness.

Zulfikar Ali Bhutto subsequently disbanded the NSC in the early 1970s on the grounds that its membership, which included the three chiefs of the armed forces alongside civilian government ministers, meant that the military continued to hold an uncomfortably powerful position in national security decision-making. General Zia did very briefly reestablish the NSC in 1985 but promptly disbanded it again just a few weeks later (Pattanaik 2000, 953–54). The chief of army staff during Benazir Bhutto's second government, Gen. Jehangir Karamat, had suggested he very much understood the importance of a strong NSC acting as a balance between military and civilian power (Haider 2017). The caretaker administration that followed the dismissal of Benazir Bhutto's government in 1997 established a Committee for Defense and National Security, to be chaired by the president, but this was also subsequently disbanded by the Nawaz Sharif government that followed on the grounds that its membership had been handpicked by the caretaker administration (Pattanaik 2000, 954). There is now a parliamentary National Security Committee, but its ability to deliver meaningful oversight and accountability of the ISI and the wider intelligence machinery, or indeed to be used as anything other than a political football by competing power brokers, should probably not be overstated.

ISI Culture

One of the most interesting recent insights into the strategic culture of the ISI was provided by its DG in the 2008–2012 period, Lt. Gen. Ahmad Shuja Pasha. Upon giving evidence to the Abbottabad Commission in Pakistan in the aftermath of the locating and killing of bin Laden in 2011, Pasha put himself forward as one of the few senior officials prepared to give evidence to the commission. His role was to comment on the ISI's position on the hugely embarrassing and controversial question of how much Pakistani intelligence had known about the presence of the Al-Qaeda leader in Pakistan. Interestingly, the commission's final report was suppressed by the Pakistani government but leaked to the media organization *Al Jazeera* shortly after its publication in July 2013. The latter subsequently claimed to have "credible evidence" that its publication of the report was quickly followed with its domain on the internet being blocked to users in Pakistan. *Al Jazeera* also reported that one page of the report relating to Pasha's testimony appeared to be missing from the leaked copy (Hashim 2013). We may never know what that page contained.

Despite the omission, Pasha's testimony represented an insight into the strategic culture of the ISI, albeit one clearly defined as a tremendous opportunity for a piece of public relations. First, Pasha noted that the ISI was the "first line of national defence" in Pakistan's national security. The agency displayed "professional standards," not to mention enormous expenditures of "blood, sweat and time," in discharging its responsibilities. Efforts by rival intelligence services (in which the CIA was included) to besmirch the ISI's name were to be interpreted as a "compliment to its achievements" (Abbottabad Commission 2013, 191–92).

Pasha also noted that, while the ISI's charter primarily concerns matters of external intelligence, its functions were "progressively extended to internal developments" during the 1980s following the invasion of Afghanistan and related subversion activities by hostile intelligence actors within Pakistan. The agency subsequently restructured and re-shaped itself into "a dynamic and modern intelligence agency suited to the requirements of the 21st century" (Abbottabad Commission 2013, 192).

Interestingly, Pasha reported that the ISI had never been formally tasked with the counterterrorism agenda but took it on through a combination of the country being run by its military masters for most of the preceding period and a general exasperation with the "dysfunctionality of the prevailing system and the ineffectiveness of other state organs." This led to a counterterrorism wing being formally established within the agency in November 2007 to support Pakistan's collaboration with the United States on the global war on terror.

Pasha noted that this "paradigm shift" by the ISI toward matters that would previously have been considered the domain of domestic intelligence agencies and law enforcement agencies had to be understood "in its proper perspective." "The people of Pakistan," he noted, "were angry because all other security organisations had failed." The subsequent condemnation of the ISI for its failure over the bin Laden episode was, in Pasha's view, "perverse" and politically motivated. He noted that senior members of other agencies such as the IB and the police had not been lambasted over the affair, when they should reasonably have been expected to have a much deeper network of informants in domestic communities than the ISI (194). On the competency of officers within the IB and the FIA, Pasha's criticism was stinging. The "vast majority of them," he proclaimed, "did not know the basics of intelligence" (199).

The CIA was also singled out for criticism for being selective in its intelligence sharing with the ISI, sometimes amounting to keeping the latter "in the dark" on key pieces of information, and for insinuating increasingly that not only did the ISI probably know about bin Laden's whereabouts but that the organization (or elements of it) were probably complicit in his concealment (196). The difficulties in this relationship are matters to which we will return.

On the question of whether the ISI should be brought under civilian control, Pasha was unsurprisingly not at all keen. He claimed that placing the ISI under the Ministry of Interior would be "disastrous" (204). He pointed out that the ISI had "no relationship" with that ministry and reported directly to the president and prime minister. Pasha went on to claim that the prime minister had asked him for a briefing only once during his tenure, suggesting a lack of interest in the ISI's activities by the civilian administration.

In assessing the DG's testimony, the commission picked up on an early observation that those who still feared the ISI were those "who should fear the ISI" (208). This indicated that, contrary to Pasha's claims that the intelligence agency had changed its "mindset, culture and methodology" following the ignominy of bin Laden's discovery and assassination, the agency was demonstrating less change to its culture than it might be willing to admit. It was further noted on the issue of the ISI deciding to become involved in counterterrorism that this was not the ISI's decision to make: it should instead have been directed by the civilian government (209).

Pasha's comments were useful in providing a shop window into many key elements of ISI's strategic culture. Interestingly, the first and most important element of its culture was barely mentioned in the report: namely, the way in which India defines every aspect of national security thinking in Pakistan. Indeed, the reason it was briefly mentioned was in the context of a risk of allowing an all-consuming obsession with India to deflect attention and resources away from other national security threats (2).

It is difficult to consider the ISI, either in material or intellectual aspects, without noting that it is very much an extension of the Pakistani military and, more specifically, the army. Pakistan's military mindset, if it can be termed such, is absolutely that of the ISI. The bonds between the two were not necessarily as concrete in the early years, when the agency was attempting to build itself from a humble starting situation and to find its place in national security strategy. By the 1965 war with India, general problems with poor intelligence gathering and coordination seemed to have led to a resolution by the leaders of Pakistan to make the ISI considerably more central to national security policy. By 1971, and the disastrous third war with India in which East Pakistan was lost, the ISI's critical role at the center of the state was set.

As already observed, the civilian PPP administration of Zulfikar Ali Bhutto, which followed the Ayub and Yahya Khan military era, had a slightly conflicted approach toward the ISI. On the one hand, the power of the agency and its hand-in-glove relationship with the army was very much feared by Bhutto. On the other, the importance and growing effectiveness of the agency, especially in confronting India, was attractive to the prime minister and saw him elevate its DG to the level of a three-star general.

One thing on which Bhutto absolutely agreed with his military compatriots was a deeply felt and oft-articulated antipathy toward India and its regional aspirations. Even before the stinging defeat to India in 1971, Bhutto had often been extremely vocal about the regional dynamic. Speaking as foreign minister at the United Nations Security Council in 1965, at the height of the conflict with India over Jammu and Kashmir, Bhutto issued a voluble attack on Pakistan's larger neighbor, describing her as "a great monster, a great aggressor." On the question of Kashmir, he declared that Pakistan would fight a "war for a thousand years, a war for defence" (Bhutto 1965). The people of Pakistan "do not want," he declared, "to be exterminated."

Such nationalistic and existential narrative represents a foundational building block in Pakistan's culture, which suggests that India always was—and always will be—working toward the collapse of its smaller brother. In the military, and by extension the ISI, a duty is felt to shoulder the burden of ensuring this can never happen and to right historical wrongs.

Bhutto was speaking in 1965 as a minister in General Ayub Khan's military government and was doing so at the point at which the initial confrontation in Kashmir was widening into a more generalized war between the two countries, in which Pakistani territory was being seized and the whites of the eyes of Indian pilots could be seen as the Indian Air Force planes flew aggressively over major Pakistani cities. As noted, Ayub was himself scarred by the terrible experiences of Partition, as were many of his military and civilian compatriots. In his autobiography, Ayub wrote about history leading up to the 1965 war:

> We crossed a river of blood to achieve Independence. . . . India's attitude to Pakistan continued to be one of unmitigated hostility. Her aim was to cripple us at birth. She denied us our share of resources and dishonoured solemn agreements for the supply of our share of stores and equipment. . . . India maintained a constant posture of aggression which meant that we had to strain our limited resources almost to breaking-point to

build up and equip an army that could contain Indian ambitions. (Khan 1967: 48)

The historical narrative can be characterized as one in which an extraordinary sacrifice to establish a state independent of the Indian hegemon has been followed by a constant need to hold and maintain Pakistan's position in the face of perpetual Indian ambition. As officers literally on the frontline of confrontation, members of the military and intelligence culture in Pakistan take the continuity of this epic, existential conflict as a given.

Even when Pakistan needs to look west toward Afghanistan, rather than east, the specter of India is always present at the feast. One of the longest-serving DGs of the ISI, General Akhtar Abdur Rahman (1979–1987), who spearheaded the majority of the period of Mujahideen operations against the Soviets in Afghanistan, was one of the last army officers to receive his commission from the British Indian Military Academy before Partition. Akhtar's chief of the Afghan Bureau for four years during the middle of the Mujahideen campaign, Brig. Mohammad Yousaf, later wrote that he believed Akhtar's taciturn and inscrutable manner was because of his experiences of fighting India three times and the "horrors" he had witnessed around Partition (Yousaf and Adkin 2001, 19).

The man who took over from Akhtar as DG ISI, Gen. Hamid Gul, was in many ways much more openly hostile toward India and much more vocal about the logic of using Islamist militant groups to undermine it. He allegedly spoke openly with PM Benazir Bhutto about the inherent logic of "keeping Punjab [in India] destabilized," not to mention being seen by many as the godfather of the militant group LeT, among many other dubious accolades (*Times of India* 2015). Indeed, Gul is the alleged author of Pakistan's strategic culture of "bleeding India with a thousand cuts" (Hasnain 2015), a strategy much favored by Gul's boss, General Zia, both in Afghanistan and in Kashmir.

The "thousand cuts" strategy could be said to be a critical subcomponent of the ISI's and army's strategic culture as regards India. Born partly from a realization that direct battlefield confrontation with a much larger enemy generally leads to disaster, but also from the Mujahideen experience in Afghanistan, in which a very well-equipped superpower was brought to heel by the use of asymmetric guerrilla tactics, the strategy is seen as the best way to confront India and spike its supposed hegemonic ambitions. Most clearly manifested in the militant strategy used in Kashmir, which, while not yet achieving the ultimate aim of "liberating" the province, has embroiled India in an expensive and continually difficult counterinsurgency; the strategy has also seen the ISI promoting the Khalistan Sikh separatists in East Punjab and offering alleged logistical support for militant and separatist movements in Sikkim and other neighboring provinces in India's far northeast (Saikia 2011). The latter is a particularly interesting strategy since it offers the opportunity to force India to deploy military resources at the other end of the subcontinent, thus having to draw forces away from Kashmir. In a sense, the whole adds up to a logical approach, in which India's capabilities are continually stretched and frustrated and in which certain agendas such as Kashmir are kept on the international community's radar, often to India's embarrassment.

Similarly, Pakistan's Afghan strategy must be seen through the lens of the India narrative. The basic logic of strategic depth in Afghanistan was well understood by the British, who saw the country as an important buffer zone between India and imperial Russia, albeit one that Britain never came close to directly controlling. For contemporary Pakistan, the risk of being sandwiched between two hostile powers was clearly evident in the Cold War, when India aligned itself broadly with the Soviet Union. A puppet communist government in Kabul—especially one that might be close to India—which was eventually propped up by a direct Soviet invasion, was viewed as a grave threat for Pakistan. In the words of Mohammad Yousaf, the ISI's Afghan Bureau chief in the 1980s, the threat was seen as an existential one in which Pakistan could have been "squeezed out of existence" (Yousaf and Adkin 2001, 21).

In the contemporary era, the emergence of Al-Qaeda in Afghanistan and the subsequent rout of the Taliban regime has also been seen in Islamabad as a very dangerous period in which India could establish some influence with the changing regime in Kabul. As the "war on terror" in the early twenty-first century unfolded, the Afghan president, Hamid Karzai, and his intelligence chief, Amrullah Saleh, frequently and increasingly saw Pakistan as the main problem in the region and pressured the United States to take a much tougher stance with Islamabad. In a classified 2006 report, Saleh allegedly characterized Pakistan's regional intelligence strategy as irretrievably "India-centric," and this had caused it to revert to supporting the Taliban more actively after 2005 (Coll 2018, 217). In July 2008 a huge car bomb was detonated outside the Indian embassy in Kabul, killing fifty-eight people, including Brig. Ravi Datt Mehta, the Indian defense attaché. US National Security Agency intercepts appeared to show that the attack had been planned between the ISI and the militant Haqqani organization (308). Richard Holbrooke, the US special adviser to the Obama administration on Pakistan and Afghanistan, later lamented that the ISI and Pakistan see "everything through the prism of India" (406). It seemed clear that the 2008 attack was aimed at sending a message to both the Indians and Afghans that a close relationship between them would not be tolerated. Such an approach did nothing to improve the already worsening relations between Pakistan and the United States.

Returning to the Abbottabad Commission report, we are reminded that the commission was concerned that seeing everything through the lens of India could both pervert national security priorities and mean that attention on other issues would be neglected. Aside from this issue, the report did not say much about India, as it was primarily focused on the bin Laden affair. A key element of ISI strategic culture that did come out very clearly, however, in the testimony to the commission given by the DG ISI, Ahmad Shuja Pasha, was a fundamental lack of confidence in the civilian government's ability to safeguard Pakistan's national security and integrity.

To a certain extent, the problematic interplay between the army and the civilian administration has been common across many postcolonial states in the early years of independence. When the colonial administrations departed, the army was often the only properly developed institution, and one in which a culture of professionalism and discipline were central. In Pakistan's case, we have seen this was less the case in 1947 in physical terms, since the army had to be split away from the British Indian Army and was initially beset with considerable problems in resourcing and capability. At the same time, the fundamental British military culture of disciplined and apolitical operations was deeply imbued in its officers, not least as many of them had studied and been commissioned alongside their British comrades at Sandhurst Military

Academy, and many had served with distinction for Britain in World War II.

Aqil Shah (2014, 31–32) considers the perplexing differences in trajectory between military regimes in such countries as Indonesia, Turkey, and Algeria and notes that, unlike in Pakistan, the military in these countries was directly involved in a war of liberation from the colonial power. This in turn meant that the military had been part and parcel of a unified and focused process of building national identity. The question is then begged as to why India and Pakistan have experienced such different histories of democratic development and different relationships between civilian government and the military and intelligence sector when both were born out of the same British military tradition.

The answer, suggests Shah (2014, 34), can be found in the fact that national identity in Pakistan was a far less developed and understood notion than was the case in India, and continues to be punctured with regional contestations and contradictions. The fractured regional picture was shown in the composition of the army itself, in the sense that most of its officers came from Punjab Province in West Pakistan, and very few from East Pakistan. Indeed, Pakistan has followed the tradition of the British, whereby Punjabis and Pashtuns were considered suitably "martial" ethnicities who made good soldiers, while Bengalis were generally considered unreliable and seditious, as evidenced by the fact that the Indian Mutiny, or Sepoy Rebellion of 1857, was spearheaded by the East India Company's Bengal regiment (54). Within the ISI, Christine Fair (2014, 110) suggests that a "pro-Pakhtun bias" has always shaped regional insurgency strategy, as evidenced, for example, by an early preference for Gulbuddin Hekmatyar as the Pakistan-backed militant of choice in Afghan operations.

These factors feed into ISI culture in several important ways. First, the external threat from India is balanced in the ISI's mission with the imperative of internal security, to guard against secessionist regional movements that could threaten the integrity of Pakistan. This approach is colored by an ethno-regional "martial" mindset, in which certain regional identities are seen as fundamentally disloyal to the concept of Pakistan. As will be explored later, this was clearly the case within the majority community in East Pakistan, allowing for a brutally repressive and uncompromising approach toward the agitators in the east by the military and its ISI handmaiden.

Furthermore, such internal and external threats can intertwine in this worldview, as regional identity movements are often seen as perfect opportunities for disruption by Indian intelligence. To be fair, allegations of ubiquitous covert Indian interference in just about every regional difficulty in Pakistan are popular fodder for the media, and vice versa in India. While apparent evidence of material support by India to militants and terrorists within Pakistan does periodically come to light, there is a great deal of smoke-and-mirror storytelling around such accounts, and many could usefully be subjected to more detailed scrutiny (Fair 2014, 105). It is also certainly the case that the army and ISI are all too willing to feed the pervasive confirmation bias within the Pakistani population about India's allegedly nefarious intentions.

The perceived tendency toward regional splintering in Pakistan allows the army and the ISI to cloak themselves with a resolute mission to ensure that incompetent and corrupt government does not add fuel to the fire and hasten a collapse of the state. We can see in Pasha's words to the Abbottabad Commission not only a clear lack of confidence in the competence and integrity of the civilian government—and indeed of its civilian agencies such as the police and IB—to ensure national security but also a somewhat arrogant notion that the army and ISI can and will step in where the civilian administration is perceived to fall short.

The three comprehensive impositions of military government in Pakistan (Ayub Khan in 1958, Zia-ul-Haq in 1977, and Pervez Musharraf in 1999) have all come on the back of real or perceived political and economic crisis and turmoil across the country. As with the fear of India, it is worth noting that the Pakistani public has generally been equally exasperated with the "kleptocratic" governments the army has removed and, initially at least, has expressed widespread support for the restoration of order and stability. As Fair (2011, 576) describes, "Pakistan's political parties are very much a part of this problem" through their frequently tumultuous, corrupt, and confrontational approaches to governance.

Part of the military establishment's difficulty with civilian government relates to the aforementioned culture of professionalism and loyalty at the center of military training. This often feels in stark contrast to the Machiavellian, freewheeling, and frankly corrupt behaviors of many civilian politicians and officials in Pakistan, and leads many in the military establishment to feel that Pakistani democracy is fundamentally flawed. Writing about the operation to support the Mujahideen in

Afghanistan, the head of the ISI's Afghan Bureau frequently lamented the corruption all around him. "Although corruption is a way of life in Pakistan," he wrote, "the military is perhaps the only organization in which it is minimal" (Yousaf and Adkin 2001, 99–100). The implication throughout Yousaf's account is that the ISI was a paragon of discipline, organization, and fairness within a pervading climate of incompetence and opportunism.

The problem with such an approach is that it can merge into a culture of authoritarianism and fundamentally antidemocratic ideals. Writing in the army's journal, the Pakistan Army Green Book, Brig. Gul Muhammad lambasted the "rampant corruption" and other problems faced by Pakistan and noted that these represented both manipulation by external foes and, more importantly, the "utter failure" of "democratic experiments" in Pakistan (cited in Fair 2014, 142).

A counterargument to the notion that the army and ISI are the only institutions to be trusted in Pakistan's governance is that they have themselves sometimes created the conditions of political instability and crisis in which martial law has had to be imposed. We have already noted how the aforementioned DG ISI in the last stages of General Zia's administration, Gen. Hamid Gul, appears to have been instrumental in forming the Islami Jamhoori Ittehad alliance that eventually unseated Benazir Bhutto's first government in 1990. In the same period, there are many allegations that the ISI was also instrumental in coordinating the anti-Bhutto activities of the rising Mohajir Qaumi Movement (MQM) in Sindh Province, whose ability to mobilize civil unrest in key southern cities such as Karachi has proved to be a major tool of disruptive influence. The question of which dark forces have been behind the MQM and other militant groups in Pakistan is murky and perennially difficult to verify. There is clear evidence that Zia's successor as chief of army staff, Gen. Mirza Aslam Beg, had occasional discussions with MQM's leader, Altaf Hussain, in the context of membership of the IJI alliance, but there is also "substantive evidence" that the Indian intelligence service, Research and Analysis Wing (RAW), provided logistical support to the movement (Kiessling 2016, 253). It is difficult to say with any certainty how much of this was in the realm of exploratory and opportunistic discussions rather than part of a coordinated and structured strategy.

A more recent example of army interference in politics demonstrates the third key strategic cultural trope of the ISI and its army sponsors. At the time of writing, the political success of Imran Khan's PTI administration has come to an end with the loss of a vote of confidence in Parliament and Khan's arrest on charges of corruption, triggering a new election. In 2013 a relatively little-known religious scholar based in Canada, Muhammad Tahir-ul-Qadri, arrived in Pakistan and almost immediately managed to mount a series of extremely well-attended rallies protesting government corruption and mismanagement. As Fair (2015, 140) noted, many in Pakistan were suspicious of how well protected and supported Qadri appeared to be and how quickly such a relative outsider managed to accumulate such large and disruptive support. This implies a degree of ISI patronage. Many also feared that the army would intervene again to establish order, but it appears they chose instead to force PM Nawaz Sharif's hand in ordering fresh elections for 2013.

Qadri's credentials are built on an Islamic set of values, which not only challenge concepts of corruption and immorality but also fundamentally challenge the notion of standard parliamentary democracy. It is notable that military regimes in Pakistan have used not only nationalistic emblems in their narratives but also Islamic ones, since these are also central to the concept of Pakistan at its formation and the reason it needed to split from India. General Zia was himself a devout Muslim and brought a renewed culture of piety to government. The Jamaat-e Islami party became a key partner in governance during this period, despite never having performed well in parliamentary elections. Controversially, Zia oversaw the introduction of Hudood Ordinances to Pakistani law in 1979, which establish a set of Sharia law elements to the penal code, including crimes of adultery and "honor." A quick glance at the Pakistan army's communications reveals the symbiotic relationship between a culture of military professionalism and faith. On its website, for example, the three principles of imaan ("faith and trust in Allah"), taqwa ("fear of Allah"), and jihad ("fight for Lordship of Allah") are prominent.[2]

The connection between these concepts is clear in external operations, where violent jihadist militants are seen as appropriate tools for pursuing national security objectives. Not only does this strike a suitable counterpoint to India's secular and predominantly Hindu identity but it also offers the benefit of uniting disparate regional and ethnic identities under one agreed identity.

Before his death in 2015, the former DG ISI, Lt. Gen. Hamid Gul, was open about his support for the LeT organization, by then recast as a supposedly charitable organization called Jamaat-ud Dawa. When Gul appeared after his retirement at a 2013 rally in Islamabad on the platform with LeT founder Hafeez Saeed, attendees were treated to a blood-curdling call for violent "holy war" against India (*Dawn* 2013). "The United States and India are very unhappy with us," cried Saeed. "This means," he went on, "God is happy with us!"

In 1992 Gen. Javed Nasir was appointed DG ISI by PM Nawaz Sharif. Described by many as the "bearded general" (Hussain 2007, 26), Nasir brought a more openly devout and orthodox Islamic outlook to the ISI. Nasir had been implicated in providing covert material support to Muslim militants in Bosnia in contravention of UN embargoes (*Orissa Post* 2021) and was closely affiliated to the Salafi proselytizing group Tablighi Jamaat. When his successor as DG, Lt. Gen. Javed Ashraf Qazi, took office, Qazi purportedly found a much less military and more religious culture in the corridors of the ISI than had prevailed before, in which long beards and Islamic dress were much more on display and the business day was punctuated by prayer times. Perhaps more importantly, the agency had become much more preoccupied with coordinating and managing militant operations in the field rather than gathering and assessing intelligence (Nawaz 2008, 467–68).

Hussain (2007, 26) suggests that the shift engendered by Nasir became "embarrassing for the military high command" and also led the United States to issue serious threats that Pakistan could be placed on the list of state sponsors of terrorism. This was ultimately avoided and Nasir was replaced as DG, but lingering concerns persist outside Pakistan that there is a dangerous underbelly of violent and orthodox jihadist thinking within the strategic culture of the army and the ISI. This, after all, would explain how the ISI developed and sponsored the Taliban not once but twice as the strategic actor of choice in Afghanistan, despite widespread revulsion at the Taliban's worldview. Not everyone in the ISI or in Pakistan in general would necessarily want a Taliban-style regime for themselves, but there is clear logic in a militant group's ability to offer both a clear counterpoint to Indian influence in Afghanistan and a supposedly uniting approach spanning factions and ethnic differences under a notion of Islamic orthodoxy and piety. This, after all, is considered by many in the region to be a fundamentally virtuous aim in the face of chaos and insecurity.

The interplay between Islamist and nationalist thinking, therefore, is a central element of ISI culture, and one that is not always fully understood among partners and protagonists who do not share the same strategic worldview. It is also a source of tension and difference between different leaders of the ISI and remains a considerably complicating factor in the general development of democracy and civilian governance in Pakistan.

Conclusions

Not only is it difficult to research the ISI given the high levels of secrecy that continue to surround its structure and operations, but it is difficult for the citizens of Pakistan to feel there is much in the way of oversight and accountability for the organization's actions. This, of course, is not a problem peculiar to Pakistan, or even necessarily to newer states in the Global South.

A large part of the problem starts with the lack of a clear statutory framework for intelligence activities. This would at least delineate the relative responsibilities of the different agencies and reduce (though not completely remove) the rivalries and turf battles between them. As it is, the ISI has become so powerful that it sometimes arrogates for itself powers that should properly be decided by Parliament and the executive. A notable example of this mindset is DG Pasha's extraordinary pronouncement at the Abbottabad Commission hearings that the ISI decided to take on counterterrorism capabilities—and even formed a whole division devoted to them—because no other agency in the country was deemed competent enough to do the job.

Very much on the list of incompetent authorities for the ISI has been the civilian governments of Pakistan, for which an evolving and deep mistrust has fed into the rationale for military overlordship of the state, especially but not exclusively at times of crisis.

In this we can see that, for all the lack of accountability that the ISI has come to display, the problems for Pakistan run much deeper and wider than this one agency alone. There is no doubt that a stronger, more balanced, more dependable and accountable intelligence community, with the ISI at its heart, probably has to start with the building of more solid processes of governance within the civilian democracy.

This is, of course, very much an ongoing project in Pakistan, as it is for many countries. In the meantime, the ISI has cloaked itself with a guardianship mission in which it does what it feels it needs to do to protect the country's national security. At the heart of this mindset is a cultural worldview in which martial professionalism is coupled with a heavy dose of Islamic evangelism perceived to be at the root of the state of Pakistan. This does not always work well in practical terms. The manner, for example, in which the ISI has grown to comprise a large element of irregular and occasional staff operating on the ground in a semi-governed manner may mean that unauthorized operations can be undertaken away from the eyes and ears of the senior management, where necessary. This surely has to be a large part of the story of bin Laden's discovery in Pakistan, about which there are two hypotheses: either the ISI leadership knew all along but chose to deny it, or they genuinely did not know and were hoodwinked by lower-level officers working toward a different agenda. The author favors the latter theory but recognizes this could be a convenient conclusion for the senior leadership, who can then deny responsibility.

It is to the question of the ISI's leadership, and how successive figures have shaped this particular intelligence organization over the years, to which we now turn.

Notes

1. The following organizational information is derived from a website operated by Pakistan Forces, a group that claims to be a "patriotic" supporter of Pakistan and the role of its armed forces.

2. See the Pakistan Army website, https://www.pakistanarmy.gov.pk/.

3

Leadership

An examination of the leadership of the ISI over the years reveals both continuity and change. As might be expected for an agency increasingly central to the fortunes of power in the state, the position of director (and later director general) of the ISI has frequently been buffeted by the storms of political change. Indeed, most of the DGs of the agency have generally enjoyed rather short tenures, lasting just two or three years or even fewer: perhaps not surprising in a country whose political history could best be described as tumultuous. But there have been some notable exceptions in certain periods where the country was consumed with a particular objective, such as the war against the Soviet Union in Afghanistan during the 1980s.

One very notable element of continuity is that, while the agency is supposed to be inter-service, as its name suggests, the top man has always, without exception, been an army officer. (The directorate board immediately below the DG does include senior navy and air force officers.) Until the 1960s, the agency was in a period of latency and was led by a director of colonel or brigadier rank. After the trauma of the 1965 war with India, in which Pakistani intelligence was felt to have performed rather badly, Director Riaz Hussain was replaced by a newly promoted two-star general, Maj. Gen. Mohammed Akbar Khan, reflecting General Ayub Khan's desire to elevate the power and importance of the ISI. This upward trajectory was continued by Ayub's successor in 1971, Zulfikar Ali Bhutto, who further elevated the position of DG ISI to a three-star lieutenant general: a situation that has pertained ever since. By this point, the agency was firmly entrenched at the very center of power in Pakistan.

In addition to the army dominance of the top job in the ISI, there has been notable continuity in the background and ethnicity of its leaders. Most of the directors and DGs have hailed from the northern Punjab Province. In a handful of other cases, such as those of Lt. Gen. Asad Durrani (1990–92) and Lt. Gen. Ehsan ul-Haq (2001–2004), the DG has been of suitably "martial race" Pashtun ethnicity. In a handful of other cases, the leader has a background in northern Indian and primarily Urdu-speaking provinces such as Uttar Pradesh (formerly United Provinces), before migration to Pakistan following independence. (This background has become known as Mohajir identity.) Notably absent in the biographies of the leaders has been a southern Sindhi or Baluchi identity, or—perhaps most significantly—a background from East Pakistan before it broke away in 1971. This is a significant factor when considering the way in which the "military state" of the army and ISI has acted in parts of the country considered to be seditious, such as Baluchistan and East Pakistan. In these places, the military has been seen by many as tantamount to an invading Punjabi (rather than Pakistani) force, not least as the Punjabi/Pashtun dominance of the leadership is generally reflected in the composition of the rank and file.

Generally, the ISI leader is appointed via a process whereby the prime minister selects from a list of candidates put forward by the chief of army staff (COAS) at general headquarters (GHQ) of the army, albeit with a clear candidate usually specified. When General Ayub Khan established martial law in 1958, this arrangement effectively changed to one in which he would decide on all senior appointments as commander in chief, although constitutionally the original arrangement modeled on British traditions has always remained in place. At times of civilian rule, the appointment process has been somewhat disrupted where the civilian government may be perceived to be making the wrong choice, or indeed where the wishes of the GHQ are not considered. This appeared to have happened with the appointment of the retired Lt. Gen. Shamsur Rahman Kallue in 1989 by the Benazir Bhutto administration. Kallue holds the distinction of being the only nonserving army officer to hold the post thus far in Pakistan's history, though, significantly, he held it for only just over a year. More recently, the DG ISI at the time of writing, Lt. Gen. Nadeem Anjum, seems to have been announced in 2021 by the COAS without having been formally endorsed by PM Imran Khan, though Anjum was on the list of candidates (Taqi 2021).

Such incidents attest both to the continual power struggle between the army and the civilian government in Pakistan and to the central importance of the ISI to the army's position in power within the state. It also shows how the long periods of martial law in Pakistan's history have led to an ambiguous political culture in which the army feels it can still call the tune, even when a civilian government with a constitutional mandate is in place. With that said, civilian governments have not always been entirely blameless in the situation. It is arguably the case that the ISI consolidated the strength and power it holds today most comprehensively under the PPP government of Zulfikar Ali Bhutto in the 1970s and through his close supporter as DG ISI, Lt. Gen. Ghulam Jilani Khan. In later years, neither the government of Bhutto's daughter, Benazir, nor that of her arch-rival in the early 1990s, Nawaz Sharif, was averse to using the ISI in Machiavellian games to undermine and unseat each other's administrations. The main conclusion to draw from such periods of history is that Pakistan's political culture is a hybrid of a civilian government that uses authoritarian levers such as the ISI to maintain a grip on power.

A further fascinating factor in the story of the leaders of the ISI over time is the waxing and waning relationship with the most important ally and partner of Pakistan, the United States. In some ways, the story is another one of continuity; a strong case can be made that no leader of the ISI, or indeed of the army, has ever really held a particular affection for partnering with the United States, given some fairly fundamental differences in ideology and worldview. But the degree to which the pragmatic logic of staying close to Washington has been on the table has risen and fallen over time, largely shaped by geopolitical realities in the region.

More particularly, Pakistan has not been able to pursue its regional strategic interests, notably those concerning the restive Afghanistan on its western flank, without considerable injections of military aid and cash from the United States during certain periods. This was most obviously the case in the 1980s but was also very significant during the post-2001 "war on terror" period. Significantly, this latter period witnessed a slow but steady deterioration in the political and military relationship between the United States and Pakistan, with much of the problem relating to perceived blockages over the sharing of vital intelligence on key targets. The United States has become increasingly unsure about Pakistan's commitment to tackling Al-Qaeda or the Taliban, a situation that reached its nadir in 2011 with the locating of Osama bin Laden in Abbottabad, and the United States' unilateral decision to remove him without warning. Throughout this period, doubts have steadily risen about the core objectives of the ISI in its fight against terror movements in the region and about its commitment to realistic partnering with the United States and its allies. As we saw in the previous chapter, the incumbent DG ISI at the time of the bin Laden raid, Lt. Gen. Ahmad Shuja Pasha, was bitter and defensive at the Abbottabad Commission hearings about the relationship with the United States. In this testimony, he revealed just how far the intelligence relationship had sunk.

To make sense of how successive leaders have shaped the ISI into the organization we know today, it is illuminating to tell the story through a series of key periods of political history in which the geopolitical environment faced by Pakistan evolved and changed. Each period can be viewed through the lens of the ISI leaders in position during crucial periods. The gallery of personalities in the ISI's top job reveals a colorful and intriguing range of personalities that have increasingly shaped the direction of Pakistan's politics over time and become one of the core powers behind the throne.

The first period is that of the foundation of the ISI in 1948 through the first imposition of martial law by Ayub Khan in 1958. The second period is that of the Ayub and Yahya Khan regime that followed, which culminated in the disastrous war with India in 1971 and the secession of the state of Bangladesh. During this period, the ISI started to change significantly from a small and very thinly resourced agency to something more akin to a key tool of surveillance and repression at the core of the authoritarian state. The third period is shorter, covering the Zulfikar Ali Bhutto government between 1971 and 1977, in which the ISI cemented its position at the center of power in the state of Pakistan. The rise of the next military ruler, General Zia-ul-Haq, whom the DG ISI had convinced Bhutto to promote above many of his contemporaries as the next chief of army staff, marked the beginning of the fourth period of analysis. The key theme of continuity in this period was the mobilization of the Mujahideen in Afghanistan to drive back the Soviets, in which the ISI and its vision of unrestricted warfare techniques were pivotal. The period ended with the death of Zia and many of his top generals (including the former but by then inactive DG ISI) in a mysterious plane crash in 1988. This presaged the ending of the Soviet occupation of Afghanistan in 1989.

There then followed the fifth period of analysis, characterized by a to-ing and fro-ing of nominally elected civilian governments headed by Benazir Bhutto and Nawaz Sharif, each of whom was PM twice between 1988 and 1999. During this period, the ISI was instrumental in electoral interference to differing degrees and was also subjected to ultimately failed attempts at reform of governance. The final chapter in Pakistan's history of military regimes to date began in 1999, when General Musharraf removed Nawaz Sharif from power and reintroduced martial law. This sixth period of analysis covers the advent of the war on terror with the 9/11 attacks in 2001, the subsequent invasion of Afghanistan by NATO's International Security Assistance Force, and a transition back to democracy in 2008. The years from 2008 to 2022 frame the final period of analysis, in which the difficult denouement of the latest Afghan campaign was mirrored politically in Pakistan by a "return to the barracks" of the army and its ISI colleagues, though this supposed ending of political interference by the ISI has not been borne out very convincingly in developments on the ground. This is perhaps best described as the hybrid regime we see in Pakistan today.

The totality of this history is told through twenty-five separate leaders of the ISI, culminating in the incumbent at the time of writing, Lt. Gen. Nadeem Anjum. This gallery of personalities includes some who stood out as pivotal in shaping not only the ISI but the political picture in Pakistan as a whole, while others have come and gone relatively quietly without troubling historians too greatly.

Period 1: Foundation and Early Years

As discussed in earlier chapters, the beginnings of Pakistan's premier spy agency were somewhat modest, and somewhat unique in geopolitical history, in the sense that they were necessarily wrought rather quickly from very frail resources. The same challenges applied across the border in India, of course, although the much greater land area and the way in which military and bureaucratic resources were doled out meant that India started independent life with a larger and more solid disposition of military officers and equipment. Its political trajectory was also rooted in a more stable and solid approach to parliamentary democracy than was the case with Pakistan, by marking a relatively straightforward continuation of parliamentary processes that had existed before in the British Indian administration. On the intelligence front, this meant that India initially kept with the civilian Intelligence Bureau as its primary agency, while the military and its associated Military Intelligence organization remained largely in the barracks. This situation prevailed until 1968, when the centralized state intelligence agency, the Research and Analysis Wing, was formally launched.

Pakistan's unique beginnings meant that, as described, the military organization necessarily retained a degree of British presence in the early years in the shape of senior officers heading up departments and detachments. The former director of Military Intelligence in Delhi from 1941, Maj. Gen. Bill Cawthorn, an Australian officer in the British administration, presided over the establishment of Pakistan's first military intelligence capability. He retained some influence over proceedings for some years after, though his exact role is ambiguous in the literature. This issue aside, as deputy chief of staff to Lt. Gen. Ross McKay, Cawthorn set about building a unit initially called the Directorate of Forces Intelligence. To head up the new unit, a senior officer who had served on the Burmese front in World War II, Brig. (later promoted to Lt. Gen.) Syed Shahid Hamid, was given the task in October 1948. He operated out of a small office in the new capital, Karachi, initially with little more than a handful of staff.

Hamid was born in Urdu-speaking Lucknow, in what was the United Provinces in northern India, and migrated to Pakistan during Partition amid horrendous scenes of communal violence. He was in an influential position and well known in the military hierarchy in the run-up to independence, having served as private secretary to Field Marshal Sir Claude Auchinleck, the last commander in chief in British India. He appears to have served in the ISI role for just under two years, ending his days in Rawalpindi writing numerous books about Partition and Pakistan.

Like many of his successors, Hamid found the task generally uncomfortable, as his primary role seemed to be to snoop on rising officers in the Pakistan military to spot any potential plots. It was also a frustrating business, as resources with which to build the new agency were desperately thin. It may be for these reasons that Hamid's early intelligence reports about a substantial communist threat in Pakistan were primarily designed to accumulate interest and funding from the early Cold War West rather than being an accurate reflection of reality (Jalal 1990, 113).

Hamid is credited with being a congenial and professional man of principle who passionately believed in the Pakistan project and was sorely disappointed by how the early political leaders of the state pursued a path of corruption and intrigue (Rashid 1993). In this way he established a critical theme within the state of Pakistan, in which the military leaders of Pakistan fundamentally distrust the competence of the civilian administration to run a stable and secure state: a state for which many felt they had fought so hard in the most difficult of circumstances.

Indeed, Hamid was close to Liaquat Ali, the first PM of Pakistan, whose untimely assassination in October 1951 is seen by many as a pivotal moment in the early failure of civilian administration in Pakistan. Ayesha Jalal (1990, 135) assesses that this was the moment when the center of power in Pakistan started to move from the first capital, Karachi, to the Punjabi-dominated military garrison town of Rawalpindi. Whatever his political capabilities, one of Liaquat's most famous gestures of defiance toward India in 1950 was allegedly inspired (according to the ISI chief himself) by a confident intelligence assessment from Syed Shahid Hamid. Having established that Indian forces were undertaking a hostile mobilization of their forces in the Meerut region, the chain-smoking Liaquat accepted the assessment from his intelligence chief and raised the famous "clenched fist" (*mukka*) against India that same evening (Hamid 2021). This set the tone for Pakistan's prevailing foreign policy stance toward India.

Hamid's move to commanding the army's Peshawar Brigade in 1950 ushered in a period of relatively short-tenure directors of the new intelligence agency, all of whom were at brigadier rank (with the exception of Colonel Afzar Malik). There is little of substance in the archives about the agency during this period, and its directors seemed to have served largely away from the limelight. It seems clear, however, that the nascent agency was slowly becoming a tool of the rising military regime, with the primary purpose of discharging a colonial-style remit to focus on potential sedition and challenges to central rule within the country. In October 1958, amid scenes of mounting political turmoil, the first president of Pakistan, Iskandar Mirza, dissolved the government and declared martial law under the commander in chief of the army, General Ayub Khan. Just under three weeks later, Mirza was himself removed from post, and Khan appointed himself chief martial law administrator.

Period 2: Military Rule, War, and Bangladesh

The reality of Pakistan's first major period of military rule had important and complex implications for the intelligence structure. Being an army general, Ayub Khan was somewhat suspicious of the civilian-led IB, though this did not preclude him from occasionally playing the agencies off against each other. A pattern seemed to emerge in which MI focused on the core battlefield intelligence task against India, while the ISI —conveniently headed by a senior army officer handpicked by Ayub— slowly eclipsed the IB and became the primary tool of regime survival in the area of internal counterintelligence (Tomsen 2011, 239). This included a focus on the rising tension in East Pakistan, which Ayub viewed as a potential focus for sedition against the center of power in the West.

Approximately a year after the military took over, Ayub replaced the director of the ISI, Brig. Muhammad Hayat, with a close loyalist in the shape of Brig. Riaz Hussain. This significant move marked an important change in the leadership of the ISI. Riaz Hussain was the first director to remain in post for a number of years, lasting until 1966 and the aftermath of the ill-fated second war against India. In time-honored fashion, he was eventually promoted out of post, to a major general commanding an army division in Sialkot. He later became the first governor of Baluchistan Province, under the short-lived One Unit Scheme under General Yahya Khan, which ended in 1971.

Riaz's success as one of the longest-serving ISI chiefs in its history to date is largely due to his unswerving loyalty to the ruling General Ayub. He also marked the consolidation of a significant shift already under way in the role and remit of the ISI, whereby it became a greatly expanded and powerful tool of political surveillance and oppression in the hands of the military establishment. Additionally, in tune with the geopolitical realities of the Cold War era, Riaz consolidated the use of Pakistan's territory for intelligence operations against the Soviets, such as the airbase in Peshawar from which Gary Powers flew his ill-fated U-2 mission in 1960 and a supporting US sigint facility in nearby Badaber, which invited a blunt warning to Pakistan from Nikita Khrushchev (Sirrs 2017, 35).

A hawk on the question of India, Riaz was one of the figures persuading Ayub that a further attempt at a strike in Kashmir using irregular militants was a good idea. By now, the ISI was starting to develop a network of informants and spies on the ground in the region, and its confidence was growing about its ability to organize a successful uprising and seize territory. Plans for the infamous Operation Gibraltar followed the formation of the Kashmir Cell at the top of government, in which the ISI had a seat at the table, if not a leading role (Nawaz 2008, 205–6).

In the end, the war proved to be something of a failure for Pakistan, and shortcomings in intelligence both in properly understanding the mood of the Kashmiri population and in the tactical battle with the Indian military on the ground were significant factors. As it became clear that a "spontaneous" uprising that would supposedly be triggered in Kashmir was not going to happen, Ayub asked Riaz what had gone wrong. He allegedly replied that his network of informants had "gone underground" (Gauhar 1997). After the war there followed a curious situation concerning attribution of blame. Ayub's press secretary at the time, Altaf Gauhar (1997), later recalled an incident in which Ayub had berated his director of ISI for focusing too much on surveillance of political opponents to the detriment of key military intelligence. This is backed up in the memoirs of Zulfikar Ali Bhutto, Ayub's foreign secretary at the time (Bhutto 1979, 62–64), and by an alleged rare show of frustration by Riaz himself (Kiessling 2016, 23). If true, this would have been a surprising show of disloyalty by Ayub toward one of his most trusted lieutenants, and somewhat hypocritical, as Ayub had been the architect of the expansion of the ISI's remit in political surveillance. But the war's failure was a tough pill to swallow for Pakistan's leaders, and mutual recriminations were rife.

In reaction to the intelligence failures in 1965, Ayub seems to have further strengthened the ISI. Riaz Hussain was promoted out of post and replaced in May 1966 by another Ayub loyalist, Mohammed Akbar Khan. The latter's appointment marked a further very significant shift in the power of the agency, since, as a serving major general, Akbar Khan was the first two-star general to head the agency. Thus began the director general moniker for the post. His appointment followed a somewhat opaque set of reforms of intelligence instituted by Ayub under a committee headed by his deputy and successor, Gen. Yahya Khan (Sirrs 2017, 66). Ayub had lamented, "we are babes in intelligence work" (Baxter 2007, 98–99) after he perceived that ISI and Naval Intelligence had failed to detect the Rawalpindi Conspiracy hatched by a group of naval officers. Ayub wrote that both the latter agencies were "fast asleep," while the deputy inspector general of police, Tareen, had done an "excellent job" (Baxter 2007, 98). In the end he was displeased with Yahya Khan's committee's work, saying it had only achieved some "tinkering here and there" (422). In particular, it had clearly failed to ensure the ISI could encroach significantly on IB's turf in domestic intelligence gathering.

An imposing Punjabi army officer who had experience of organizing militants in Kashmir in the run-up to Operation Gibraltar, DG ISI Mohammed Akbar Khan was a hardliner. He displayed an opposition to the transfer of power back to civilians (Ziring 1974, 411) and was a key figure in the brutal approach to the insurrection in East Pakistan that eventually led to the breakup of Pakistan. Various cables from the British High Commission cited Akbar's uncompromising approach on such issues as the restriction of reporting on events in East Pakistan and the possible use of torture on Mujibur Rahman, the leader of East Pakistan's dominant political party, the Awami League (Sirrs 2017, 75). There are also suggestions that Akbar Khan presided over the betrayal of specific Bengali journalists and intellectuals to Maj. Gen. Rao Farman Ali (Kiessling 2016, 25), an artillery commander in East Pakistan and then adviser to the governor of East Pakistan who is widely credited with orchestrating the killings of Bengali citizens during the East Pakistan crisis, including an alleged massacre at Dhaka University of more than one hundred people on March 25, 1971, conducted under the Pakistani army's Operation Searchlight.

Interestingly, the long-suppressed report of the Hamood-ur Rahman Commission Inquiry into the circumstances leading to the dismemberment of Pakistan in 1971, conducted at the beginning of the Zulfikar Ali Bhutto government, gave Farman Ali the benefit of the doubt on direct involvement in the murder of civilians during the crisis (Government of Pakistan 1972). This runs counter to many contemporary reports. Either way, there seems little doubt that the DG ISI Mohammed Akbar Khan was instrumental in the military's brutal approach to the East Pakistan crisis in 1970–71, which did nothing to ensure the peaceful consolidation of the state across its diverse communities. It is also notable that the ISI found itself up against a formidable foe for the first time during this period, in the shape of the Indian RAW intelligence agency established in 1968. It seems clear that one of RAW's first major successes was the mobilization of the resistance in East Pakistan to the military's suppression, including the direction of the Mukti Bahini militia force that eventually spearheaded the foundation of Bangladesh. For the first time in a concerted way, Pakistan was being played at its own game of unrestricted warfare, with disastrous consequences for Islamabad.

Period 3: A Brief Return to Democracy in the Zulfikar Ali Bhutto Era

By 1969 it had become clear that Ayub's rule was over, as protests by a burgeoning number of civil organizations began to grip the streets (Jalal 1990, 307–8). In March he decided to hand over power to the commander in chief of the army, General Yahya Khan. History did not judge Yahya's rule kindly, commencing as it did with the launch of the ill-fated Operation Searchlight in East Pakistan and ending after the military's surrender to Indian forces at Dhaka racecourse on December 16, 1971.

This military failure and humiliation looms large in Pakistan. In some ways, it could be said to have had the effect of emboldening the military—once it had licked its wounds—to continue its perpetual confrontation with India and to right the wrongs experienced on the battlefield. One of the last major acts in the unraveling of the situation was the holding of parliamentary elections to the National Assembly in December 1970—the first comprehensive elections in Pakistan since independence—and the refusal of the military government to honor the results. The outcome of the vote was an almost perfect east–west split, with Sheikh Mujibur Rahman's Awami League delivering an almost clean sweep of seats in East Pakistan and Zulfikar Ali Bhutto's PPP emerging as the largest party in the West.

Technically, the Awami League should have formed the national government, as it won more than half the seats overall (167 out of 313, against the PPP's second place with 86). But the Yahya Khan regime was in no mood to cede any power to the East. Prevarications and delays in constituting the government led to rising protests in East Pakistan, which were met with violent suppression by the security forces. In March 1971 Sheikh Mujibur Rahman was arrested and taken back to an ISI facility in Karachi, where, he was probably tortured into taking a more conciliatory position on the call for secession from Pakistan. He would later become the first president of independent Bangladesh.

In September 1971, as it was becoming clear that the tide was turning against West Pakistan, Akbar Khan was replaced as DG ISI by another highly pivotal figure in the ISI's history, Lt. Gen. Ghulam Jilani Khan. Akbar Khan had ultimately ended up on the wrong side of history with his uncompromising approach to the East Pakistan crisis. As a brigadier in the Pakistan army, Ghulam Jilani was Eastern Command chief of staff in 1971 before his promotion to the ISI role. While he had argued for a more pragmatic "hearts and minds" approach to East Pakistan, his solution was oriented toward a somewhat hostile conception of the "un-Islamic" nature of East Pakistani society and the need to expunge it of dangerously Hindu and Indian influences, such as use of the Devangari script (Sirrs 2017, 83). In this he shared with many of his colleagues a fundamentally exclusivist, Punjabi/Pashtun conception of martial-race supremacism at the heart of Pakistani identity and governance.

One of Jilani's first assessments upon assuming his new role accurately predicted that a comprehensive Indian military move against both West and East Pakistan was imminent (Sirrs 2017, 85). He also set about establishing, under Bhutto's command, a unit of Afghan guerrillas that could be used to disrupt the Pashtun nationalist movement across the border in Afghanistan. This became the Special Operations Bureau, established in 1973, and included such figures as Gulbuddin Hekmatyar, Burhanuddin Rabbani, and Ahmed Shah Massoud, who would later become highly significant as leaders of different factions in the Mujahideen force confronting the Soviet Union (Kiessling 2016, 34). Thus began the ISI's forays into a next-generation strategy of unrestricted warfare and the birth of the Afghan Bureau. It also established a connection with certain virulently Islamist strands of regional militancy. Brig. Raza Ali was brought in to head this bureau toward the end of Jilani's tenure, continuing on to successfully mobilize the beginning of the Mujahideen operations until Jilani was replaced in 1983 by a subsequent DG ISI, Akhtar Rahman.

Ghulam Jilani Khan represented a further elevation in rank of the DG ISI to a three-star general, a level at which it has remained ever since, with a couple of cases of four-stars briefly holding the post immediately before onward deployment. He was a Punjabi officer not particularly pietistic in his religious outlook and suspicious of the "feudal" power of wealthy landowners in Pakistan. This allowed him to curry favor with the supposedly socialist PPP of Bhutto, even though the Bhuttos were one of the largest landowning families in southern Pakistan. Ghulam Jilani urged Bhutto to hold fresh elections in 1977 as general political unrest grew on the streets. He is credited with realizing that Bhutto was fatally vulnerable to flattery and with using a seemingly sycophantic approach to remain in power through a period of extreme distrust of military generals. Perhaps ironically, Bhutto was so fearful of the military taking over again that he elevated and strengthened the ISI in internal political surveillance, much as General Ayub Khan had done in the previous decade.

One of the most noteworthy elements of Ghulam Jilani's period at the top of the ISI was the manner in which he was instrumental in persuading Bhutto that Zia-ul-Haq should be promoted to major general and COAS above others (Bhutto 1979, 82). He did so possibly having realized this was the preference of the United States and the CIA, which had been impressed with Zia during his time in Jordan as a brigadier in a Pakistan army detachment (Kiessling 2016, 36). Like Ghulam Jilani, Zia always cannily recognized that strong relations with the United States were important, not least as they ensured the army and ISI received funds and material support at critical times. This was despite the fact that many in the rank and file of the military and intelligence services were fundamentally suspicious of the Americans (Kiessling 2016, 48). For Washington, Zia's loyalty was critical at such times as the crisis with Iran in 1979 (when Pakistan became the new site for eavesdropping facilities previously located in Iran) and the Soviet invasion of Afghanistan the same year.

In July 1977 Zia launched Operation Fair Play, in which Bhutto was arrested and his government deposed in a military coup. A few months later, Ghulam Jilani joined the new Zia administration as secretary general of defense and thereafter served as governor of Punjab Province. This might have been seen as a betrayal by the incarcerated former PM, but Bhutto always maintained his belief in Jilani's loyalty. In his account of the period, Bhutto (1979, 81) justified this belief by noting that, if Ghulam Jilani had been considered by the military regime as a "supine flatterer" of his and worthy of exploitation, he would have been arrested alongside numerous other officials on the fateful night of July 5, 1977, when Bhutto was removed. Instead, Jilani was left in place for some months afterward. We will never know whether this was an accurate reading of the situation or a very deft act of deception by Ghulam Jilani and his army paymasters.

Period 4: A Return to Military Rule under General Zia, and Afghanistan, 1977–89

Ghulam Jilani was succeeded in post by Lt. Gen. Muhammad Riaz Khan, whose relatively short tenure of approximately two years was cut short by untimely death from a medical condition around the same time that Bhutto was executed. It is notable that one of the key aspects of Zia's regime was an increasing "Islamization" of politics and administration in Pakistan. This included Zia's propensity to use Islamic political parties such as Jamaat-e Islami, which has typically fared very poorly in democratic polls, as key advisers in his administration. One of his most controversial moves was the promulgation in law of the Zina (Hudood) Ordinance of February 1979 by presidential decree, which brought certain aspects of Sharia code into Pakistani law, specifically the punishment of adultery by stoning to death (Government of Pakistan 1979). DG ISI Muhammad Riaz Khan shared Zia's interest in the application of Islam to governance and administration. It is alleged that, upon assuming his post, he asked for guidance on whether intelligence gathering was Islamic. The newly instituted Religious Directorate at army HQ responded with confirmation that all was well and that intelligence could be interpreted as being sanctioned by the Koran and the Sunnah (Sirrs 2017, 110). This may have been the beginning of the more open expression of what might be interpreted in the West as Islamic extremism within the corridors of the ISI: a situation that had appeared to develop considerably by the early 1990s.

Riaz Khan was followed in post in 1979 by Lt. Gen. Akhtar Abdur Rahman, who was notable for being the longest-serving DG ISI to date. The length and continuity of his reign is attributable in large part to the fact that it coincided with the Mujahideen mobilization against the Soviet Union and its client government in Afghanistan, in which the ISI was elevated to center stage as the front company for the Cold War's last major confrontation. In this, he could be said to have presided over a successful operation, though he did not see it all the way through, being succeeded in post in 1987 and then dying alongside General Zia in the as-yet-unexplained 1988 plane crash.

Kiessling (2016, 51) describes Akhtar as one of the "most successful but also the most controversial" of DG ISIs. A taciturn but efficient man, he agreed with Zia's general strategy of bleeding the Soviet Union in Afghanistan through an insurgency, and using this general approach to ensure both the support of the United States and "strategic depth" to the west of Pakistan. In the early days of the Afghan operation, he imposed his control by making sure the chain of command from the chief of the Afghan Bureau, Brig. Raza Ali, to the COAS, General Zia, was rerouted through him as DG ISI. In 1983 he replaced Raza at the helm of the Afghan Bureau following an incident in Quetta in which ISI officers were found to be selling arms illicitly to the Afghans. (Ali was implicated not in the sales directly but in failing to manage the situation; Kiessling 2016, 53.)

Raza Ali's successor as head of the Afghan Bureau for most of the subsequent campaign in Afghanistan was Brig. Mohammad Yousaf. While he found Akhtar to be not the easiest to work with, he considered his DG to be a highly professional and trustworthy individual, at a time when the millions of dollars flowing in from both the United States and from the Saudi royal family were offering enormous opportunities for corruption (Yousaf and Adkin 2001, 19). Yousaf remained the loyal and dependable servant of Akhtar to the end, which is poignant considering the cloud of allegations of serious personal enrichment that dogged Akhtar in his later years.

Akhtar was promoted to a four-star general in 1987 to become chair of the Joint Chiefs of Staff Committee. An upward move into this largely ceremonial position has proved common for outgoing DG ISIs. Theories abound as to why Zia removed Akhtar at the time, including those corruption allegations and the idea that the Americans were worried he was too close to such figures as Hekmatyar and could have become a dangerously Islamist influence in the region after the war (Kiessling 2016, 56–57). The explanation could also be a simpler one, that it was time for him to move toward retirement: he was sixty-three at the end of his tenure at the ISI.

Akhtar was succeeded by Lt. Gen. Hamid Gul for what turned out to be the last chapter of the war in Afghanistan. Described by Aditya Sinha as the "most infamous" ISI DGs (Dulat et al. 2018, 28), Gul was a flamboyant and outspoken character who represented a marked change from his inscrutable predecessor.

A Pashtun and previous chief of MI, Gul was close to the CIA station chief in Islamabad and was probably their preferred incumbent to the somewhat fundamentally Islamist Akhtar. Within the constellation of Mujahideen commanders, Gul was thought to have favored Massoud over Hekmatyar, which would have suited Washington (Kiessling 2016, 62). Ultimately, however, he proved himself to be a "patron" of extremist Islamist elements such as Hekmatyar and the Taliban and generally of the use of elements of the "global jihad" for strategic gain (Tomsen 2011, 245). He was noted for his closeness to the violent militant group Lashkar-e-Taiba, occasionally appearing openly after retirement on the same stage as its leader, Hafeez Saeed (*Dawn* 2013).

Gul's checkered and relatively short tenure as DG included presiding over ill-advised attacks within Soviet territory at the end of the Afghan war and being the man in post at the time of the spectacular Ojhri Camp disaster in Rawalpindi in 1988, when a significant proportion of stockpiled arms for the Mujahideen went up in flames, killing more than a hundred people. The corps commander at the camp, General Imranullah, blamed both Akhtar and Gul for the disaster, much to General Zia's consternation (Aziz 2016). But like so many things in Pakistan, the cause of the incident remains a mystery. The likeliest explanation is that it was a case of poor storage conditions in a camp ill-advisedly located within a heavily populated urban area.

Gul also presided over an ill-conceived assault on Jalalabad in Afghanistan in the closing stages of the war with the Soviets, which failed spectacularly and, in the words of Brigadier Yousaf, was one of the key reasons the "Mujahideen snatched defeat from the jaws of victory" (Yousaf and Adkin 2001, 252). Significantly in light of future events, bin Laden was also present at the ill-fated battle (Nawaz 2008, 536).

In a review of a curious book jointly authored by a later DG ISI and his Indian counterpart (on which more below), Gul is described as an "ultra conservative" and the Pakistani equivalent of Ajit Doval: an infamous former Indian intelligence officer who worked undercover in Pakistan and was a hawk on counterinsurgency and counter-Pakistan operations (*Business Recorder* 2018). Asad Durrani also describes Gul as "a professional intelligence man. Very brainy," even if he "liked to sex things up for the necessary impact" (Dulat et al. 2018, 28). Whatever the verdict on this most colorful and nakedly anti-Indian of DG ISIs, opinion remains divided ultimately on whether he was "angel of jihad or windbag provocateur" (Walsh 2011).

Period 5: Return to Democracy, Bhutto and Sharif, 1989–99

Hamid Gul was not present on the mysterious military aircraft disaster that killed General Zia and many of his top officials on August 17, 1988, though the former DG ISI, Lt. Gen. Akhtar Abdur Rahman, did perish in the crash. Gul remained in post through the transition to the next phase of democracy under Zulfikar Ali Bhutto's daughter, Benazir, enabled by the sudden end of Zia's military regime. But he was not favored by Benazir, not least as he allegedly held very conservative views about whether a woman should be leading an Islamic country at all (Nawaz 2008, 424).

Benazir Bhutto then appointed a new DG ISI: retired lieutenant general Shamsur Rahman Kallue. His was a controversial appointment, and a unique one, being the only nonserving military officer to date in the post. He had voluntarily resigned from the army during the previous regime, disagreeing with General Zia's Islamization policies (Tomsen 2011, 291). A humble man, Kallue's time in post was a short and somewhat unhappy one. He was generally known as "No Clue Kallue" by his critics, particularly when a coup conspiracy dubbed the "Midnight Jackal" case broke under his nose (Bakhtiar and Abbas 2018).

The Midnight Jackal case unfolded in 1989, when the head of the ISI's internal security department, Brig. Imtiaz Ahmed, was forcibly removed on suspicion of plotting against the Benazir Bhutto government. This revealed a number of things. It showed the degree to which the intelligence agencies were involved in political machinations and the way in which the different agencies were played off against each other (Imtiaz was appointed chief of IB when Nawaz Sharif took over from Benazir Bhutto as PM). It also appeared to show that Kallue did not know much about what was happening on his watch.

The brief Kallue episode was significant to the story in a number of ways. It was clear that, through his appointment, Bhutto was trying to shift the balance in the appointment of the most important intelligence chief toward the civilian administration and away from the army, by appointing someone who had not been expressly proffered by Zia's successor as COAS, General Mirza Aslam Beg. But, being retired, Kallue lacked a current powerbase and network within the military. It was also the case that Beg and Kallue did not get on personally, all of which caused Beg to start working primarily with his MI chief, Maj. Gen. Asad Durrani, and to freeze out Kallue (Nawaz 2008, 425).

Kallue's appointment had been the result of a newly instituted committee set up to review the role of the intelligence agencies in an attempt to change the direct appointment of the DG ISI by the army. But the experiment failed. Nawaz (2008, 425) attributes this to the fact that Bhutto "failed to understand the culture of the Pakistan army." It could also be said that she failed to fully understand the hybrid nature of the civilian-military regime that was emerging.

Kallue's successor was another Pashtun in the shape of the aforementioned former chief of MI, Lt. Gen. Asad Durrani, who was appointed by the new Nawaz Sharif government following elections in 1990. A fascinating and somewhat Machiavellian character, Durrani's most important legacy is as something of a puppet master who used his influence within the intelligence community to shape and derail both the Benazir Bhutto and Nawaz governments (Jayaram 2011). In this, he could not have been more different from his predecessor.

The extent of the army's and ISI's manipulation of the 1990 elections began to emerge during a subsequent investigation of suspicious transfers of money through Mehran Bank, which became known in Pakistan as the Mehrangate scandal. After a long investigation Pakistan's Supreme Court eventually delivered a judgment in 2012, in which former COAS Beg, former DG ISI Durrani, and former president Ghulam Ishaq Khan were found guilty of distributing millions of rupees to opposition Islamic Democratic Alliance politicians in the run-up to the 1990 elections, unseating Benazir Bhutto's PPP government. The head of the Islamic Democratic Alliance and new PM, Nawaz Sharif, was a prime beneficiary (Boone 2012). Durrani was careful not to directly implicate the ISI itself, claiming that he acted on direction from the army.

Although the 2012 judgment marked an interesting reassertion of civilian constitutional power by delivering a humiliating judgment against the military establishment, it was all somewhat after the event, and its overall effect on the strength of the hybrid regime in Pakistan should probably not be overstated. For Durrani, the humiliation did not stop his coauthoring a surprising book called the *Spy Chronicles*. Published in 2016, this book documented a series of congenial conversations Durrani had held with his counterpart at the time, the RAW chief, A. S. Dulat. Probably aimed partially at rebuilding Durrani's image as a pragmatic statesperson of historical significance, the book was generally judged to be one in which nothing of major substance was revealed. This, however, did not prevent Durrani being called into GHQ in Islamabad to explain his actions over the publication (*Hindustan Times* 2018).

Before Benazir Bhutto's PPP returned to power in October 1993, Durrani was replaced in post by the avowedly Islamist Lt. Gen. Javed Nasir. Dubbed by some the "bearded general" on account of his fulsome facial hair (Kiessling 2016, 105), Nasir served for just over a year. As described, he had previously been implicated in providing covert material support to Muslim militants in Bosnia (*South Asia Tribune* 2002), and subsequently in ISI's involvement in a major terrorist attack in Mumbai in March 1993, thought to be a response to the destruction of the Babri Masjid in Ayodhya a year before (Rahman 2013). He was closely affiliated to the Salafi group Tablighi Jamaat (Evangelizing Party) and undoubtedly brought this culture to the ISI. Upon taking office, his successor as DG, Lt. Gen. Javed Ashraf Qazi, purportedly found a much less military and more religious culture in the corridors of the ISI than had prevailed before, in which long beards and Islamic dress were on display, and the business day was punctuated by prayer times (Nawaz 2008, 467). Perhaps more importantly, the implication was that the agency had become much more preoccupied with coordinating and managing militant operations in the field rather than gathering and assessing intelligence.

Nasir's replacement was in many ways a more orthodox DG, combining all of the same principles of a strong intelligence sector in Pakistan with a pragmatic and politically skillful approach, unlike the somewhat alarming and robust approach of his predecessor. His role was largely to steady the ship, both for the Pakistan government and for its supporters in Washington. Like many before and after, this allowed Lt. Gen. Javed Ashraf Qazi, who took up the post of DG ISI in late 1993, to transition into a political career. Ashraf Qazi was both MI and ISI chief in his time, and then moved into politics as a senator for the Pakistan Muslim League (PML), Nawaz Sharif's party and the main, Punjab-centered secular party in opposition to the PPP. He also served in two ministerial posts under the Musharraf government that took power in 2008.

Ashraf Qazi's military heritage was strong, being one of only two DG ISIs to hold the prestigious Hilal-i-Imtiaz (Crescent of Excellence) medal for outstanding service. His legacy was subsequently somewhat besmirched by a National Accountability Bureau investigation, which implicated him in a corrupt deal to sell land in Punjab Province to a Malaysian golf course developer (Raza 2018).

Two further DGs served during the Nawaz government until the tumultuous sequence of events that led to the military resuming power in 1999 under General Musharraf. The first was Lt. Gen. Naseem Rana, who served as DG ISI from 1995 to 1998. One of Rana's most notable moves was to persuade the Nawaz government to formally recognize the Taliban government in Afghanistan, alongside the UAE and Saudi Arabia, once it was becoming clear that the Taliban were establishing control over most of the country. This was a pragmatic move on which not everyone in Pakistan agreed, notably army chief Jehangir Karamat (Nawaz 2008, 542).

The second DG ISI in this period was Lt. Gen. Khawaja Ziauddin. Kiessling (2016, 141) claims that, like Kallue, Ziauddin's appointment was a similarly ill-fated attempt by the civilian administration to appoint a DG ISI that had not been anointed by the military establishment. As before, the situation became factional, whereby the COAS, Musharraf, decided to work more closely with an alternative in the establishment, Lt. Gen. Muhammad Aziz Khan, chief of general staff at army GHQ and deputy DG at the ISI, thus sidelining the DG (Kiessling 2016). By then one of the main foreign policy and intelligence objectives was determining whether and how to deal with the emergent Taliban government in Afghanistan, and indeed the figure of bin Laden, whose importance the Americans were starting to fully realize. But a schism was developing between COAS and PM in Pakistan, which gave Ziauddin little room for maneuver.

The period ended in almost comedic fashion when Sharif dismissed Musharraf as COAS while the latter was in the air returning from a trip to Sri Lanka and attempted to appoint Ziauddin as the new COAS. This did not become apparent to Musharraf until air traffic control refused to allow his plane to land. The die was cast: Musharraf eventually landed and took over in a military coup, dismissing Sharif and sending him into exile in Saudi Arabia.

Period 6: The Army under Musharraf, War on Terror, and a Slow Return to Democracy, 1999–2008

Although martial law had returned to Pakistan in 1999, its character was notably somewhat different from that of earlier periods under Ayub Khan and Zia-ul-Haq. This was not least as the geopolitical realities— and rising crisis—in neighboring Afghanistan meant that Washington was forced to bite its tongue and work with Musharraf as a key ally. (This, of course, had also been the case with General Zia in the 1980s, although he was much more interested in the Islamization agenda than was Musharraf.) General Musharraf, like Zia, was a shrewd politician who recognized the importance of keeping the Americans firmly on his side, although one could argue he had little choice in the focused post-9/11 environment.

With that said, one of the key features of the final period of analysis was a complex and increasingly untenable walking of the tightrope in Islamabad between a behind-the-scenes support of the Afghan Taliban and selected other militants for purposes of strategic depth and an outwardly expressed support for the United States in tackling Islamist insurgency in the region. This proved to be an increasingly complex and painful challenge both for Pakistan and for the United States, with the depths of the relationship eventually plumbed by the discovery of bin Laden in Pakistan, just a few hundred yards from a military base.

Musharraf's first DG ISI, Lt. Gen. Mahmud Ahmed, perhaps typified the situation. Visiting the CIA at the very time of the pivotal 9/11 attacks, Ahmed attempted to walk the line between agreeing with the Americans that Pakistan was 100 percent on their side and simultaneously trying to suggest that the Taliban chief, Mullah Omar, was essentially a peaceful man with humanitarian instincts (Abbas 2006). The problem was that Ahmed was a "zealot" who fundamentally distrusted the American worldview (Scott-Clark and Levy 2017, 10), favoring instead that of the Taliban. Eventually, the relationship with Musharraf became too strained, and Ahmed was removed from post in November 2001.

His replacement was Ehsan ul-Haq: another Pashtun, like Ahmed, and former MI chief, but much more to Washington's liking. He remained close to Musharraf through the difficult early period of the so-called war on terror, presiding over several important interdictions of high-value terrorist targets in Pakistan, such as that of Khalid Sheikh Mohammed in 2003, the alleged mastermind of the 9/11 attacks.

The period was one in which Musharraf twice nearly paid with his life for sticking close to the Americans, surviving two concerted attempts at assassination by the Tehrik-e Taliban Pakistan (Pakistan Taliban Movement, TTP) in December 2003. The strain was showing for Haq, however, who became angry about creeping compromises of sovereignty and secrecy through the flying of US drones from Pakistani bases and the inevitable penetration of US eavesdropping and intelligence assets within Pakistan that would limit the ISI's independent room for maneuver (Scott-Clark and Levy 2017, 222).

Like many of his predecessors, Haq was eventually promoted to become chair of the Joint Chiefs of Staff Committee. He was replaced as DG ISI in October 2004 by General Ashfaq Pervez Kayani, the second four-star chief of the ISI after the short-lived Ziauddin in the 1990s. A veteran of the 1971 war with India, the chain-smoking Kayani eventually succeeded Musharraf in 2007 as COAS when the latter retired from the army. Steve Coll (2018, 146) described Kayani as one of a new breed of "yes but" senior officers who increasingly challenged the United States over their policy in the region.

Kayani appeared at least outwardly to find a way to work with the Americans through the early period of the war on terror, when cooperation was initially effective in terms of curtailing the operations of Al-Qaeda and there appeared to be some degree of trust between Washington and Islamabad on central shared objectives. He initially reassured the Americans that the Pakistani officer corps was "completely reliable . . . liberal and moderate" (Coll 2018, 149). Having studied at Fort Leavenworth himself, he was considered a man of a more worldly view than many of his contemporaries (Scott-Clark and Levy 2017, 546).

However, the longer-term view was that Kayani was presiding over a period in which the ISI was increasingly working with the Taliban behind the scenes, seeing it as the sensible long-term strategic asset to be used once the Americans and their allies had gone or, indeed, if they became inextricably distracted by the situation in Iraq. Bruce Riedel, a former senior NSC official in the US government and policy adviser to President Barack Obama, later noted that it was clear by 2006 that the Taliban were receiving material support and coordination from the ISI (cited in Sirrs 2017, 228).

By 2007 the Musharraf military regime was starting to unravel under mounting pressure on several fronts. Musharraf reluctantly swapped his uniform for civilian clothes, promoting Kayani to COAS in his stead. New elections were announced, and Lt. Gen. Nadeem Taj was appointed DG ISI. A close Musharraf loyalist who had been with the general both during the infamous flight in 1999 that launched the military coup and during the first of the two assassination attempts in 2003, Taj was not accorded much respect by the Americans, who considered him little more than a "bag man" for Musharraf (Coll 2018, 310). His warnings to Benazir Bhutto about her safety following her tumultuous return to Pakistan in 2007 to contest the elections took on a sinister significance when she was assassinated by a suicide bomber in Rawalpindi on December 27, 2007. Unresolved theories about the incident include—perhaps inevitably—that the military establishment, or rogue elements within it, were to blame. At any rate, the elections went ahead, and Bhutto's husband, Asif Ali Zardari, swept to power as president to initiate the latest period of democracy.

Period 7: Hybrid Democracy, 2008–2022

The general election of February 18, 2008, which formally ended the Musharraf military regime, was a significant development in Pakistani politics. Despite being "neither free nor fair," according to the UN and European Union (Department for International Development 2008), the election achieved a largely peaceful transition of power from military to civilian regime. The PPP secured power under the late Benazir Bhutto's husband, President Asif Ali Zardari, in part riding a wave of sympathy over her assassination the year before. More importantly, it began the most continuous period of parliamentary democracy in Pakistan's history, including largely peaceful transitions of power in 2013 and 2018. While none of these polls were without electoral irregularities, the process has been a significant one of steps toward a more robust democratic future (Richards and Miraj 2015).

Still, Pakistan's current system of democracy has proven to be an amalgam of civilian democracy with continued military influence behind the scenes (and sometimes not very far behind them). Such civilian-military assemblages are not uncommon in many parts of the world and have become known as hybrid democracies (*Economist*, 2021). In Pakistan the civilian administration has continued to find itself somewhat at loggerheads with both the army and the ISI over certain key decisions and policies on national security.

The first DG ISI in this period was Lt. Gen. Ahmad Shuja Pasha, appointed by the newly installed COAS and former DG ISI Kayani in October 2008, who moved Pasha across from the role of director general of Military Operations. His appointment proved, in the words of Steve Coll (2018, 325), to be a "momentous choice" for Pakistan-US relations, and not in a good way. Unlike many of his forebears, Pasha neither had studied in the United States nor had a history of close contact with US military or intelligence officials until he headed up Military Operations in 2006. As we have seen, he held a fairly dim view of traditional civilian politics in Pakistan, considering the dominant Bhutto and Sharif families to be elitist and ill equipped for professional government. He also bristled increasingly at American pressure on Pakistan to distance themselves from militant organizations, including the Taliban, seeing such groups as strategic actors in the region with whom the ISI should and would have contact (Coll 2018, 328).

The tension in the relationship ultimately contributed to the erosion of Pakistan-US military and intelligence relations toward a breaking point. Incidents such as the Raymond Davis affair in January 2011 led to growing anger on Pasha's part that the United States was taking liberties with Pakistani sovereignty. When Davis was arrested after a shooting incident in Lahore, but then found to be a contractor working for US intelligence for whom pressure was brought to bear for diplomatic immunity to be applied, Pasha fell out with CIA chief Leon Panetta, with whom he had previously held relatively cordial relations (Scott-Clark and Levy 2017, 384). The situation worsened two months later when the United States conducted its raid against bin Laden's Abbottabad compound without any recourse to the Pakistan military or government. By then the intelligence relationship was virtually in tatters.

The bin Laden incident has also been at the center of another scandal in Pakistan, known as "Memogate," in which allegations have been made that the Zardari government went behind the back of the military establishment to the Americans and that the army and ISI secretly protected bin Laden in Pakistan (Shah 2012). In this highly convoluted and complex case, the suggestion has been that the military considered another coup but felt it was too soon after the restoration of civilian government. The US deputy national security adviser, John Brennan, claimed on the day of bin Laden's capture that it was "inconceivable" that bin Laden had not had a support system inside Pakistan. The official Inter-Services Public Relations (ISPR) office in Pakistan initially said nothing, adding to theories that the army and ISI had indeed been caught on the hop by the raid (Scott-Clark and Levy 2017, 427–28). The likeliest prognosis here is that elements below the senior leadership of the ISI did know about bin Laden's whereabouts but kept the situation secret from their superiors.

The bin Laden raid and subsequent fracturing of Pakistan-US relations proved to be something of a watershed. The key features of the following years included a gradual denouement of Western desire to remain involved in Afghanistan, eventually leading to the initiation of the Doha talks with the Taliban in 2018 and the withdrawal of NATO forces in August 2021. The Taliban talks followed President Donald Trump's "reset" of relations with Pakistan, after a frosty start in which he accused Islamabad of "lies and deceit" and cut off £1.3 billion in military aid (Afzal 2020).

In Pakistan the key political development in this period was the rise and fall of a new political party, Pakistan Tehrik-e Insaf, under former international cricketer Imran Khan, which successfully formed the government of Pakistan following the 2018 elections. Despite being a potential harbinger of a new style of postmodern politics in Pakistan (Richards and Miraj 2015, 4), allegations have swirled around the PTI as being a creature of the military establishment, for its apparent ability to break the dynastic hold on politics of Nawaz Sharif's PML party. For the ISI, the relationship with the Nawaz Sharif and Imran Khan governments has been a key feature of the latest period, in which there has been a succession of relatively short tenures of DG ISIs.

Pasha was replaced as DG ISI by Lt. Gen. Zaheer-ul-Islam in March 2012. Sporting floppy hair, a bushy mustache, and tailored suits, Islam has been linked to the PTI and its agenda. A whiff of conspiracy has been reported in the media, whereby he has been indirectly accused of having sought the downfall of the Nawaz Sharif government in 2014 by organizing behind the scenes a series of disruptive marches and sit-ins on the streets of Islamabad by the PTI and a movement called the Pakistan Awami Tehrik (Pakistan People's Movement; Abbasi 2020). Islam has denied the allegations, but the theory is a familiar one of the military establishment effecting indirect influence on the fortunes of a sitting government by encouraging widespread disruption and unrest.

The Nawaz Sharif government replaced Islam with newly promoted Lt. Gen. Rizwan Akhtar in November 2014. Akhtar retired prematurely because of "pressing family commitments" and to focus on his role as president of the National Defense University in 2016 (*Express Tribune* 2017). He was replaced by Lt. Gen. Naveed Mukhtar in December 2016. Previously commander of V Corps in Sindh, Mukhtar was an experienced intelligence officer, having formerly headed the counterintelligence division of the ISI (*Dawn* 2016a). Mukhtar also retired relatively early, less than two years into the job, but his successor, Lt. Gen. Syed Asim Munir Ahmed Shah, served for one of the shortest tenures of any DG, only eight months. Shah was the second DG ISI to hold the prestigious Hilal-i-Imtiaz award, after Ashraf Qazi. A former chief of MI, Shah was promoted to a four-star general and became the COAS in 2022. Although the defense minister in the Imran Khan government asked citizens to "refrain" from viewing the reshuffles of senior army officers "through a political lens" (ANI 2022), it seems clear that behind-the-scenes machinations between army and government could well be responsible for the changes.

Lt. Gen. Faiz Hameed replaced Asim Munir in June 2019, retiring from post just over two years later. He was considered to be on the list of candidates for becoming COAS but was apparently sidelined through his apparent closeness to the PTI, who were falling out of favor with the army during his tenure as DG ISI. (Hameed also became a source of ire for the opposition Pakistan Muslim League–Nawaz party.) He found himself the subject of a curious pronouncement by the ISPR in 2022, which complained that it was "imprudent" for politicians to cast aspersions on the "illustrious formation" of the Peshawar Corps, of which Hameed had become commander. The DG of the ISPR, Maj. Gen. Babar Iftikhar, said the army was showing "tolerance and restraint" by avoiding being "dragged into politics" (Siddiqui 2022). That the military's official PR office should make any comments about whether it should or should not be involved in politics—or indeed on what the elected politicians should or should not say on the matter—seems remarkable and emphasizes the complex interweaving of civilian and military power at the heart of the state. It is also worth mentioning that the tussle between the army establishment and the government over Hameed's appointment consumed much time and energy for the PTI government at a time when other issues were arguably much more important.

The incumbent DG ISI at the time of writing, and the twenty-fifth appointment to date, is Lt. Gen. Nadeem Anjum. He has also found himself at the center of recriminations between the civilian government and the military. PM Imran Khan was unhappy about the ISPR's announcing Anjum's appointment as the new DG ISI before Khan had decided on the list of candidates put forward by the COAS, as the process normally goes. A scathing article in Indian media about the nature of the hybrid regime in Pakistan and the notion that Khan was merely a puppet PM for the military suggested that Hameed's continuation in post would have been preferred (Taqi 2021). For now, civilian governmental processes are holding, with new elections due in 2023 following the loss of a confidence vote by the PTI government. But an almost daily tussle between a civilian government and the military establishment, if the former falls out of favor with the latter, seems to be the order of the day.

Conclusions

The characters who have served as director and director general of the ISI have varied over the years, often reflecting the nature of the regime in place at the time, whether it has been avowedly military or more civilian oriented. All postholders have shown a degree of continuity in being senior army officers, and most have hailed from the same regions in what was West Pakistan, namely, Punjab Province; Pashtun districts or Northern Areas such as Gilgit; or northern, Urdu-speaking parts of India, before migrating to the new state of Pakistan. Within these patterns, some have been relatively hardline Islamist characters such as the "bearded general" Javid Nasir in the 1990s or the taciturn Lt. Gen. Akhtar Abdur Rehman of the previous decade. Others have presented as more urbane, civilian suit-wearing individuals, such as Lt. Gen. Zaheerul Islam or Lt. Gen. Faiz Hameed in the contemporary era.

Inevitably, some DGs stand out as having been pivotal in the development of authoritarian power within the state and of a foreign policy of using militant groups in unrestricted warfare, both against India in Kashmir and in Afghanistan. Others have come and gone relatively quietly, sometimes with short tenures, often because Pakistan was in one of its rare periods of relatively static politics.

The more significant names have tended to coincide with major crises and transformations in Pakistan's history, usually with major conflicts, whether against India or in Afghanistan. The 1965 war with India saw the hitherto longest-serving director, Brig. Riaz Hussain, presiding over a period of development in an ISI that proved to have been patchy at best in providing useful battlefield intelligence. He was then followed by an elevation in rank of the organization's head to a two-star general with the appointment of Maj. Gen. Mohamed Akbar Khan.

The war that followed in 1971—in many ways a much more significant setback for Pakistan—was followed in turn by a further elevation of the DG's rank to a three-star general with the appointment of Lt. Gen. Ghulam Jilani Khan by the civilian administration of Zulfikar Ali Bhutto. These increases in rank reflected two important developments. First, the perpetual confrontation with India drove the hardening of a military-led, repressive model that centered a strong intelligence service. Second, this authoritarianism was replicated across both military and civilian regimes.

Other key figures in the ISI's history include the long-serving Lt. Gen. Akhtar Abdur Rahman through the major part of the war against the Soviets in Afghanistan and the short but tumultuous leadership that followed of Hamid Gul, described by many in India as one of the most notorious of Pakistan's intelligence chiefs for his use of violent Islamist militants for strategic power.

We have also seen how the waxing and waning relationship with the United States has been a key factor, with Washington's approval or disapproval of the incumbent ISI head sometimes being pivotal. Where certain DGs have proven too close to Islamist elements such as Gulbuddin Hekmatyar in Afghanistan, as was the case with Akhtar in the 1980s, concern in Washington has been a significant factor in promoting reshuffles from time to time. In the contemporary era, the slow and tortuous unraveling of Pakistan-US relations over an increasingly obvious support for the Taliban by Islamabad has been highlighted by the difficult tenure of DG ISIs such as Ahmad Shuja Pasha.

Throughout all these key periods, the men leading the ISI have generally favored a continuous ideology on certain key issues: an often ambiguous attitude toward civilian rule in Pakistan, veering from naked distrust of the competence of elected politicians to a willingness to interfere with the electoral process. Underpinning these approaches is a culture of military supremacy as the only trusted vanguard of national security and cohesion in Pakistan. Central to this notion is continuity in the use of militant organizations for the perpetual confrontation against India. In the most recent hybrid phase of politics, we seem to be witnessing a process in which the ISI appears outwardly to conform to proper process and ministerial jurisdiction, but only when it suits, and sometimes with thinly veiled warnings to the civilians about the risks of going too far. In this, there is a degree of continuity that is likely to be sustained for some time to come.

4

Activities, Operations, and Analysis

Initially established as a body to coordinate tactical and strategic intelligence across the armed forces, the ISI increasingly became central to intelligence power in the state of Pakistan in both internal and external contexts. As we have seen, this process accelerated at the end of the 1950s, when the tumultuous initial experiment with parliamentary democracy collapsed and the first martial law regime of General Ayub Khan took over. While the other two main state intelligence agencies, the MI and IB, remained in place, by the 1970s and the ill-fated loss of East Pakistan, the ISI had become the preeminent intelligence agency at the very heart of power in Islamabad.

The ISI has sometimes been described as the "most effective intelligence agency in the third world" (Yousaf and Adkin 2001, 12). Such a reputation was greatly enhanced during one of the final major chapters in the Cold War, when the ISI was instrumental in facing down the Soviet Union's military by organizing and deploying the Mujahideen forces in Afghanistan. By this stage, it has become apparent that the ISI was no longer just an intelligence gathering and assessment agency along the lines of the British state intelligence agencies, for example, but was more a "full-spectrum" agency, covering everything from gathering intelligence of importance to Pakistan's national security to the deployment of that intelligence in the organizing of covert action both within and outside the country.

In this sense the ISI had become more akin to the CIA, whose 1948 mandate under the National Security Directive included everything from propaganda to "subversion against hostile states" and assisting resistance movements pitted against communism (Richards 2010, 21). With this said, a critical way the ISI differs from many agencies within and beyond the West is in how it has developed both an internal and external mandate, involving itself not only in subversion and infiltration abroad but also in the monitoring—and manipulation—of internal political processes within Pakistan. This is perhaps where a powerful and centralized intelligence agency can start to become dangerous to the political development of a democratic state, and where a state such as Pakistan struggles to break free of the hybrid military-civilian nature of power.

While the ISI employs many civilians in analytical and administrative roles, we have seen how it is essentially a military organization. The top directorate board is composed of senior military officers, with the chief always being a senior army officer, rising to the rank of three-star general with the tenure of Lt. Gen. Ghulam Jilani Khan in the 1970s. This has meant that the ISI's mission and purpose is inextricably linked to the army's conception of national security in Pakistan, and to the military barracks rather than to the halls of civilian bureaucracy. External national security in Pakistan has been characterized by the perpetual conflict with India, with Kashmir at the epicenter, and, increasingly, by the notion of establishing "strategic depth" to the west in Afghanistan. Internally, the mission seems to have been to ensure an administration tied to the above objectives was always in place.

Conflict with India is central to the story of Pakistan's development, with major battlefield confrontations occurring in 1947–48, 1965, and 1971, plus a smaller but no less dangerous skirmish in the lofty peaks of the Siachen Glacier in 1999. The ISI's initial performance in these conflicts, in terms of its ability to drive strategy with good intelligence, could best be described as patchy, but this seems to have served only to cause successive leaders to further develop its power and capability. The military-led national security imperative also ensured that the democratic interlude in the 1970s under Zulfikar Ali Bhutto was, perhaps ironically, a period in which this trajectory of empowerment of the ISI continued on an upward path. While subsequent civilian governments have attempted to reshape the intelligence culture in Pakistan to one in which power is more balanced and oversight and accountability of the agencies more structured, none have so far managed to dent the ISI's fundamental power within the state.

If intelligence assessments have not always been an area of strength in the ISI, one area where it could be said to have developed a strong capability is in the organization and mobilization of proxy insurgent forces to achieve Pakistan's strategic aims. Again, initial forays into this field of activity were not entirely successful, as the ill-fated infiltration of irregular Pashtun militants into Kashmir shortly after Partition demonstrated. However, this operation served only to embolden Pakistan in pursuing the strategy of asymmetric or "unrestricted" warfare as the best way to confront the much larger and better-equipped military foe of India. The same strategy is inextricably linked with operations in neighboring Afghanistan, where the ISI has developed and used militant factions including the Taliban to achieve Islamabad's strategic aims on its western flanks. Arguably, this strategy has been so effective over the years that Pakistan has suffered blowback from militant forces who have become powerful and independent actors in their own right, such as the Lashkar-e-Taiba organization, or, indeed, the Taliban, in both of its "Afghan" and "Pakistani" (TTP) forms. (It should be noted that the blowback in these two cases is slightly different: while the TTP directly attacks the Pakistani state, the LeT has generally remained loyal to the domestic establishment. But its reckless ventures in India have landed Islamabad in hot diplomatic water on several occasions.) In this sense, a myopia that develops from an exclusively military conception of national security may prove to be the undoing of Pakistan's development as a stable and economically active state. This, in turn, may argue for continued efforts to bring the ISI eventually under the heel of democratic process.

The ISI and the Machinery of Intelligence

The standard, Western-originated conception of the intelligence cycle as the central business model for intelligence agencies within governmental machinery suggests that the production of intelligence should happen only in response to specific questions being raised by policymakers who will have identified the key strategic gaps in knowledge. The model describes a somewhat sequential, production-line process that may not necessarily be suitable for dynamic contemporary environments (Hulnick 2006, 959). Perhaps more importantly in the current context, the cycle is essentially modeled around intelligence assessment-based models that do not account for covert action operations and around models of machinery that are more likely to be found in settled and developed states, where intelligence agencies are firmly rooted in clear processes of legal mandate, oversight, and accountability. (With this said, the West showed that the process does not always work the way it should; the case for invading Iraq in 2003 in pursuit of alleged weapons of mass destruction was a prominent example of institutional intelligence failure.)

The Pakistani intelligence environment has never satisfied these bureaucratic criteria, being more akin through most of the state's existence to a process of firefighting through episodes of military emergency. Perhaps for these reasons, a clear and neat process of intelligence machinery as described by the intelligence cycle model has not pertained to the shape and operation of the PIC, including the ISI. For a start, we have seen how the ISI has tended to treat civilian politicians, who would normally be providing direction in the intelligence process, with "suspicion if not contempt," in the words of Robert Johnson (2009, 122). We have also seen how there is no law specifically governing the day-to-day activities of the ISI, other than the general definition of the Constitution (which has been suspended several times under martial law) or under the standard stipulations of civil law in Pakistan covering the activities of law enforcement bodies. In the case of the latter, there is essentially no mechanism for bringing the ISI to account for its actions given the lack of a formalized oversight process, other than the periodic efforts to form commissions of inquiry.

As noted in chapter 2, Pakistan has made various generally short-lived attempts to establish a national security council at stages in its history, but none of these have led to major steps forward in clearly coordinating and directing the activities of the ISI and its system agencies. There is some evidence that, in the very early years of the establishment of the ISI, considerations were made as to whether Britain's

Joint Intelligence Committee, which had itself been established only a few years before but had found its feet during World War II (Goodman 2008, 47), should be a suitable model for newly independent Pakistan. Britain had established a Commonwealth Joint Intelligence Bureau and Joint Counter-Intelligence Bureau in an attempt to coordinate intelligence across its current and former realm, particularly on the question of the rise of the communist threat, but the denouement of the empire and schisms between India and Pakistan in particular meant these bodies proved to be inconsequential in the long run. There is evidence that the first director of the ISI, Syed Shahid Hamid, spent some weeks in the UK in 1949 studying its intelligence and security architecture (Sirrs 2017, 29–30). Contact between the Joint Intelligence Committee and the ISI appears to have continued for some years, with ISI chief Brig. Syed Ghawas asking London for help in 1956 in setting up Joint Intelligence Committee–style structures in Pakistan (Sirrs 2017, 30). But these do not seem to have led to any particular institutional changes. Within Pakistan, the need for counterintelligence activities to focus in part on potentially seditious military officers led to a power struggle between the IB and ISI, in which the latter came out on top.

As the former DG of both the ISI and MI, Lt. Gen. Asad Durrani has said intelligence agencies "have to use unconventional means. And, to neutralize similar methods by the other side, they will be seriously handicapped if they were to strictly operate under the law" (Pakistan Institute of Legislative Development and Transparency 2007, 9). This mindset perhaps helps to explain Durrani's approach to scuppering the PPP's performance in the 1990 election, as was revealed subsequently in the 1994 Mehrangate financial fraud trial. Difficult questions of human rights abuses by Pakistani intelligence agencies, such as those exposed by the Commission of Inquiry on Missing Persons (Anjum 2011), and evidence of the severe intimidation of journalists (Waraich 2011) merely reflect the degree to which the intelligence agencies feel they can operate with autonomy and impunity. While these are serious questions in themselves, they are also arguably signs that there is a fundamental lack of a culture of challenge and accountability for decision-making within the PIC, which is likely to contribute to failed assumptions about enemies and targets as much as it affects domestic affairs.

Capabilities

Signals intelligence operations in Pakistan have a long history dating back to the British era, when signals intercept stations were located in what is now Pakistan to gather intercepts from the Far East and from British India's Persian and Afghan neighbors. The strategic importance of the northwest frontier of India had ensured the Indian army's intelligence corps were headquartered in what was an otherwise somewhat far-flung outpost in the subcontinent, in the city of Karachi (Ball 1996, 45). Immediately after independence, tactical military sigint units were established, primarily around the border in Kashmir, focusing mostly on Indian military radio signals. At times during Pakistan's four major conflicts with India, these sigint units have provided intelligence on Indian military maneuvers and on discussions by Indian ministers and senior military personnel about war plans (Ahmed 1967, 67). During the 1965 conflict, sigint provided a key capability for Pakistani Air Force operations and identified a radar station at Amritsar in Indian Punjab, which was subsequently incapacitated by Pakistani airstrikes (Ahmed 1967, 179–80). In the 1971 conflict, a sigint station in Dacca in East Pakistan was also used to monitor political radio traffic, notably that of the leader of the secessionist Awami Party, Sheikh Mujibur Rahman (Salik 1977, 43).

The strategic considerations of the Cold War led to the establishment of a very large US sigint station at Badaber, near Peshawar in northwest Pakistan, between 1958 and 1970. This facility was also an important base for U-2 imagery aircraft flights. There is evidence that some of the operations conducted at this site were carried out jointly with the Pakistanis, including airborne electronic and imagery intelligence overflights of Indian territory, capturing intelligence on Indian radar installations and other sites, which proved of tactical advantage to Pakistan in the 1965 conflict (Ball 1996, 52). The reestablishment of the station in the 1980s also allowed the ISI to receive substantial sigint assistance from the United States in monitoring the war in Afghanistan, in the shape of access to tactical radio interception and direction-finding equipment (Yousaf and Adkin 2001, 94). However, the more recent experiences of the Raymond Davis affair and the capture and killing of bin Laden have led to an effective freeze in intelligence cooperation between the CIA and ISI (*Dawn* 2011c). How much this will have affected technical cooperation between the two agencies is uncertain, but it is bound to be having an impact.

Ashley Tellis (2008, 25) notes that sigint assets are "disproportionately oriented toward targeting India," despite the recent counterterrorism activity on Pakistan's western flank. Such interception activities have served the ISI well, but increasingly more sophisticated forms of communication such as use of the internet coupled with encryption software will test such aging sigint capabilities and require further investment in more modern and costly capabilities. As Tellis (2008) observes, it is not clear yet how much progress the ISI has made into these newer sigint challenges.

Interestingly, a retired major general in the Indian army, Yashwant Deva (1999), has suggested that India made slower progress toward technical intelligence gathering, preferring to focus for too long on a "sprawling network of spies and human analysts." Occasional reports of operations on the ground reveal clues as to capability. Ramesh Vinayak (1998) describes an episode when the Indian army used intercepted covert radio transmissions from a militant cell in Srinagar to home in on a particular building. A gunfight ensued in which a group of militants were killed, following which an important discovery of radio equipment was purportedly made in the property. The discovery found that the militants were using encoded messages transmitted from a master control located in Pakistan, sent over HF radio using complex and difficult-to-intercept frequency-hopping and "burst" transmissions. At the time of the Srinagar discovery, Vinayak, quoting Indian security agency sources, claimed there were four hundred covert militant radio calling stations operating in the Kashmir Valley alone.

The equipment described marks a considerable improvement in capabilities and tradecraft over the early stages of ISI and MI operations. As described, the first confrontation with Indian forces in Kashmir in 1947–48 was peppered with problems such as troops on both sides of the fence using radio communications on the same frequencies, and often en clair (Nawaz 2008, 71). These episodes also illustrate how much effort the ISI has subsequently put in over the years to the coordination of asymmetric, militant operations in Kashmir and elsewhere.

Operations: Death by a Thousand Cuts

Alongside technical capabilities such as imagery intelligence, interception of radio signals, and access to domestic communications within Pakistan (for which the process of warranted authorization is distinctly shady), there is no doubt that India's strategy of maintaining a "sprawling network" of human assets in the shape of informants, spies, and militants has also become a mainstay of the ISI's capability. Such humint capabilities mark the intersection between intelligence gathering and the discharge of covert action on the ground. Aside from other considerations, humint tradecraft obviously has a much longer history than technical approaches and, significantly, is both cheaper than sophisticated technical capabilities and less dependent on key relationships with advanced intelligence partners.

For Pakistan, there is the additional logic of proxy militant operations when confronting a foe such as India, whose conventional military capabilities are much larger and more likely to prevail in a straight battlefield confrontation. Lt. Gen. Javed Nasir, who commanded the ISI between 1992 and 1993, has shown himself to be something of the General Gerasimov (McKew 2017) of Pakistan, through his writings on the strategy of militant operations. In an article on the military confrontation with India in Kashmir, Nasir (1999) wrote that proxy militant operations "are a bottomless bucket, a super sucker of more and more troops." The effects of sustaining an extended low-level counterinsurgency operation are both physical and psychological: "These operations sap energies and resources with such rapidity that even the strongest economies and the best of soldiers start wilting under it very quickly."

Outside Kashmir, there is some evidence that Pakistani intelligence has supported covert militant operations across India for many years. Some commentators in India feel that the ISI has an almost ubiquitous presence in its country, with active or "sleeper" agents in every Indian city (Wilson 1999). The truth of this is hard to verify, but there is no doubt that the ISI has become increasingly well versed in running clandestine operations in parts of India. Throughout the 1960s, Pakistan and the ISI exploited the zeitgeist of the Cold War by supporting destabilizing and secessionist movements in India (which allied itself to the Soviet Union), such as that of the Sikhs' Khalistan movement in Punjab, receiving patronage in so doing from the CIA (Gregory 2007a, 1014). Meanwhile, in the far northeast of India, in Assam, a collection of revolutionary and separatist groups under the umbrella of the United Liberation Front of Seven Sisters (one of the main elements of which is the United Liberation Front of Assam) are purportedly receiving training and assistance from the ISI (Saikia 2011, 190). In some cases the training is conducted locally in the border area close to Bangladesh, while in others it is suggested that United Liberation Front of Assam militants have trained in Islamist militant camps in Afghanistan (Verghese 1996, 60). If true, this reflects another key logic in the notion of strategic depth in the hinterland of Afghanistan.

Afghanistan in the 1980s: The Mujahideen Operation

The DG of the ISI in later stages of the Mujahideen operations against the Soviet Union, Lt. Gen. Hamid Gul, has been credited with authorship of the infamous "bleeding India with a thousand cuts" strategy (Hasnain 2015). Whether he is rightfully credited with this description, Gul was building on a pattern already established, in which the ISI had become pivotal in acting as the go-between for the United States and the "Seven Parties" of Afghan militias who formed the Mujahideen coalition.

General Zia, who took over in a military coup in July 1977, was always clear about the strategy when he was thrown into the center of the final major Cold War confrontation after the Soviet Union's invasion of Afghanistan in 1979. As Brigadier Yousaf described, Zia "wanted the water warm, not boiling hot" (Yousaf and Adkin 2001, 65). By this he meant that the strategy was first to hit the Soviet forces with a multitude of pinprick, hit-and-run attacks that would tie them up in expensive and destructive operations without ever achieving full control of the difficult terrain and that would alienate them from the population. Second, the ISI would position itself as the one and only interlocutor with the Mujahideen rebels, keeping the Americans out of the explicit picture and thus avoiding the whole situation becoming too obviously a confrontation between East and West. (It would instead be cast as a religious insurgency against the godless invaders.) Third, the ISI's support to the militants would need to be covert so that the Soviet Union could not establish a solid justification for attacking Pakistan itself. This included

ensuring that meetings between ISI officers and Mujahideen commanders would be generally held in Pakistani territory, lest an officer be cap-
tured in Afghanistan. There were times where this complex equation
almost failed, such as in the aftermath of a destructive attack north of
the Amu Darya River inside Soviet territory in 1987, which brought
the water dangerously close to boiling (Yousaf and Adkin 2001, 217).
Hamid Gul sanctioned this attack upon his arrival as DG ISI and almost
upset the applecart so painstakingly constructed under his predecessor,
Lieutenant General Akhtar, over the previous years.

Zia's vice chief of army staff, Gen. Khalid Mahmud Arif, explained
that an "Afghan cell" had been set up in Foreign Office in 1973 on
the direction of PM Zulfikar Ali Bhutto, who was increasingly worried
about the political situation in Afghanistan under President Mohammad
Daoud Khan, who was setting himself against Pakistan and promoting a
path of Pashtun nationalism in the frontier region and in Pakistan's Baluchistan Province. The Afghan cell fell into abeyance somewhat when
Bhutto was dismissed in 1977, but Zia restored it the following year
(Arif, cited in Fair 2014, 121). In the meantime, DG ISI Ghulam Jilani
Khan and the inspector general of the Frontier Constabulary had been
working to establish key intelligence networks on the ground in Afghan-
istan, developing close links with Hekmatyar and Rabbani in particular
(Fair 2014).

After the Soviet invasion of 1979, in which Moscow aimed to prop
up the People's Democratic Party of Afghanistan government that had
unseated Daoud Khan in a coup in 1978, the ISI set about coordinating
the training and supply of a constellation of militant groups. By 1984,
with the help of substantial injections of cash from the United States
and Saudi Arabia, the operation had coalesced around the Seven Parties, who constituted a putative Afghan Interim Government sitting in
exile in Peshawar. Of these seven groups, four were avowedly Islamist
in their outlook (such as Gulbuddin Hekmatyar's Hezb-e-Islami and
Burnahuddin Rabbani's Jamiat-e-Islami), while others were more motivated by local ethnonationalist considerations and ambivalent about the
Islamist, jihadist cause (notably Ahmed Shah Massoud, a Tajik from the
northern Panjshir Valley). It became clear that the ISI generally favored
the avowedly Islamist group, for the main reason that Pakistan saw
merit in a strongly orthodox Muslim power in Kabul after the end of the

war, which would achieve the multiple objectives of keeping India out, acting as a strategic regional ally, and overcoming the regional Pashtun nationalism that had always threatened to disrupt the national project in Pakistan. At the same time, we have seen how the political and intelligence relationship with the United States at the time was sometimes affected by how avowedly supportive of characters such as Hekmatyar were the DGs of the ISI, such as Akhtar. A delicate line had to be danced by Zia and the ISI with Washington, and the tune occasionally changed.

History shows that the operation was, in many ways, a huge success for the ISI and for Pakistan's allies such as the United States in that it contributed significantly to the end of the Soviet Union, which collapsed less than three years after its 1989 withdrawal from Afghanistan. For Pakistan, the whole operation brought spectacular amounts of military aid into the coffers. In 1979 an initial offer of $400 million in military aid from President Jimmy Carter was famously dismissed by General Zia as "peanuts." The gamble paid off as in 1981 Ronald Reagan upped the offer to $3 billion, and Zia pledged full cooperation (Kiessling 2016, 49).

For the ISI, the operation also allowed for several continuous years in which covert action tradecraft using proxy militant groups for infiltration across borders could be further perfected. The skills acquired, and indeed training camps and some of the personnel used, have subsequently been used for preparing operations in Kashmir and in other parts of India. Viewed a different way, however, the strategy could be seen to have been a failure in the longer term. The ISI and Pakistan were not able to follow through with the installation of a permanent administration of their choosing in Kabul following the departure of the Soviets. During the war itself, the strategic objective of capturing the capital, Kabul, which DG ISI Akhtar had once said "must burn" (Yousaf and Adkin 2001, 163), meant that the ISI was instrumental in driving the relentless shelling of the city by Mujahideen factions, causing untold civilian deaths and the displacement of refugees eventually numbering in the millions. (Most of these internally displaced people ended up in refugee camps in Pakistan, placing a huge extra burden on its economy.) Finally, the fundamentally disparate and competitive nature of the Mujahideen coalition plunged post-Soviet Afghanistan into a brutal and appalling civil conflict for some years afterward as the different parties vied for control of the capital, Kabul.

It was into this melee that the Taliban movement stepped. By the early 1990s, Afghanistan was in turmoil as various "warlords" wreaked their havoc. The leading factions were the Northern Alliance of primarily non-Pashtun factions and groups, led by Ahmed Shah Massoud, and Gulbuddin Hekmatyar's Hezb-e-Islami, which cloaked itself in leadership of the majority Pashtun community but had a distinct, Islamist vision for the country. It soon seemed apparent that neither had the strength to strike the decisive blow and capture the state.

In the early 1990s, a movement of young, primarily Pashtun men schooled in the austere and fundamentalist Deobandi madrassas of the frontier districts began to organize themselves as a counter-warlord faction under the leadership of Mullah Omar, a veteran of the Mujahideen conflict in the Kandahar region. The Taliban (meaning "scholars") started to make a name for itself with a simple vision of stability, security, and a swift and brutal justice against the insurgent and criminal elements that held sway over most of the country. Through a combination of military conquest and the co-opting of various regional factions, the Taliban had driven the Northern Alliance out of Kabul by 1996 and took control of most of the country other than Massoud's Panjshir Valley by 1998. (It should be noted here that my use of the "Taliban" generally refers to the core group based in Afghanistan, initially led by Mullah Omar, and sometimes called the "Afghan Taliban." The TTP group, often referred to as the "Pakistani Taliban," are a different organization, which split away from the main group, and are generally focused in and around Pakistan itself.)

There is no doubt that the ISI had a heavy hand in the rise of the Taliban and that it viewed the Taliban as probably the only organized force in the region that could realistically impose control over Afghanistan (a correct assessment, as it transpired). They have also always seen the Taliban as a sympathetically Islamist movement whose worldview is antagonistic both to predominantly Hindu India and to regional ethnonationalist identity such as that of the Pashtuns. An Afghanistan ruled by the Taliban might have been unpalatable for many around the world, but for Pakistan, it would theoretically be a stable, peaceful, and nonexpansionist regime with whom coexistence would be straightforward. It also offered Afghan citizens a period of stability after years of brutal insecurity.

It is probably not right to say that the movement was completely a creature of the ISI, but it did emerge from a network of Deobandi madrassas largely funded by the Pakistanis through the 1970s and 1980s (with heavy financial support from Saudi Arabia, which was sympathetic to an austere, Wahhabi-style strand of Islamism with some similarities to the local Deobandism). The direct links probably emerged via connections with the Pakistani Jamiat Ulema-e-Islam party, whose leader Maulana Fazal-ur-Rehman was close to Benazir Bhutto's government in the early 1990s. He appears to have facilitated links between the emerging Taliban movement and Maj. Gen. Naseerullah Babar, Benazir's interior minister and the former head of the Afghan cell during her father's administration in the 1970s (Fair 2014, 128).

From this point on, it appears to be the case that Pakistan, through the ISI, began to heavily back the Taliban and to see it as a long-term strategic partner in the region. This was, of course, doubly significant in the period that followed, when Al-Qaeda took up residence in Afghanistan under the eye—if not complete support—of Mullah Omar's regime. As we have seen, it seems clear that, at least from 2006 onward, the Pakistani establishment was starting to lose confidence in the long-term political and military relationship with the United States and was reverting to fully backing the Taliban as the partner of choice in Afghanistan.

A parallel and complex element of the Taliban's rise is its relationship with a group called the Haqqani Network, which emerged in 1996 under Jalaluddin Haqqani, an infamous former Hezb-e-Islami commander in the Mujahideen. The Haqqanis are based in North Waziristan in an area that was previously the Federally Administered Tribal Areas of Pakistan before being subsumed administratively into Khyber Pakhtunkhwa Province. Although it operates as a semiautonomous group, mounting violent attacks across the border in Afghanistan (facilitated by geographical proximity to Kabul), and demonstrates potential links with both Al-Qaeda and the regional Khorasan Province branch of Islamic State, the Haqqani Network has declared allegiance to the Taliban and has effectively become one of its more violent armed factions (Lurie 2020, 1). In August 2015 Jalaluddin's son Sirajuddin Haqqani was formally declared the deputy to the emir of the Taliban, cementing the links between the two organizations. Following the Taliban's resumption of power in Afghanistan in 2021, he is now acting interior minister in its government, despite being on the FBI's Most Wanted list in connection with a terrorist attack on a Kabul hotel in 2008 that killed six, including an American citizen (*Voice of America* 2022).

The importance of the Haqqani Network to the ISI's evolving strategy of unrestricted warfare through the use of militant proxies is central. Taking its name from a prestigious and historic Deobandi madrassa in Akora Khattak, Pakistan, called the Darul Uloom Haqqania, the group has long roots in the region and represents not only a militant faction but also a broad network of religious schools and community organizations. Its wealth and logistical capabilities caused it to be one of the most important organizations facilitating Mujahideen operations throughout the war with the godless Soviets, establishing very close ties to the ISI. Indeed, Coll (2018, 154) describes the network as the "linchpin of ISI's covert policy."

In many ways, the Haqqani Network demonstrates the paradox of the ISI's militant strategy, and indeed of the United States' support for Islamabad through various periods of crisis in Afghanistan. Once a logistical partner receiving money and arms from the CIA, the Haqqanis are now a proscribed terrorist organization in the United States and a source of ire between Pakistan and the United States for the former's supposedly Machiavellian and deceptive narrative on connections with such militant groups through the period of the war on terror. At the same time, for Pakistan, it could be argued that a group such as the Haqqanis cannot be ignored given their central significance to the region and to the complex network of families and clans around the Durand Line. The situation could never be black and white for Islamabad.

The link between the Mujahideen and Al-Qaeda eras contained a complex element of continuity. The Makhtab-ul Khidmat-ul Mujahideen (Service Bureau for Holy Warriors, MKM) was established by radical Palestinian cleric Abdullah Azzam in the 1980s as an NGO facilitating the movement of funds and personnel to assist in the fight against the Soviets (Zahid 2022). The MKM managed to recruit wealthy Saudi Arabian citizen Osama bin Laden during the 1980s and brought him to the conflict zone in Afghanistan. He in turn took over from Azzam after the latter's death in a bomb blast in Peshawar in 1989 and renamed the movement Al-Qaeda wul Jihad (The Base of the Jihad; Zahid 2022). It is not known how far the future Al-Qaeda leader was personally involved in combat as opposed to logistics, although there are suggestions that he participated in the ill-fated assault on Jalalabad at the end of the war, which showed the Mujahideen was ill equipped to establish control over Afghanistan after the Soviets' departure (Nawaz 2008, 536). A tentative link was clearly established with Mullah Omar and the Taliban thereafter, allowing Al-Qaeda to retain its presence in Afghanistan after the war, until its forcible removal in December 2001.

Aside from being the forerunner of Al-Qaeda, the MKM was instrumental in facilitating a raft of other violent jihadist movements in the region by bringing a diaspora of largely non-Afghan radical fighters from across the Muslim world. The organizations springing out from this period include Lashkar-e-Taiba, thought to have been established in 1987 as a broad charity and proselytization group called Markaz-ud-Dawa-wal-Irshad (Center for Preaching and Guidance). The armed wing of this group was used in Mujahideen operations, receiving support from both the CIA and ISI, and was retained by the ISI as a militant partner after the war (Clarke 2010, 1). Its connection with the Pakistani state has been much debated, but it seems clear there have been close links between it and the ISI at various stages in its history, especially in military operations against Indian troops in Kashmir. In 1999 LeT militants allegedly assisted Pakistani troops in the Kargil Heights confrontation with India (Clarke 2010, 2), and there appears to be ample evidence in Indian counterintelligence files of LeT militants communicating with ISI "Directorate S" handlers in Pakistan during numerous violent attacks in Kashmir (Coll 2018, 344).

Probably the most controversial operation in which LeT has been involved was the Mumbai terrorist attacks of November 2008, in which an amphibious infiltration of militants originating from Pakistan killed 164 in a brutal swarm attack on the Indian city. The DG ISI, Lt. Gen. Ahmad Shuja Pasha, initially denied that the attack had anything to do with Pakistan, but by then the relationship with the United States was so poor that no one in Washington (and certainly in New Delhi) believed him. Indeed, Gen. Michael Hayden, the director of Central Intelligence, declared there was "no doubt" it was the work of LeT and that "mounting evidence" showed operational direction from Pakistan. Some weeks later, in a tense Christmas Day meeting between Hayden and Pasha, the latter offered a slightly more nuanced assessment, in which he admitted that some former ISI officers may have been involved in some "broad training" of the militants (Scott-Clark and Levy 2017, 315–16). Pasha's words were instructive, as they indicate that initial ISI sponsorship of militant groups may not always mean there is full and direct control over time: a point to which we will return.

LeT is not the only militant group operating in Kashmir by any means, with other significant elements including Jaish-e-Mohammed and Harakat-ul-Jihad al-Islami (which operates also in Bangladesh), to name just two of many. There are subtle differences between them in terms of underpinning ideology and character, but one thing uniting many of the groups is that they have formed the bedrock of the "death by a thousand cuts" strategy against India under the operational direction of the ISI.

It is also worth noting that operations against India by ISI-sponsored militant groups are not confined to Kashmir or to India. Former Afghan president Hamid Karzai frequently expressed suspicion of the ISI's meddling in the country, not least following an assassination attempt in April 2008, thought to have been undertaken by the Haqqani Network (Lurie 2020, 3), and the suicide bombing of the Indian embassy in Kabul in July 2008 (Thottam 2008). The CIA has backed up these claims, pointing out to Pakistani prime minister Yusuf Raza Gilani during his visit to the United States in July 2008 that it had solid evidence of the ISI's role in the Indian embassy bombing (Janes 2008). In the context of Afghanistan, a pro-India stance on its western flanks is seen as greatly undesirable by Pakistan. Strategic depth in Afghanistan will not work if Kabul becomes a key ally of New Delhi and thus effectively encircles Pakistan and prevents it from concentrating its forces on its eastern border with India.

In the meantime, Pakistan continues to accuse India of undertaking destabilizing covert action in return. In early November 2009 Pakistan's information minister and a senior military spokesman announced in a press conference that "concrete evidence of India's involvement in militancy in South Waziristan" had been found in the shape of Indian arms and ammunition, literature, and other equipment uncovered in military raids in the region (*Dawn* 2009a). The interior minister, Rehman Malik, had gone further a week before by accusing India of involvement in "almost every terrorist activity in Pakistan" and raising a thinly veiled threat of nuclear retaliation (*Dawn* 2009b). This may be a fine example of "mirror-imaging" within the intelligence community in Pakistan. V. Yadav and C. Barwa (2011) argue that the Indian intelligence agency, the Research and Analysis Wing, which is often invoked in Pakistan's claims of destabilizing activity, simply does not have the resources and capability to undertake an extended operation of covert destabilization in such places as Baluchistan. But this assessment, of course, could be merely subtle deception in the shape of plausible deniability, as is standard fare for intelligence services around the globe.

Internal Political Operations

As we have seen, the ISI's remit was primarily external-facing in the early years, though the first director, Syed Shahid Hamid, made it clear in his memoirs and notes that he was tasked with the uncomfortable mission of covertly monitoring his colleagues in the military for signs of sedition. A tension and ambiguity between the ISI and the police-led IB on the question of institutional primacy over investigation of internal figures has never been completely resolved, but the ISI's supremacy over most aspects of intelligence, internal and external, was eventually established. Many of the changes in this area were accelerated during the first military regime of General Ayub Khan, who established martial law in 1958, suspending the first post-independence constitution of 1956.

Despite having a very loyal DG ISI in Riaz Hussain and elevating the post to a two-star general, the frustrating aftermath of the 1965 war with India, in which Pakistan failed to achieve its objectives of driving India back and "liberating" territory in Kashmir, was a period in which the ISI's limitations were laid bare (as were, indeed, the limitations of the whole Pakistani intelligence capability). Z. A. Bhutto's memoirs recount an incident touched on in chapter 3, in which Riaz Hussain was berated for an episode during the war in which Military Intelligence had been unable to pinpoint the location of the Indian Armored Division. Its whereabouts were established only by chance when an Indian dispatch rider was intercepted. "With a quivering voice," Bhutto (1979, 85) recounts, Riaz suggested to an angry General Ayub that the intelligence apparatus had been too distracted by "political assignments on elections and post-election repercussions" rather than focusing on tactical military objectives.

This episode underlines two key factors. First, in critiquing the ISI's involvement in domestic political processes, one must appreciate that Pakistan's system of democracy remains extremely underdeveloped, and most of its political history to date has been dominated by military regimes. Until the post-Musharraf period commencing in 2008, Pakistan had enjoyed few elections worthy of the name. Indeed, the first proper broad-mandate election after independence did not happen until 1970, and these did not deliver a fully sitting Parliament and government until the constitution was redrafted in 1973 and Zulfikar Ali Bhutto took up position as prime minister. There was a further election at the end of this administration in 1977, but the results were never honored by General Zia, who seized power. There were no further democratic elections until nearly two decades later, in 1988, when Zulfikar's daughter, Benazir, won under the PPP party of her father. These, and other elections up until 2013, were heavily subjected to electoral manipulation and interference by the state and could not be said to be particularly close to being free or fair.

During the lengthy periods of martial law, the military leaders of Pakistan have tinkered with various methods of plebiscite and endorsement, such as Ayub's "basic democracies" system, which resembled early elections in democratic countries such as Britain in which the voting constituents were severely limited by type and number, excluding women and most other citizens other than certain elite and landowning men. General Zia held a referendum in 1984 about his central policy of Islamization of the Pakistani state. As Mansoor Kundi (2003, 29) recounts, *The Economist* dubbed this a "heads I win, tails you lose" choice, which not surprisingly heavily endorsed the constitutional changes Zia wished to make.

Taking Huntington's definition of *praetorianism* as a situation in which the military intervenes in politics (Ziring 1974, 403), Pakistan has clearly qualified as a praetorian regime for most of its existence. At the time of writing, it is arguably only now a hybrid regime, on a pathway to something resembling a free and fair civilian democracy. It is also the case that a Western, Westphalian notion of state and society is not something on which every leader—military or civilian—has agreed on as the vision for Pakistan. To some extent, this is partly down to the extraordinary and unusual circumstances in which the state was born in 1947. The period of General Zia's regime in particular highlighted a confusion about the state's definition as either some form of Islamic emirate or a more Westphalian and secular democracy. Such debates are far from resolved at the time of writing.

Taking the example of postcolonial Cameroon, Achille Mbembe (1992, 3) pondered the "banality of power" in a raft of postcolonial states, in which the structures and procedures of constitutions, courts, parliaments, and elections are retained and curiously fetishized but are at once continually manipulated by predatory and praetorian rulers to suit their ends. It is almost as if some degree of legitimacy is given to authoritarianism if it appears to follow a ritualized form of bureaucratic process, even if the results are preordained.

Pakistan's history certainly accords with this picture, whereby successive military leaders have attempted to legitimize their actions in various ways by amending the constitution, securing judgments in the Supreme Court, and holding various plebiscites and votes. For the ISI, as its power began to rise as well as its centrality to acting as the vanguard of national security and army rule, the agency was inevitably involved in a number of operations to shape the political picture in ways that the military rulers preferred.

The primary techniques used in ISI internal operations seem to be to target major elections by assembling broad-based political coalitions sympathetic to the army, which would challenge whichever of the main parties were likely to otherwise prevail at the election (usually either the PML or PPP, depending on the period in question). In so doing, the ISI uses the range of humint tradecraft motivations perfected by the KGB (money, ideology, compromise, or ego; Petkus 2010, 99) to persuade particular individuals to participate in the relevant political coalition aimed at unseating or frustrating the undesirable party. Such broad-based coalitions have often been unwieldy and fragile in their composition, which, in turn, has often meant political turmoil in their aftermath. From time to time, certain parties have effectively acted as "kingmakers" through their decision as to which side to back on the urging of the army and ISI, with the MQM in Sindh Province probably being the most notable example: a party not large enough in itself to form a government but one commanding enough seats in the critical urban area of Pakistan's largest city, Karachi, to swing the balance.

In the 1977 elections, a broad alliance of religious and primarily right-wing parties formed the Pakistan National Alliance to oppose Bhutto's PPP. Shahid Javed Burki (1988, 1088) suggests that the army under Zia did not have the time or resources to organize this coalition and that it was a largely spontaneous assemblage of disaffected middle class and other interest groups who felt alienated by Bhutto's increasingly authoritarian and socialist policies. Indeed, Bhutto (1979, 96) was himself receiving intelligence assessments on how the elections were going from both the ISI and IB, and these suggested he was going to secure a majority for the PPP despite the Pakistan National Alliance's best efforts to challenge him. Once this became clear, Zia launched Operation Fair Play to remove Bhutto and his government, riding the wave of public disaffection with his rule in many quarters. Bhutto was eventually hanged, in 1979, on charges of the murder of a political opponent.

The 1988 elections happened in the immediate aftermath of the death of Zia and many of his top generals in an air crash, and this again seemed to mean that there was little time to organize comprehensive interference in the polls. Benazir Bhutto eventually achieved the mandate to form the new government, albeit with a smaller-than-expected majority, under the eye of COAS Aslam Beg. Nawaz (2008, 416) describes the latter as the first representative of the "new Pakistan army," having been the first army chief to have been born after Partition and, to boot, a Mohajir who had work to do to prove himself to the Punjabi/Pashtun military elite.

The 1990 elections were a very different situation, however, and were probably the most ISI- and army-orchestrated polls in Pakistan's history. The operation was directed by Lt. Gen. Asad Durrani, the new DG ISI replacing the hapless Kallue, and the only DG to simultaneously hold the position of chief of MI for a period. The first step was to form an opposition alliance of right-wing parties to oppose the PPP, which was called the Islami Jamhoori Ittehad and included Nawaz Sharif's PML as its largest single element. A significant amount of finances to the tune of 140 million rupees was raised from Habib and Mehran banks, and this was then moved into secret ISI accounts for Durrani to manage in enticing various political actors to participate in the anti-Bhutto alliance (Nawaz 2008, 434). In a subsequent court affidavit in the 1993

Mehrangate investigation, Durrani revealed that payments included 3.5 million rupees to Nawaz Sharif, 0.5 million rupees to the aforementioned MQM in Sindh Province, and 5 million rupees to Jamaat-e Islami, among many others (Cowasjee 2002). He also claimed he had been directed in the operation by COAS Beg.

Benazir's PPP had attempted to establish a rival Pakistan Democratic Alliance for the election, but this achieved only 45 seats compared to the IJI's 105, allowing the latter to sweep into power. The operation showed not only a core technique used by the ISI to manipulate elections but also a complicity in those activities by civilian politicians, including three-time PM Nawaz Sharif, who was himself later unseated by the next military regime under General Musharraf. In general terms, while electoral malpractices seen in many countries such as the manipulation of ballots and voter lists are not entirely absent from the scene in Pakistan from time to time, the process of electoral manipulation has tended to comprise two main strategies. One is the buying-off of oppositionists prepared to form a loose political alliance, as seen in the 1990 case, while the other is the mobilization of disruptive and crippling protests and sit-ins, which generate a general sense of political crisis for the incumbent regime. Operation Wheel Jam in 1958 was one of the earliest examples of disparate protest groups being brought out onto the streets to create a sense of crisis, on the back of which General Ayub dismissed the government and imposed martial law. In more recent times, "million-men marches" have delivered a similar effect, with one of the most notable examples being the protests and sit-ins orchestrated by Imam Qadri and Imran Khan in 2014, targeted at the third Nawaz Sharif government. (Khan's PTI later prevailed in the 2018 elections.) The manner in which the relatively obscure, Canada-based cleric Qadri was able to so quickly mobilize considerable numbers of people for street mobilization on his return to Pakistan led many to believe that the army and ISI must have been behind the scenes organizing the opposition to Sharif's government. For his part, Qadri vehemently denied such connections to the military establishment (Jillani 2014).

Conclusions

In a curious twist to the 2014 agitations, the army chief, Raheel Sharif, intervened and quickly and efficiently secured a stand-down by the protesting parties. Some observers found this a disturbing intervention by the army in the political situation, representing something of a "soft coup" (Boone 2014a). The intervention perhaps underlined the hybrid nature of the new era, in which the army plays a continued role in politics but one short of direct seizure of power. The fact that the army was able to achieve such a quick resolution of the crisis raised fears of connections and orchestration with the protesting protagonists behind the scenes.

The episode underlined the essential praetorian culture of the army and ISI, which had formerly included direct intervention in the country's governance in the pursuit of national security and the development of national political identity. When specific operations have broken out into the public consciousness, such as the Mehrangate scandal, details are revealed of how the ISI has gone about the process of political manipulation. This reveals an application of standard humint tradecraft, not only in the external intelligence sphere but also in the internal political situation in Pakistan.

Meanwhile, aside from the bread-and-butter activities of establishing intelligence assessments of importance to the leadership, and in managing the internal political situation, the covert action strategy at the center of external operations is the most important of the agency's operational activities. This strategy has, in many ways, represented both the extraordinary capability and achievement of the ISI as an intelligence power but also, arguably, its most controversial and flawed approach to regional geopolitics. It may be that, in continuing to support groups such as LeT and Haqqani Network, Pakistan may have in mind the strategic value to Iran of the Hezbollah organization. While the latter is larger than the LeT, for example, it shares many of its characteristics in terms of being much more than a military force, also encompassing community and ideological activities and capabilities. Hezbollah's significance to Iran's strategic interests in the Gulf region is enormous, as it is to regional allies such as Assad's Syria. On paper, the LeT and other groups such as the Haqqanis have the potential to serve the same purpose for Pakistan, but the miscalculation may be that such groups become semi-independent of the ISI's control and start to cause problems for Pakistan itself.

The notion of "rogue elements" within the ISI who—unbeknownst to the agency's top leadership—pursue a more radical pathway that includes covert sponsorship of radical elements such as Al-Qaeda or indeed the Taliban is hotly debated. This question was never more pertinent than in the aftermath of the discovery of bin Laden within Pakistan, which the ISI leadership continue to maintain was a complete surprise and, indeed, an intelligence failure on their part (Coll 2018, 559). The CIA's assessment is that the strictly covert and compartmented nature of Directorate S within the ISI allows it to undertake operations with radical militant groups in a way that affords plausible deniability among the agency's leadership (Scott-Clark and Levy 2017, 314). Whether this is a conscious strategy or not, the problem is that it seems to land the ISI in hot water in Washington when it has to deny connection with a situation for which evidence of complicity appears strong. There is also the risk that the ISI has over time unleashed monsters that later come back to bite the hand that fed them. It is clear that the war on terror has been a challenging period for Pakistan, in which it has been fighting within its own borders extreme militancy wreaked by organizations, such as the TTP, that are not within the ISI's constellation of strategically useful partners but are uncompromisingly hostile to Islamabad. If this is the price for a strategy of proxy militancy, it poses serious questions for the state and its citizens about whether that strategy is the best way to proceed in the long term.

5

International Partners

In July 2021 Indian media reported that the DG ISI, Lt. Gen. Faiz Hameed, was accompanying Pakistan's foreign minister, Shah Mahmood Qureshi, on an official visit to Beijing (Yousaf 2021). The visit was to discuss deepening defense and security cooperation, including counterterrorism operations, between Pakistan and China. A Foreign Ministry statement declared that the bilateral relationship was one of "unparalleled mutual trust, understanding and commonality of interests" (Yousaf 2021). It was also clearly the case, however, that one of the key agenda points was likely to be a terrorist attack a short while before the visit in which nine Chinese engineers had been killed by a suicide bombing of a bus near a hydropower plant in Khyber Pakhtunkhwa Province. Interestingly, Qureshi later declared that the attack was carried out by Pakistan Taliban (TTP) militants "backed by the Afghan and Indian intelligence agencies" (Sadaqat 2022).

This vignette of international diplomacy is illuminating in a number of ways. First, any large and self-respecting state intelligence service such as the ISI is likely to have a number of bilateral intelligence relationships with regional governments and their equivalent intelligence services, based on a pragmatic liaison over issues of mutual interest, even if the topics of discussion are selective—a point to which we will return. Such relationships will be shaped by an extraordinarily complex interweaving of ideological, regional, practical, and political considerations on both sides, not all of which will always be precisely aligned. In the case of China, an interest in establishing a relationship with Pakistan relates to highly significant economic potential in the region, not least the development of the China–Pakistan Economic Corridor and related neo–Silk Road initiatives that pave the way for regional economic development in such areas as infrastructure and energy. The projects also deliver strategically significant access to the Indian Ocean. At the same time, a political and ideological counterbalancing of the power and development of India within the region will be significant to both sides, as will be a balancing of a potentially overdependent relationship with the United States and its Western allies.

To set against such positive drivers, however, Beijing will be wary of ways in which support of regional jihadist movements could exacerbate the problems with insurgents in China's western Xinjiang Province, and, as demonstrated in the 2021 killing of Chinese engineers in Khyber Pakhtunkhwa Province, of the power of factional militants within Pakistan to disrupt and derail regional economic projects. Qureshi's claim that the 2021 Kohistan bus attack was authored by Afghan and Indian intelligence actors is impossible to verify, and likely to be more political machination than objective truth. At the same time, India (and, to a lesser extent, Afghanistan) will also be strategically motivated by complicating and curtailing the profit obtained by rivals through their alliances with hostile powers. Given that, a process of support for destabilizing militant proxies is an important part of the playbook of intelligence services on all sides of the borders in South Asia. Intelligence on the motivations behind such attacks will be crucial for all concerned and will drive the logic of regional intelligence relationships.

The northwest frontier of India was always an extremely complex and restive place for the British colonialists, and this means that both Pakistan and Afghanistan (between whom the borders are contested and blurry in places) now find themselves in a particularly dangerous and complicated zone on the global map. The zone is one in which major powers have met, clashed, and tried but failed to establish supremacy. As Tim Marshall (2021, xiii) has noted, "Politicians are important, but geography is more so."

To understand how the ISI has operated in such a complex environment since the establishment of the state of Pakistan in 1947, this chapter considers the waxing and waning of a set of international partners with whom the agency has had to work. The story is a multifaceted and complex one shaped by intersecting ideological, economic, and political factors.

Unsurprisingly, the story begins with the British, who initially envisaged the Pakistani intelligence community as being part of a wider regional grouping of Commonwealth partners, united under joint intelligence and counterintelligence boards, with London at the hub of the wheel. However, as revealed in governmental archives, considerable British concerns over "virtually non-existent" security in Pakistan or India led to extreme caution over the level of intelligence sharing, to such an extent that it soon became apparent that the new South Asian countries were considered second-class intelligence partners (Sirrs 2017, 39). The formation of the inter-service and supposedly coordinating ISI was modeled on such a trade in intelligence, and efforts continued into the 1950s to enhance the relationship, as evidenced by visits to London by successive directors of the ISI (41). The fact of the matter, however, was not only that London remained extremely cautious over security but also that Britain was becoming much less important to strategic geopolitics than the United States, particularly in the new Cold War environment. The intelligence relationship with Washington became much more significant from a relatively early stage.

The rise and fall of the relationship between the ISI and the US intelligence community is the most important element of the history of the former's intelligence relationships, and probably the most tumultuous and complicated. In all cases, the relationship has been shaped by the relative power of pragmatic mutual interest, against a fundamental difference in ideology. In many ways, the two states would never normally be destined to be close friends, but circumstances have driven them together on many occasions, despite strong evidence on occasion that the relationship is unpopular among the Pakistani population at large. It is also the case that the closeness of the relationship is usually dictated by external factors, particularly by events across the border in Afghanistan. When the political temperature in Kabul is hot, Pakistan and the United States work closely together.

The significance of this relationship plays partly into the question of China. In some ways, an intelligence relationship with both Washington and Beijing would seem anathema to a realist notion of Cold War (or indeed the "new Cold War" to which Beijing often refers) geopolitical considerations. In other ways, however, intelligence relationships can cover some or all of many regional considerations, and a pragmatic and non-ideological approach to politics can mean a state can work with a partner on some, if not all, issues. It is also the case that the complex multipolar world in which we all live after the collapse of the Soviet Union in 1991 means that political and military relationships can be less binary than they used to be.

Bruce Riedel, the key security adviser to US President Obama, once described Pakistan's security outlook in very telling ways. As a "powerful soft power" within the Muslim world, he noted, not to mention a nuclear power with two hundred million citizens, Pakistan should be a significant player in the diplomatic and intelligence world (cited in Nawaz 2020, 67). The fact that it sits within South Asia, whose strategic significance for the United States is very different from other parts of the world such as the Middle East or Asia-Pacific, however, means that it tends to fall "into a chasm between Iran and India" (Nawaz 2020). But for Pakistan itself, the regional considerations of India, Afghanistan, and indeed China need to be set against the state's role within the wider Muslim world. This means that intelligence relationships with Iran (with whom Pakistan shares a complicated border in Baluchistan) but also with Saudi Arabia and Turkey to some extent (fellow Sunni Muslim powers with strong regional significance) shape the picture of the ISI's international intelligence relationships as well. Indeed, the Pakistani writer Zulfikar Khalid characterized Pakistan's international partnerships as being underpinned by a trilateral picture of China, the United States, and Muslim world powers headed by Saudi Arabia (cited in Fair 2014, 174). This chapter considers case studies of these relationships.

The Logic and Theory of Intelligence Relationships

In many ways, the basic logic of intelligence sharing is clear in a world beset with complex transnational issues such as weapons proliferation, organized crime, and terrorism. Indeed, in some ways such intelligence sharing is a responsibility, as was underlined by the passing of UN Security Council Resolution 2396 in 2017, reminding member states of the need for "timely information sharing, through appropriate channels and arrangements" to disrupt the planning of terrorist attacks (3).

The advent of Al-Qaeda and the subsequent war on terror substantially elevated the importance of the ISI to a range of intelligence agencies across the globe, especially those in the West. By this point, it was recognized that the ISI had developed a considerable humint penetration of the key region of interest in Pakistan's opaque northwest border with Afghanistan, with a huge network of connections among militant organizations and their foot soldiers. Such networks of informants had been directly developed and orchestrated by the ISI since Pakistan's birth, accelerating through the 1980s and the Mujahideen operations against the Soviets. As the erstwhile director general of Britain's MI5 intelligence agency, Eliza Manningham-Buller, noted, the 9/11 attacks marked a watershed following which "the need for enhanced international cooperation to combat the threat from Al-Qaida and its affiliates" was taken as a given (Intelligence and Security Committee 2018, 134).

In the intelligence world, the "Five Eyes" relationship that flowed from shared experiences in World War II, encompassing comprehensive intelligence sharing between the United States, UK, Canada, Australia, and New Zealand, is a unique example of a multilateral intelligence relationship with no real parallels. In some cases, a collection of states will participate in semi-structured multilateral agreements for sharing intelligence. At the tactical level, particular agencies will also sometimes participate in multinational intelligence "hubs" or "fusion centers," usually dealing with specific issues such as regional counter-crime or counterterrorism efforts. Pakistan, for example, has observer status at the Central Asian Regional Information and Coordination Center, which focuses on organized narcotics trafficking across the region, and this may entail a limited degree of intelligence sharing between the ISI and the center's member states on such issues. More significantly, Pakistan was granted full member status of the China-led Shanghai Cooperation Organization in 2017 (whose members also include Russia), having previously been an observer (Ministry of Foreign Affairs 2017). One of the organization's purposes is to provide an intelligence-sharing mechanism between member states, again primarily on such issues as counterterrorism (Fayaz 2019, 96), in which the ISI is the lead coordinating intelligence agency for Pakistan. Beneath all of these more formal relationships, a myriad of bilateral or multilateral intelligence relationships will operate between states with very focused objectives and mechanisms.

Forging a relationship with a partner can often involve a complex web of mutual interests in which intelligence is just one standard currency. Geography is usually crucial in prompting a relationship. The ISI has found itself more recently a factor in what critical analysts in the West are calling "remote warfare" (Knowles and Watson 2018, 1). Here, a fatigue with deadly involvement in "boots on the ground" operations in complex theaters in Asia and Africa has led to an increasing willingness to achieve national security objectives by working through intelligence and military partners already well established in the regions in question. A notion of "capacity-building" is part of the equation, whereby intelligence partners will see more value in investing in the resources and capabilities of agencies such as the ISI in the interests of making them more effective in the longer term than in taking on complex operations in-theater themselves. This, of course, carries with it a number of challenges. These include the potential compromise of sensitive sources or capabilities and pressure at home from human rights lobbies critical of the ethical integrity of agencies such as the ISI. Working with such agencies can be characterized as supping with a long spoon (Richards 2018, 3).

Such relationships may be asymmetric in the sense that the state reaching out to establish the partnership may receive benefits in a different area in return. These might not even be about intelligence capabilities per se but could encompass military aid or other economic investments. A sense of this complex interweaving of policy areas was reflected in the DG ISI and Pakistan foreign minister's Beijing visit in 2021, whereby discussions clearly involved a mixture of closely related economic and security issues. This factor also means that such relationships can work both ways and that threats can be made to "turn off the tap" if there are political or diplomatic problems, as Pakistan, for example, has frequently suggested to the United States (Bokhari et al. 2018).

The utilitarian notion of "mutual shared interests" can be understood in various ways in different parts of the world. For Western countries, national security is fairly clearly defined around broad ideological axes, namely, countering violent extremism and terrorism, promoting human rights, and confronting antidemocratic powers such as China and

Russia. In some cases, as numerous examples demonstrate, the imperatives of one may temporarily trump another, as seen in how the West deals with partners on counterterrorism for whom attitudes toward adherence to human rights or democracy are distinctly ambivalent (Richards 2018, 3).

For many other countries, including Pakistan, if national security is explicitly defined at all, it is generally about a more limited set of objectives in ensuring the territorial integrity of the state, confronting key foes (with India in pole position), and ensuring the survival of the military regime at the center of power. The same grand ideological factors that outwardly drive the West are not explicitly mentioned, and this allows for a more pragmatic, local, and consequentialist approach to intelligence operations and sharing. It also allows for a focus on internal insurrection in such areas as Baluchistan or the Pashtun areas, where developments are perceived to threaten territorial integrity.

This can lead to complex intelligence-sharing relationships with some partners, such as Iran, for example, which is important on certain issues such as stemming cross-border militancy and crime across the shared border in Baluchistan but sharply divergent on other issues, such as support for the Taliban in Afghanistan. Such complex calculations work in both directions: on the issue of developing a nuclear capability, for example, there is evidence that Iran worked with Pakistan once it became clear the latter had become the first Muslim country with a nuclear capability (Traynor 2003). How far the ISI was involved in such connections seems unclear, but it will have given the intelligence relationship a much greater currency at the time on such a sensitive and covert issue. At the same time, intelligence interests in a particular country or region can be defined rather myopically by one party, at odds with the worldview of the other. Buzan (1988, 1) raised the example of "relative security indifference" in the United States' definition of "Southwest Asia" in the latter stages of the Cold War, in which Iran was considered much more important than Pakistan. Such regional security definitions tell us "very little about the pattern of security relations generated among the local states themselves."

As noted, it is also important to consider Pakistan's stuttering progress on defining its core mission as a state and on developing robust democracy in a form that would be understood in the West. Zulfikar Ali Bhutto revealed in his memoirs some interesting thinking about China, for example. Drawing an unfavorable parallel with the Zia military regime that had imprisoned him, Bhutto (1979, 206–7) said, "The Chinese people have been taken to pristine heights by political leadership and through political motivation." Developing the point, he suggested that while the Chinese military is a significant element in central power in Beijing, the effective interplay between it and the Communist Party allows for a more robust and effective polity than was the case in Pakistan. Further parallels were drawn with other military regimes such as Turkey, demonstrating that the notion of an authoritarian regime is not necessarily anathema in a country such as Pakistan. This, in turn, means that the calculations over intelligence partnerships with states such as China will be different from those in Western countries.

At the same time, in considering intelligence partnerships, it is also important to note the warning within the academic discipline of foreign policy analysis that focusing on "actor general" theories, in which states are seen as unitary actors, can be dangerous (Hudson and Vore 1995, 210). As is sometimes said about Russia, "the Kremlin has many towers" (Matthews 2022, 153). Thus, we should not assume that intelligence services, military chiefs, and civilian politicians will always agree on the direction of strategy or on the merits of a particular relationship within any given state. This applies on all sides of a partnership. For the United States and Pakistan in the most recent era of counterterrorism cooperation, Nawaz (2020, 64) notes that the State Department in Washington, which became increasingly uncomfortable about the military and intelligence relationship with Pakistan, was at odds with the CIA and Department of Defense, who were driving the more limited focus on "finishing off the Taliban," for which maintenance of the relationship with Pakistan was crucial. Within the international partnership, therefore, neither actor could be seen as unitary in its views.

A Brief History of the ISI's Intelligence Partnerships

The ISI emerged from a British-conceived model of intelligence structures in the Indian subcontinent, in which tactical military intelligence stood alongside the police-led Intelligence Bureau. Britain had itself discovered through World War II that coordination of assessment across the military services was crucial, as was the interplay between fast-moving tactical assessments and more strategic views of developing conditions in and beyond the immediate region. This had led to the creation of the Joint Intelligence Committee in London as a model, and some thinking that this could be expanded into the Commonwealth through the creation of hub-and-spoke joint intelligence and counterintelligence boards across the realm. We have also seen how the latter element in particular never quite made it off the ground, foundering on a strong sense in London that the security and counterintelligence risks in countries such as India and Pakistan were just too significant to allow for an equitable and broad-based intelligence exchange. In short, the intelligence institutions in the subcontinent was too underdeveloped and too leaky in the British view.

The Cold War, coupled as it was with the unraveling of the British Empire, delivered a changing set of circumstances through which the early ISI developed. The communist threat was probably never a significant one in Pakistan, but the ISI certainly spent some time initially considering the risks and presenting an almost certainly overblown set of assessments to the United States, inviting much-needed investment and assistance (Jalal 1990, 112–13). What was beyond doubt was the favorable geographical position of Pakistan for the United States on the southern fringes of the Soviet Union, and the opportunities this afforded for military and intelligence coordination. The most significant early manifestation of this factor was the establishment in 1959 of a major airbase at Badaber, near Peshawar in the North-West Frontier Province, which the Pakistanis made available to the Americans for a range of activities, including overflight of Soviet territory by the high-altitude U-2 spy planes. In return, the Pakistani Air Force received a squadron of F-104 fighter jets (Fair 2014, 181).

This set the scene for a pattern of major US assistance to the Pakistani military and the ISI, waxing and waning over the years in a tumultuous relationship. There is no doubt that this particular relationship has proved to be the most significant for Pakistan, in terms of numbers, if not the most straightforward. At the same time, bumps in the road in the relationship in the early years led Pakistan to consider developing parallel military and intelligence relationships with China and, to a lesser extent, the Soviet Union (though the latter relationship did not develop very far). Two key drivers for such hedging were headed by the risk of inviting adverse reactions from Moscow through hosting the Americans in Pakistan: a risk underlined when U-2 pilot Maj. Gary Powers was shot down in Russia after setting off from the Badaber airbase in 1960. Further risks became apparent during the Mujahideen operations in Afghanistan in the 1980s, particularly after an attack within Soviet territory in 1987 directed by DG ISI Hamid Gul. On all these occasions, the Soviets made it clear that Pakistan could be at risk of inviting direct attack from Moscow: a threat that underlined the importance to Pakistan of a policy of obfuscation and denial over the exact nature of its connections with the US military on several occasions (Fair 2014, 181).

The second driver for hedging over the partnership with the United States has been the latter's persistent reluctance to take sides between India and Pakistan during disputes and, indeed, to occasionally offer military assistance to both sides. The Sino-Indian conflict of 1962 was a particularly indicative episode. President John F. Kennedy informed General Ayub Khan that the United States was providing military assistance to the Indians in repelling the threat from communist China, but assurances had been sought from Nehru that this military equipment would not be used against Pakistan (Nawaz 2008, 198). Ayub was allegedly furious that he had not been consulted on the aid beforehand. Cannily, Pakistan subsequently managed to secure a further disbursement of two squadrons of F-104 fighter jets under a military assistance package totaling $143 million, driven in part by Kennedy's nervousness about alienating Pakistan (Nawaz 2008, 199). It proved to be something of a false dawn in the relationship, however, as military aid to both India and Pakistan was cut off by the United States during the 1965 war over Kashmir (Fair 2014, 182).

In the meantime, there is some evidence that the Sino-Indian conflict of 1962 also allowed Pakistan to establish a military and intelligence relationship with Beijing, primarily aimed at coordinating militant activities against the shared target of India. In or around 1963, evidence suggests, a "coordinating bureau" was established between the ISI and Chinese intelligence to assist China in arming and organizing anti-India insurgent groups such as the Nagas in India's far northeast (Sirrs 2017, 43). It is not clear how extensive the intelligence relationship was at this time, but it clearly set the scene for a partnership for the ISI that would both enhance strategic operations against India and hedge against fluctuating assistance from the United States.

Regional developments during the 1970s led the ISI to strike further significant intelligence partnerships. A rebellion by Baluchi separatists in 1973, which threatened both southwest Pakistan and southeast Iran and in which antagonistic actors in Iraq and Afghanistan seemed to be playing a disruptive role, led the ISI to develop operational ties with the shah of Iran's Sāzmān-e Ettelā'āt va Amniyat-e Keshvar (State Intelligence and Security Organization, SAVAK) intelligence agency in Tehran. It received help in so doing from the CIA (Kiessling 2016, 33). Operations were successful in the sense that they drove the Marri tribal militants into a long period of exile in Afghanistan, though this only served to bring them under the wing of the KGB and its brutal and much-feared protégé intelligence service in Afghanistan, the Khadamat-e Aetla'at-e Dawlati (State Intelligence Agency, KhAD), with long-term consequences for militant operations in Baluchistan (Kiessling 2016).

It appears that around the same time the covert Afghan Bureau was established within the ISI, not least as the above episode was demonstrating that Afghan president Daoud Khan's Moscow-backed regime represented a major strategic threat to Pakistan, particularly over the manipulation of separatist ethnonationalist forces such as the Pashtuns and Baluchis. By the end of the decade, when Soviet tanks rolled into Kabul to prop up the failing regime, an important new partnership for the ISI emerged with Saudi Arabia. Cultural, political, and economic ties had been important between the two countries, with full diplomatic relations being established in the 1960s and Pakistani pilots being involved in a Saudi military operation against Yemeni insurgents in 1969 (Panda 2019, 4). Saudi Arabia has also frequently bailed out the Pakistani economy, most recently in 2019 with the announcement of a $3 billion package to alleviate a balance of payments crisis (Khan 2018).

When General Zia assumed power in 1978, Saudi Arabia proved to be an important ally for his Islamization agenda, not least as the Saudis' Wahhabi creed fit well with Zia's favored strands of Sunni Islam for Pakistan, in the shape of Deobandism, and the Ahl-e Hadith creed espoused by the Darul Uloom Haqqania. (These represent more fundamentalist strands of Islam when compared to the Barelvi Sunni strand generally favored by many Pakistanis, particularly those in the Indus Valley areas.) The convergence of the Iranian Revolution of 1979 and the Soviet invasion of Afghanistan undoubtedly led Saudi Arabia to develop a more robust and forward-leaning balance-of-power strategy in the region to set against the rise of Shia Iran. It was at this stage that a new intelligence relationship was struck with the ISI, supplementing a previous low-level tactical exchange with the IB on criminal matters (Nawaz 2008, 372). Millions of Saudi riyals flowed into Pakistan to assist with the Mujahideen operations—and, indeed, to invest in fundamentalist madrassas in the frontier region—much of those funds flowing through accounts in the subsequently discredited Bank of Credit and Commerce International and via facilitating agents such as Azzam's MKM.

The ISI has retained intelligence links with both Iran and Saudi Arabia subsequently, though the power contest between the two Gulf states has often placed Pakistan (a country that has a significant Shia Muslim population alongside the majority Sunni community) in a delicate position.

The 9/11 terrorist attacks in the United States and the subsequent launching of the so-called war on terror led many Western countries to expand and enhance their intelligence relationships, especially with Muslim countries. The ISI already had well-developed relations with many of the major Western intelligence services, including Britain's MI6 and domestic counterterrorism intelligence agency MI5, with whom the long historical connections bolstered by the presence of a significant Pakistani community in the UK increased the significance of intelligence partnering. The relationship's importance was underlined when three British Pakistani individuals (within a group of four) undertook a major suicide bombing operation on the London transport network in July 2005, killing fifty-six people and injuring many more, and when a further major operation in 2009 to bomb transatlantic jets by a group of individuals with apparent connections in Pakistan was narrowly averted.

Meanwhile, closer to home, the ISI finds itself at the time of writing with a set of changing intelligence dynamics. Through the most recent conflict in Afghanistan, the intelligence relationship with the United States has been through probably its most difficult and damaging of periods to date, and it remains to be seen how matters can be reset. At one level, the United States is willing and able to step away from Islamabad, but on the other hand, all of the same regional factors in which the relationship was forged are likely to remain for the foreseeable future.

Transnational terrorism sponsored by Islamist groups within and around the region is not likely to disappear; and the reinstallation of the Taliban regime in August 2021 will mean the ISI will remain a highly significant—if problematic—intelligence shop window into the dynamics across its border.

In Afghanistan itself, while there was some degree of tactical interaction between the ISI and the National Directorate of Security in Kabul, the relationship became severely strained as the latter became increasingly convinced the ISI was directly sponsoring many of the militant groups undermining Afghanistan, such as the Haqqani Network and wider Taliban. In the case of the latter, despite DG ISI Pasha's increasingly implausible suggestions that the "Quetta Shura" was a myth (Nawaz 2020, 65), it was obvious that the Taliban's operational headquarters were located in the capital of Baluchistan Province and could not have operated largely unmolested for so long without Pakistan's cover. The former chief of the National Directorate of Security, Amrullah Saleh, once claimed in an interview with Germany's *Der Spiegel* magazine that there were "piles and piles of evidence" of the ISI's supporting militants engaged in the insurgency within Afghanistan. He also said that he had been supplying the ISI with a great deal of information about militant targets but received little in return (Richards 2011, 29). The whole situation has since been upended by the Taliban's takeover in Afghanistan and the presumed disbanding of the former National Directorate of Security. As noted, many of the militants with whom the ISI has a long historical connection, not least the Taliban's interior minister, Sirajuddin Haqqani, are now in positions of power in Kabul. This means there are very likely continuing intelligence connections between the ISI and the Taliban government, but the nature and extent of these connections are not yet clear.

Case Studies

It is interesting to delve deeper into some of the issues surrounding the ISI's intelligence relationships by focusing on various case studies that have emerged at least partially into the open domain. These cases often help to shine a light into the opportunities, and indeed the risks, of intelligence partnering and on the factors that have shaped the ISI's worldview.

The United States: Continuity or New Direction?

Much has been written about the extraordinarily complex intelligence relationship between the United States and Pakistan, and its general downward spiral in the years leading up to the International Security Assistance Force withdrawal from Afghanistan in 2021. Despite the diplomatic anguish of this period, it may be that an opportunity is arising for some form of resetting of the relationship.

During the tumultuous Trump administration in Washington, signs of a new, more hardline approach to the intelligence relationship with Pakistan started to emerge. While, in the words of Joshua White, US NSC adviser to President Obama, an acceptance of "duplicity" was "baked into" institutional understandings of the intelligence relationship with Pakistan, President Trump had changed the traditional tenor of dialogue by tweeting on New Year's Day 2018:

> The United States has foolishly given Pakistan more than 33 billion dollars in aid over the last 15 years, and they have given us nothing but lies & deceit, thinking of our leaders as fools. They give safe haven to the terrorists we hunt in Afghanistan, with little help. No more! (Schmidle 2018)

Whether the US president had woken up that morning with a new and unilateral resolve to change the decades-long nature of the bilateral relationship, an influential paper published shortly before by Husain Haqqani of the Hudson Institute, a former Pakistan ambassador to the United States, and Lisa Curtis of the Heritage Foundation, a former CIA and State Department official, had suggested a similarly tough approach to the situation. Noting that US military aid to Pakistan had declined ever since the bin Laden raid in 2011, when it had reached an annual peak of $3.6 million, Haqqani and Curtis suggested that the Trump administration should hold firm on the Pakistani government's cracking down on *all* militant organizations in its midst, not just the ones Islamabad considers not to be direct threats to itself (Haqqani and Curtis 2017, 3). Such an injunction, it was suggested, should be backed up with various measures, including imposing travel restrictions on selected military and ISI officials, retaining the right to unilaterally conduct drone strikes in Pakistani territory, and stripping Pakistan of its status as a major non-NATO ally, among other sanctions (9–12). At the same time, the report recommended some nuance in the approach, including not yet designating Pakistan officially as a "state sponsor of terrorism," for which some members of Congress had called. Interestingly, the report also suggested working with other intelligence partners of the ISI, such as China and Saudi Arabia, that share some of Washington's concerns and could bring their influence to bear on Islamabad (10, 12).

Subsequently, the Pakistan Study Group of scholars in the United States has published a report proposing a more careful resetting of the relationship. "There is a need to acknowledge that inducements or threats will not result in securing change in Pakistan's strategic direction," the assessment suggested (*Dawn* 2022a). This implies that any change should be very gradual and that Pakistan continues to hold many strategic cards that the United States will not be able to ignore. Reflecting that the "Kremlin has many towers," one US official noted on the question of whether Trump's hardline suggestions would signal a major policy change that "there are many people involved in the policy process. This is a deliberative process" (Schmidle 2018). With a subsequent change of government in the United States to the Democrats under Joe Biden, little appears to have changed in the relationship other than a relative lack of immediate interest in Pakistan following withdrawal from Afghanistan. Indeed, the main issue seems to be concern over Pakistan's relationship with China, with media reports circulating that a dangerous dependency on Beijing will ultimately be disadvantageous to Islamabad (Wintour 2018). From all these developments, we can reasonably assume that little of substance in the difficult intelligence relationship between Pakistan and the United States is likely to change fundamentally, not least because the underlying web of interests and dependencies at the root of the relationship have fundamentally not changed and are unlikely to do so. We can also see that the relationship is seen as much through the lens of other regional considerations, such as the rise of China, as to those relating to Pakistan itself.

The UK: Ethical Complications and Differing Priorities

As with the United States and many other countries, especially those in the West, the UK's main intelligence dialogue with Pakistan currently concerns day-to-day exchanges on terrorist investigations connected to

Pakistan. For UK intelligence agencies, this is a somewhat more frequent dialogue than is the case with many other countries, given the close historical connection with Pakistan and the considerable interplay between communities in both countries.

While the intelligence partnership between MI6/MI5 in the UK and the ISI could probably be considered crucial to the success of many counterterrorism operations, two particular problems bedevil the relationship. The first is the question of human rights abuses and the implication that the ISI frequently presides over the serious mistreatment of certain detainees. For a partner country such as the UK, this brings opprobrium on its intelligence services from human rights groups, which claim that having a formal intelligence relationship with the likes of the ISI is tantamount to being routinely complicit in the use of torture, despite official claims of an ethical and "rules-based" stance.

In 2018 the UK government's parliamentary Intelligence and Security Committee published a long-awaited report into alleged cases of complicity in the mistreatment and non-legal rendition of terrorist suspects in the post-9/11 period (Intelligence and Security Committee 2018), a report resulting from an inquiry first announced by the British PM in 2010 but lamentably late in its production. The report focused on a number of specific cases, notably that of Binyam Mohamed, a British national who was arrested in 2002 and then spent seven years in detention, eventually ending up in Guantanamo Bay. During this period he alleges he was tortured not only in Pakistan (the implication being at the hands of the ISI) but also in Afghanistan and Morocco. It was further alleged that British intelligence officers facilitated his questioning in Pakistan at a time when they must have been able to see he was being tortured and were thus complicit in the mistreatment (Richards 2012b, 776). The cost to the UK was not just reputational but also financial since Mohamed eventually received an out-of-court settlement thought to amount to millions of pounds (Hutchison 2010).

The conclusion to the Intelligence and Security Committee's damning report, which posed some difficult questions for the UK government, albeit more than a decade after the events in question, was that the situation had improved subsequently with the issuing of improved guidance for intelligence officers working with foreign partners on the ground. It also highlighted the fact that much of the problem in the early

2001–2004 period was as much to do with the UK's intelligence relationship with the United States (to whom British intelligence officers felt somewhat subordinate in the white heat of the post-9/11 period) as with its relationship with Pakistan (Intelligence and Security Committee 2018, 117–19).

This is not, of course, to absolve the ISI of any responsibility for mistreatment, numerous other cases of which were coming to light at the time (Cobain 2009). A highly critical report titled "Cruel Britannia," published by the influential NGO Human Rights Watch (2009, 2), claimed that "in Pakistan, torture often follows illegal abductions or 'disappearances' by the ISI, other intelligence services, the military or other security services." Such incidents, it claimed, were "systematic and routine."

The second difficulty in the intelligence relationship between the UK and Pakistan is a relatively common one in intelligence partnerships, namely, the problem of differing intelligence priorities. In particular, the ISI—as with many other intelligence services—has a strong interest in receiving intelligence on dissidents and oppositionists living in exile in London. The UK has less interest in providing such intelligence if those dissidents are not directly involved in any criminal activity in the UK, and, indeed it does not want to set precedents that will compromise the liberty of dissidents on its soil through bowing to pressure from overseas intelligence services. But to keep the flow of counterintelligence of high value from Pakistan, such investigations will inevitably be part of the mix.

One particular case has involved the Karachi-based MQM party, which, as discussed, has proved over the years to be a highly disruptive force, not only in the political picture but also in involvement in racketeering and ethnic-sectarian violence in Pakistan's southern cities. Its founder and erstwhile leader, Altaf Hussain, has spent many years residing in London to escape various criminal charges in Pakistan. The MQM has been indicted by the British authorities in three areas in recent years: once for alleged involvement in the murder on a London street of a dissident activist, Imran Farooq (Bennett-Jones 2013); once for alleged money laundering (*Dawn* 2016d); and most recently, for the remote orchestration of serious political violence, including murder within Pakistan through pronouncements made in London by Altaf Hussain. Bringing a charge on this issue became possible after a change to the UK counterterrorism laws covering the promotion of terrorism. Frustratingly for the Pakistani police and intelligence services, Hussain was acquitted of the latest charges (*ThePrint* 2022), and he and his organization have generally managed to avoid prosecution thus far. For the British, the problem is that the MQM are not a domestic intelligence priority since they pose a limited threat to local security.

Similarly, the ISI's interest in Baluchi insurgents and dissidents living in London is a frequent area of interest in the intelligence exchange but is another case in which interest from the UK's intelligence services will be low, on the grounds that such dissidents are of little consequence to the UK itself. During a visit by the COAS General Raheel Sharif to counterparts in London in 2015, the issue of "UK-based organizations creating security problems in Pakistan was forcefully raised." Specifically, the Hizb ut-Tahrir organization (whose global headquarters are in London) and "Baloch dissidents" were identified as being of particular interest (*Economic Times* 2015). Of particular concern is that the ISI might go further than merely seeking intelligence on such exiles. A British media report in 2021 claimed that several European intelligence services had recently warned exiled Pakistani individuals in their countries to be wary of threats from Pakistan. Of particular concern were Baluchi dissidents, journalists and human rights activists, and individuals connected with a Pashtun nationalist organization called the Pashtun Tahafaz Movement (Baloch and Townsend 2021). The suspicious deaths of two female Baluchi activists in Canada and Sweden suggest that the threat may not be misplaced (*BBC* 2020). Given that the UK has been the scene of dissident murders by Russian intelligence services in recent years, the threat of extrajudicial intimidation and murder is taken very seriously and will complicate intelligence relationships with supposed partners and allies such as the ISI.

China: A Delicate Economic Dance

There is no doubt that China has developed into a significant partnership for Pakistan on all issues, including intelligence exchanges, through a combination of factors. The potential for substantial economic investment into Pakistan, especially on energy and infrastructure projects, looms large in the equation. China has also been a significant strategic hedge against both the "cyclical marriage of convenience" with the United States (Kuszewska and Nitza-Makowska 2021, 235), against whom Beijing is seen as a more dependable and constant ally, and the aspirations of India as a regional hegemon.

We have seen how Pakistan and China worked together from the early days of Pakistan's independence on jointly mobilizing Naga insurgents in India's far northeast. Operations in that region may have become more difficult logistically after the loss of East Pakistan in 1971, but the central principle of intelligence cooperation on covert operations was established (Fair 2014, 16). The nuclear factor has also been an important connection between Islamabad and Beijing. When India unexpectedly tested a nuclear weapon in 1974 at its Pokhran complex, Pakistan became determined to establish its own capability. Zulfikar Ali Bhutto (1979, 21) was already interested in nuclear power but declared that Pakistanis would "eat grass" if they had to, to establish Islamabad's own nuclear bomb. In this endeavor, in which the nuclear scientist A. Q. Khan was tasked with developing an indigenous Pakistani capability, it seems clear that China was a key partner, especially on weaponization technology (Nawaz 2008, 552). With that said, it is not clear how far the ISI was directly involved in or supportive of this endeavor in the early years, with some reports suggesting they flagged concerns about Khan's independent activities on nuclear proliferation in the 1980s (McCalman 2016, 113).

We have also seen how a strategy of promoting militant insurgency as a strategic tool can be a double-edged sword for the promoter. The nature of the ISI's relationship with China in recent years seems to be driven by the need for periodic assurances to Beijing that Pakistan has nothing to do with militant groups such as the East Turkestan Islamic Movement, which has authored a number of terrorist attacks in China. The ISI also feels it needs to give the impression to Beijing that it will assiduously investigate attacks within Pakistan on Chinese personnel and infrastructure. Meanwhile, the ISI's intricate involvement with Afghanistan and with the Taliban has been seen as a strategic asset for China on such issues, for example, as ensuring Afghanistan does not become a base for the training of Uighur Islamist militants (Cornell 2003, 14).

The flagship economic element of the China–Pakistan Economic

Corridor project is the large port facility at Gwadar in Pakistan, which is situated to the west of Karachi on Baluchistan's coast, in which China is the majority shareholder. This provides the maritime terminus for trade and energy links from the central Asian republics of Kazakhstan and Kyrgyzstan down through Xinjiang Province in China and into Pakistan. Similar to the Niger Delta militants in the oil-rich southern region of Nigeria, Baluchi militants see Gwadar as a project from which the local population derives no benefit. The Baluchi Liberation Army has orchestrated a number of serious terrorist attacks in and around the port, such as the attack in 2019 on the Pearl Continental Hotel at the port (Kuszewska and Nitza-Makowska 2021, 236).

In August 2011, at a time when the intelligence relationship between Pakistan and the United States was reaching its nadir following the bin Laden raid, DG ISI Ahmad Shuja Pasha visited Beijing in a "secret" trip that was interpreted by the media as an effort to calm China's fears over Pakistan's training of Islamist militants in China. The visit came after a particularly violent attack in Kashgar, Xinjiang, in which at least fourteen people were killed (Tharoor 2011). It seems that in so doing, Pasha repeated many of the tropes in the relationship, including that China was considered an "all-weather friend" of Pakistan (as opposed to the fair-weather friend in Washington) and that most Pakistanis are sympathetic toward China and would not want to hurt it (Tharoor 2011). To be fair to the ISI chief, there is some evidence from opinion polling that the Pakistani public does hold China in much higher esteem than it does the United States (Kuszewska and Nitza-Makowska 2021, 236), an important factor in both directions for Islamabad's considerations over the relative merits of its political and military relationships. Aside from this, the timing of the DG ISI's trip and the fact that he felt he needed to make it demonstrate the complex interplay and hedging between its relationships with China and the United States: its two most important partners.

What the ISI receives in terms of intelligence in return for its connections with Beijing is shrouded in secrecy. Likely, the main focus will be on intelligence about India, particularly intelligence concerning troop dispositions in and around Kashmir, of which China would have a mutual interest in monitoring.

Partnerships in the Muslim World: Sectarian Machinations

As a fellow Sunni Muslim power with aspirations of forging significant regional soft power status—not to mention as a fellow military regime for much of its existence—Turkey has been one of the Muslim-world partners with whom the ISI has developed links. Reports suggest that the ISI has sought assistance with militant fighters in Kashmir and has been interested in promoting Turkey's diplomatic stance on Kashmir, which is sympathetic to Pakistan's cause (Sharma 2020). Indeed, Indian media suggest the ISI's ties with Turkey have generally deepened in recent times as a hedge against the more traditional Gulf allies of Saudi Arabia and the UAE, which have shown signs of developing stronger diplomatic leanings toward India (*Tribune* 2023).

However, as the bipolar world of the Cold War has moved to a more multipolar world in which regional powers are more significant, intelligence relationships with partners across the Muslim world are colored by a complex web of geopolitical and, indeed, sectarian considerations. Saudi Arabia has been the leading intelligence partner for Pakistan in many ways, given the deep political, economic, cultural, and religious connections between the two states. This includes not only the obvious fact that Saudi Arabia houses the most holy sites in Islam to which all Muslims conduct pilgrimage but also the fact that migrant worker remittances from the Gulf for all South Asian countries, including Pakistan, have tended to be a highly significant element of the economy. At the same time, Pakistan has a significant Shia minority in its population, and, with a long and troublesome shared border in the Baluchistan district, it cannot ignore the need for intelligence relations with Iran.

The problem for the ISI is that the regional power contestation in the Gulf sometimes places Pakistan in a difficult position between Saudi Arabia and Iran. One issue has been the nuclear weapons capability. With the collapse of the Joint Comprehensive Plan of Action on Iran's nuclear aspirations following President Trump's announced withdrawal in 2018 and Tehran's subsequent hardening of its approach on the issue, Pakistan's status as the only Muslim country with a viable nuclear capability could be useful to Saudi Arabia, should it wish to take the step of quickly acquiring its own. The Saudi diplomat Muhammad Khilewi, who defected to the United States in the 1990s, suggested that

Saudi Arabia had been developing illicit relations with both Pakistan and Iraq since the 1970s on the possibility of putting in place an accelerated nuclear capability. Notwithstanding the reliability or otherwise of Khilewi's testimony, some analysts suggest Pakistan would not be keen to fulfill such a role because of the international acrimony it would generate (Panda 2019, 6–7).

In the meantime, incidents such as the 2016 execution of a prominent Shia cleric in Saudi Arabia, Sheikh Nimr al-Nimr, put pressure on Pakistan, which was one of the many places in which angry demonstrations against the execution took place (*BBC* 2016). Unlike other countries with significant Shia populations, such as Bahrain, Lebanon, and Iraq (not to mention Iran, of course), it appears Pakistan chose to stay quiet on the diplomatic front. A similarly delicate situation has arisen over the military action by the Saudi-led Gulf Cooperation Council forces in Yemen since 2014 against the Shia Houthi militant forces. Despite previously supporting Saudi Arabia militarily in Yemen, Pakistan's Parliament initially voted to stay neutral over the conflict, though in more recent times, there is some evidence of a greater willingness to show sympathy with Riyadh in the conflict (*TRT World* 2019). While these are political and diplomatic decisions in part, the military and intelligence interests in the hybrid regime of Pakistan may mean that such considerations will have a larger bearing on strategy than might be the case in more conventionally democratic countries.

During the war on terror, one of Iran's contributions was to temporarily "detain" members of bin Laden's family and close associates in Iranian facilities (*Los Angeles Times* 2009) as a political calculation. (US intelligence appeared to know they were there from an early stage and that some of the attacks by Al-Qaeda in Iraq were being orchestrated from Iran, which led to back-channel negotiations over various potential deals; Scott-Clark and Levy 2017, 205–7). The equation is complicated for Iran, since the anti-Western stance of both Al-Qaeda and the Taliban is not necessarily unattractive in utilitarian terms, despite both organizations being violently antagonistic toward "rejectionist" Shias (especially in the case of Al-Qaeda). However, in the thinly populated and poorly policed region of Baluchistan, which straddles the border between Pakistan and Iran, the presence of a Sunni Islamist Al-Qaeda offshoot called Jaish al-Adl (Army of Justice) has caused considerable tension between

Tehran and Islamabad over the latter's perceived inability (or unwillingness) to curb the group's cross-border activities. In some cases this has amounted to explicit threats by Iran to carry out operations against the group across the border in Pakistani territory (Panda 2019, 9).

Separately, the India factor is inevitably never far away in intelligence discussions about Baluchistan. In March 2016 news emerged that an alleged Indian spy named Kulbhushan Jadhav had been detained by the Pakistani military in Baluchistan after an infiltration across the border from Iran. Jadhav has subsequently been sentenced to death in a Pakistani court and is the subject of a considerable ongoing diplomatic and legal spat between India and Pakistan. Pakistan claimed that Jadhav's arrest was "proof of Indian interference and state-sponsored terrorism" (*Dawn* 2016b).

In the meantime, notwithstanding movements of militants and spies, the porosity of the Baluchistan border is also beneficial for transnational organized crime groups, particularly those moving opium from the poppy fields of southern Afghanistan toward Western or regional markets. Shortly after Jadhav's arrest, the media reported that the Iranian government had formally responded to a request for information about Indian intelligence activities in Iran (Khan 2016). Unsurprisingly, there was no detail about what that response had said, but it was reported that the Iranian ambassador to Pakistan, Mehdi Honardoost, had "stressed the need for strengthening monitoring of the border between the two countries and timely exchange of information" (Khan 2016). Although obviously not too much should be read into such a diplomatic statement, it demonstrates that Iran and Pakistan's unavoidable shared interests in monitoring the Baluchistan region will ensure that intelligence channels are likely to remain open through the difficulties, both in terms of IB intelligence on policing issues such as organized crime and with the ISI in terms of managing the liaison more generally and exchanging intelligence on cross-border terrorism and militancy. The ISI will also remain intensely interested in any signs of Indian intelligence activity in the region.

Conclusions

All major state intelligence agencies with an overseas focus have within their remit the role of coordinating intelligence "liaisons" with equivalent partners in other countries. They also sit within a wider inter-governmental process in which the exchange of key intelligence might supplement—and be balanced against—a broader set of political and economic considerations. In a multipolar world, the nature and range of such relationships is often broader than might be supposed, with tactical intelligence being exchanged with countries on such issues as fighting organized crime or tracking terrorists, when dialogue with the same partners might otherwise be difficult or strictly limited on broader political issues.

The ISI's intelligence relationships are numerous and ever-changing, but key priority relationships can be characterized as falling into a broad trilateral pattern of the United States (and allied Western partners), China, and Muslim-world partners. This disposition of partnerships is shaped by a complex web of strategic considerations and balancing acts that epitomize the challenging region in which Pakistan is situated. At the same time, as with most issues of concern in Pakistan's world-view, the guiding influence of the perpetual contestation with India is a highly significant factor. This was the main driver for the developing intelligence relationship with China in the 1960s, for example, and is likely to remain an extremely significant factor as all the major pow-ers increasingly "pivot" toward the burgeoning Asia-Pacific region (or the "Indo-Pacific" as the UK calls it). It also ensures that intelligence relationships with the likes of Iran remain critical, despite political and tactical differences and clashes across the shared border.

As is the case with the ISI's main operations and capabilities, a large proportion of the interaction with foreign partners is to do with the use of proxy militant forces, in several ways. As the agency with an unpar-alleled knowledge of, and connection with, the complex tapestry of mil-itant groups and factions in and around Afghanistan, the ISI finds itself virtually indispensable to China, the United States, and any number of other countries within and beyond the immediate region. Conversely, the tendency of other regional powers to adopt exactly the same strategy to achieve their strategic aims, whether it be Iran, China in the case of sponsoring rebels such as the Nagas or Maoist Naxalites in India, Af-ghanistan, or—indeed—India, means that a constantly evolving chess game of who is supporting which group in the name of any number of local and regional aims is very much the dominant agenda for the ISI and governs whether and how it interacts with other partners.

Such a covert militant strategy does, of course, represent a double-edged sword and can often complicate as much as enhance relationships. This is perhaps most notably the case in the context of China, and its battle in Xinjiang with the East Turkestan Islamic Movement, which undoubtedly has connections with Islamist militants in and around the border zone between Pakistan and Afghanistan. While the ISI may represent an invaluable intelligence channel on this particular movement, it can also bring accusations of duplicity when it appears to sponsor a wide myriad of interconnecting Islamist groups, in such a way that it is not always clear which group is on whose side. In the relationship with China, this constantly threatens the critically significant and rapidly developing economic relationship with Beijing, which Pakistan can ill afford to compromise. The ISI finds itself in the middle of the situation, with much of its recent activity in China seeming to involve repeated assurances that there is no sponsorship of the East Turkestan Islamic Movement and that attacks on Chinese workers in Pakistan are probably authored by other nefarious actors such as Afghanistan or India.

This factor is the key difficulty at the heart of the strategic relationship with the United States, which represents Pakistan's most important foreign liaison historically in terms of the sheer amount of military aid it has represented. The love-hate relationship between these countries seemed to plumb new depths from 2008 onward, when it increasingly became clear that the ISI was returning to sponsorship of the Taliban while simultaneously helping Washington and its allies to fight the same movement. The Raymond Davis affair and discovery of bin Laden in Pakistan seemed to precipitate a crisis in the relationship rarely before seen to quite the same extent, and President Trump seemed to signal that something radical and potentially terminal was about to happen with the partnership.

Subsequent history has shown, however, that little has changed, and this is for one key reason. Intelligence partnerships are based on utilitarian calculations on both sides about strategic priorities. To differing degrees, there may be questions of ideological alignment on issues such as adherence to human rights, but in most cases the considerations will be consequentialist and tactical ones to do with the ends justifying the means. For the US and other states, the fact that Afghanistan and its surrounding areas are still hubs for a variety of extremist movements, including remnants of Al-Qaeda and the Islamic State–Khorasan Province organizations—a situation exacerbated by the return to power of the avowedly anti-Western Taliban—means the need for a capable and comprehensive intelligence presence on the ground in this difficult region will be paramount for the foreseeable future. The ISI's extremely well-developed intelligence networks in the region, built up over many years of engagement with regional militant actors, will make them an essential and unrivaled intelligence partner without whom the pursuit of strategic national security priorities will be impossible. The picture of intelligence relationships we see currently, therefore, is likely to persist.

6

Cultural Representations

Recent academic work in international relations and intelligence studies has seen a slowly increasing interest in the connection between popular cultural representations and the state's organs of governance and control, including intelligence agencies. Much of this work has focused on the notion of "intelligence culture" in different societies, that is, how the concept of "intelligence" is viewed by society in terms of its aims, performance, and responsibilities. Popular views of intelligence agencies and personnel tend to be situated across a spectrum from the negative (repressive, shadowy, unaccountable) to the positive ("patriotic" and heroic; as epitomized, perhaps, by the fictional character James Bond). How such agencies and their operatives are seen often relates to particular local and regional history and to the manner in which intelligence has played a role in that story. In societies with a repressive and authoritarian past, for example, intelligence may be seen as synonymous with secret police and internal oppression. In societies with a different historical trajectory, the characterization may be more uplifting.

Cultural expression and the consumption of media is, of course, an ever-changing landscape to set against historical developments. To differing degrees in different societies, media has increasingly proliferated beyond controlled and "mediated" services to user-driven content generation in the form of social media and private commentary on internet-based channels such as YouTube. At the same time, the entertainment industry has changed and developed in terms of the subjects considered to be entertaining and the ways in which fictional stories and characters can help us understand and interpret the political environment around us. The mode of delivery is also important in this analysis, considering cinema, television, and internet streaming, not to mention print and other media. In all of these cases, the state is playing an increasingly complex role in terms of how far it can control the message and which messages it wishes to see promulgated. Set against this is the question of how far consumers of media use it to form their opinions.

Louise Pears (2016, 78) describes the "narrative turn" in international relations, in which there has been an increasing interest in analyzing and interpreting popular and mediated narratives for their significance to political opinion-forming. In a sense, security studies has increasingly had to consider the importance of the "everyday," that is, not just the statements political leaders make but the television shows and movies watched or the books and newspapers read (Pears 2016, 76). In the South Asian context, the movie industry is particularly important to this story and is subjected to a particular examination in this chapter.

In intelligence studies, it is interesting to note how states have increasingly recognized the importance of direct engagement with their public in developing a more positive "intelligence culture," particularly in situations where the past has been problematic and negative. Rubén Arcos (2013, 340) raises the interesting example of Spain. Here, a complicated history of authoritarian rule under Gen. Francisco Franco, which ended in 1975, led many to be inherently suspicious of the central notion of "intelligence" within the state, and particularly that undertaken by the national police. As with many Western countries in the aftermath of the 9/11 attacks, a new, centralized, and coordinating intelligence agency was formed for the twenty-first-century era in the shape of the Centro Nacional de Inteligencia in 2002. One of the agency's first actions was to launch a nationwide Intelligence Culture Initiative, which hoped to reset and improve how state intelligence was understood and supported by the population. This included such activities as the sponsoring of university programs in intelligence studies in a form that had not been seen before in Spain.

In many other countries, there has been similar recognition that intelligence chiefs should occasionally come out of the shadows to reassure the public that the activities happening behind closed doors are virtuous and in the interests of the population at large. In the UK, the three main state intelligence agencies were not publicly avowed until the passing of parliamentary acts in 1989 and 1993. In recent years, the heads of all of these services have increasingly been heard commenting in the media on current events, or even appearing at academic events and discussions—a situation that would have been unthinkable just a few years ago.

In Pakistan, it is interesting that the current DG of the ISI, Lt. Gen. Nadeem Ahmed Anjum, appears to be spearheading a new era of openness, which some have described as a "quiet revolution" in intelligence affairs (*Intelligence Online* 2022). Signs of this revolution include appearing in person—allegedly an all-time first for a serving DG ISI (*Dawn* 2022b)—at a news conference, in which he directly addressed questions about the mysterious death of a Pakistani journalist, Arshad Sharif. The DG appeared alongside the chief of the Pakistani military's official public relations office, Inter-Services Public Relations. The press conference, reported as being "explosive and unexpected" (*Dawn* 2022b), could indeed herald a new awareness in the ISI and its army sponsors, in which attempting to positively shape the public narrative about their activities and offering some element of accountability (both of which have been given short shrift historically) may be the new way forward. Anjum underlined at the conference that a decision had been made the previous year for the military and ISI to undertake a more "constitutional role" in political affairs than had been the case previously: a surprising and far-reaching admission (*Dawn* 2022b). The fact that he was speaking so openly about such issues with the media is a potentially very positive development, but, at the same time, it might only signal a public relations counteroffensive on the part of the military establishment. Either way, the relationships between the ISI, the executive, and civil society in the shape of the media and its consumers appear to have taken an interesting new direction. This, in turn, underlines the perceived significance of interactions between these actors in the modern era.

Intelligence Culture

In a volume considering intelligence "outside the Anglosphere," a region that has tended to dominate academic discourse in intelligence studies, Philip Davies and Kristian Gustafson (2013, 287–88) make the case for appropriately applying theories of culture to the business of understanding the intelligence world. First, culture informs how people think and how they might act but does not necessarily determine those thoughts and actions: "Culture tells us less what people will do than how they will go about doing it." When pondering this in relation to the business of intelligence, there are implications both for those working in intelligence roles and for those looking on from the sidelines. In the case of the former, intelligence "is ultimately about managing uncertainty where one must and mitigating it where one can" (288). Interestingly, this applies to all intelligence services, whether they find themselves in authoritarian or liberal-democratic systems. In the case of the message for the onlookers, it is not just about managing uncertainty but being seen to have done so in a reasonably competent way.

At one level, therefore, many of the core considerations are generic. This might include an understanding, as suggested in these various examples, that intelligence services ultimately cannot operate effectively if they do not have the support of large parts of the population. In an authoritarian system, this may not matter immediately, but it will make life increasingly complicated over time, and perhaps more so in the modern era, when the relationship between the state and the media landscape is more complicated than before and more difficult to control. It is also the case that the core function of public relations is for governments to control the message. Driven by influential work in the 1920s, such as that by Edward Bernays (1923), a recognition of the importance of the link between public opinion and the driving of political agendas set the scene for the sciences of communications and PR in the modern age of mass communication.

In Pakistan, it appears that the ISI's creation in 1948 was followed shortly afterward by the establishment of an inter-service PR unit in the shape of the ISPR. Like the ISI, the rank of its chief has risen over the years, becoming either a major general (two stars) or lieutenant general (three stars). (Lt. Gen. Babar Iftikhar was the ISPR chief accompanying ISI DFG Anjum in the aforementioned press conference, while the DG ISPR at the time of writing is the slightly more junior Maj. Gen. Ahmed Sharif Chaudhry.) The seniority of the post, rising from a colonel or brigadier in the early days, reflects its importance to the military establishment, but it also attracts charges of the unit being an overly influential actor within the hybrid regime. In 2016, for example, a high-profile lawyer and chair of the Human Rights Commission in Pakistan, Asma Jahangir, filed a High Court petition in Pakistan for the release of information about radio stations allegedly controlled by the ISPR without the oversight or control of the broadcast regulator (*Daily Pakistan* 2016). The outcome of the petition is not clear; Jahangir died of a heart attack in 2018.

In the meantime, it is clear that the ISPR has always been an important mouthpiece of the military regime, providing supportive narratives for the legitimacy of army power within the state. This has included—as is the case with many governments—having a community of sympathetic newspaper editors. During the military regime of General Yahya Khan in the late 1960s, for example, the ISPR chief, Col. A. R. Siddiqui, noted that the editor of the *Pakistan Times*, one Z. A. Suleri, was not only very supportive of the military regime but "lent it a depth and dimension beyond the dreams of the junta" (cited in Nawaz 2008, 251).

In the contemporary era, the ISPR has clearly understood the importance of using a variety of modern mechanisms for promulgating the narrative. A glance at its website (www.ispr.gov.pk) reveals not only news items about the activities of the armed forces but also patriotic songs, everyday TV dramas about military life such as *Ehd-e Wafa* (Pledge of Allegiance), documentaries about Pakistan, an online TV show called *Pakistan Army Team Spirit*, and even a "shoot 'em up"-style video game called *Glorious Resolve*. In all these cases, the production quality could be described as professional, and the target audiences are clearly a wide spectrum from the academic to the mainstream youth and the aspiring middle class. In this sense, the ISPR clearly understands the importance of the "everyday" in its signaling. The degree to which it aims to control this narrative, however, is a point to which we will return.

War on Terror and Western Narratives

The 9/11 attacks in the United States in 2001 and the political firestorm they prompted in the shape of the so-called war on terror have been subjected to much scrutiny subsequently. While there is debate about how much the attacks actually changed the security picture, given that they were a culmination of developments that had been initiated some years before, there is little doubt that they did deliver significant developments in political myth-making and discourse on all sides of the equation.

For many commentators, such as Francis Fukuyama (1992) and his "End of History" thesis, the mood at the beginning of the 1990s, when the Cold War came to an end, was somewhat triumphalist, in that Western liberal capitalism appeared to have won the day and shown the rest of the world the ideal final destination for political development. During the same period, Huntington's (1993) "Clash of Civilizations" thesis attempted to predict the new global security environment by drawing new "battle lines" between civilizational groupings.

The 9/11 attacks were the largest single terrorist act witnessed in living memory and seemed to call for a similarly epic response. In the UK the prime minister of the time, Tony Blair, spoke about the "calculus of risk" having changed (Peter 2010). For constructivist and critical security scholars such as Barry Buzan (2006, 1101), the 9/11 attacks allowed the United States and its allies such as Britain to elevate their response in the shape of the global war on terror to the existential level of the Cold War, both of which "have been staged as a defense of the West, or western civilization, against those who would seek to destroy it." In the United States, M. S. Hirshberg (1993) described the continuation of the Cold War "patriotic schema," which framed the world in terms of good versus evil, allowing for a continuation of America's historical "duty" to be the vanguard of freedom and democracy.

Much critical analysis has been undertaken of the high-level political discourse following the 9/11 attacks using speech act theory and critical discourse analysis. Richard Jackson (2005), in his extensive critique of the discourse surrounding the global war on terror, picks up on an apparent similarity with the dichotomous principles of the Cold War.

Then, the oppression and lack of democracy in communist states were counterposed against the West's freedom and respect for human rights in defining who was right and who was wrong. Similarly, "terrorists" in the contemporary era are characterized as espousing inverse mirror-image values to those of the West through their barbarism and inhumanity (Jackson 2005, 59).

For Pakistan and its policy of seeing militant groups as strategic tools as well as potential enemies, such a black-and-white schema is problematic and could be said to considerably complicate the relationship with Western powers. The difficulties in the polarizing shift in Western discourse about "terrorists" following the 9/11 attacks manifest themselves at two levels. One is the strain placed on counterterrorism military and intelligence relationships between Western and non-Western countries such as Pakistan, as discussed in the previous chapter. The second is that, in Western societies, community relations have come under increased strain in the contemporary era, and particularly those between majority communities and Muslims. Such delicate inter-community balances were clearly further pressurized post-9/11 by "counterterrorism" and "counter-radicalization" policies in Western countries (many of which have been recast subsequently under the general rubric of Countering Violent Extremism). In these policy areas, Muslim minority communities were seen as "risky" elements within society. An interesting academic literature and set of competing debates have emerged over the "threat within" thesis that has been a central aspect of comparative periods of heightened terrorism risk, in which certain communities are considered both "risky and at risk" (Heath-Kelly 2012, 78) from radicalizers or terrorist recruiters. Such thinking owes much to Paddy Hillyard's (1993) "suspect community" thesis about the way in which the British state supposedly viewed the Irish at the height of the Troubles between 1969 and 1998.

In an interesting empirical study about conceptions among minority communities in the UK and France of terms such as *radicalization*, evidence suggested that many Muslims saw the term as inextricably linked to Islam and to Muslim communities rather than being generally about all forms of extremism. They also saw a disconnect between normative media and government narratives around such issues relating to counterterrorism strategy and their own views and conceptions of the problem as members of a minority Muslim community (O'Loughlin et al. 2011, 153).

In studies of media and culture, there is evidence that not only are portrayals of Muslims generally negative in the Western media but that, in countries where Pakistani communities are present, a similarly negative portrayal of national identity is merged with that of Muslims. In a study of selected US daily print media in the 2001–18 period, for example, Hassan Naseer and Abdul Khan (2020) found a strong preponderance in editorials toward a negative rather than positive portrayal of Pakistan.

There has been much interest in how post-9/11 Western tropes of Muslims and indeed Pakistanis are promulgated in the media and how this is received by different groups of viewers. In one study Khan (2020) found that "Islam on TV is still largely centered around terrorists and oppressed women." Some valiant attempts have been made to shift the balance, such as the US TV comedy *Ramy*, which attempts to show the lighter side of life as a Muslim in the West. But critical opinions suggest such attempts have a long way to go in shifting the normative balance.

One of the most striking examples of the growing significance of popular culture to society and politics was the briefing delivered to the UK Parliament in 2017 by the British Pakistani TV star and rapper Riz Ahmed on the dangers of a lack of diversity on TV fueling radicalization (Stolworthy 2017). In his address, Ahmed warned not only of the dangers of young Muslims in the West being alienated by the way they were being portrayed in popular culture and media but also about the high production values offered by organizations such as ISIS, which had the power to seduce angry young citizens. Interestingly, Ahmed likened the lure of violent action and excitement as akin to wanting to be "the next James Bond" (Stolworthy 2017), thus repeating the trope of intelligence agent as action hero.

Western cultural representations of such issues post-9/11 have inevitably come under much scrutiny. One of the most studied examples is the blockbuster US TV series *Homeland*, a winner of six Emmy awards with a viewership of millions across the globe. Covering eight seasons between 2011 and 2020, *Homeland* focuses on the CIA's fight with Al-Qaeda, centered on the key protagonist, US intelligence agent Carrie Mathison (played by Claire Danes). Given its subject matter, *Homeland* makes frequent reference to the ISI as a tricky and shadowy partner of the United States, perhaps accurately reflecting the increasingly difficult relationship between the two agencies over the period in question.

Once described in the *Washington Post* as "the most bigoted show on television" (Edwards 2017), *Homeland* has attracted its fair share of criticism, especially in the Muslim world. In one unfortunate incident of misunderstanding, some Arabic graffiti used as a backdrop in one episode to add authenticity was found to say, *"Homeland* is racist" (Edwards 2017). Beyond the charges of suggesting that Muslims and Arabs are generally terrorists, the ISI is portrayed throughout the series as a ubiquitous actor to whom all investigations and clues inevitably lead, whether those concern the Western partners in the global war on terror or the Taliban with whom they are fighting (Narasaki 2014). Through a variety of incidents, the fact that the CIA can never completely trust the ISI to be on its side at all times is made very clear, as is the fact that some of the senior ISI officials with whom they are dealing are not necessarily cognizant of everything that is going on within their own agency (as exemplified by the character of the ISI's Colonel Aasar Khan; International Movie Database n.d.).

In many ways, given the Machiavellian strategy developed over many years by the ISI, such portrayals are not necessarily very wide of the mark, and it is interesting that the makers of *Homeland* chose to promulgate them in this way. However, the military establishment in Pakistan does not see it in quite the same manner. In 2014 the government in Islamabad, which was under the third civilian premiership of Nawaz Sharif at the time, formally complained about the US TV show. Notwithstanding *Homeland*'s portraying Pakistan as a "grimy hellhole," Nadeem Hotiana, a Pakistan embassy spokesperson in Washington, complained in an article in the *Washington Post* that "maligning a country that has been a close partner and ally of the US . . . is a disservice not only to the security interests of the US but also to the people of the US" (Denham 2014).

This statement is a revealing one in that it portrays a theme that gathered steam increasingly in Islamabad through the problematic years of the war on terror. In particular, many in Pakistan have felt that the military establishment there has paid a heavy price for operations against militants in the tribal areas but that this has not been accorded sufficient respect by Pakistan's Western partners. By June 2009, for example, it is estimated that more than a thousand military and intelligence officers had been killed in such operations within Pakistan (Fair 2009, 39). In 2014 a major army offensive against militants in North Waziristan, named Operation Zarb-e-Azb (Strike by the Sword of the Prophet) was launched. This marked a significantly more robust approach to the "bad militants" threatening Pakistan itself, such as the TTP, and was dubbed by the ISPR a "war of survival" (Sareen 2014, 3). The operation was precipitated in December 2014 by a major terrorist attack on a military school in Peshawar that killed 141, most of them children. In response, Zarb-e-Azb marked a major shift in strategy toward concerted Pakistani military operations in the tribal areas and is credited with reversing an upward trend in terrorist casualties within Pakistan itself. At the same time, significant numbers of military officers, not to mention local civilians, have laid down their lives in the struggle.

In an article significantly titled "A Tale of a Valiant Army against Terrorism," Khurram Ali Khan wrote about the operation in 2015, in *Hilal*, the magazine of Pakistan's armed forces:

> The perception at global level about Pakistan's alleged double game in the war against terror is now totally eradicated as the operation gave a clear message to the world that Pakistan takes war against terrorism very seriously. The concept of good or bad Taliban does not exist at all. The military has carried out air strikes against every militant faction, whether it is against Pakistan or any other country. There are allegations on Pakistan that it has a soft corner for the Haqqani Network or Afghan Taliban but the reality is different from such allegations. (Khan 2015)

Here we can see a familiar refrain from official circles in Pakistan, that not only are the charges of duplicity that form a central theme in Western analyses of the ISI and military in Pakistan incorrect, but that it is morally dubious to criticize a partner country in such a way when it has sacrificed so many of its own officers and citizens in the struggle. As described, collected evidence pours a degree of cold water on some of the claims, but the counternarrative to the normative post-9/11 assessment of the ISI and its colleagues is very clear in this example.

Bollywood, Hollywood, and Tollywood

At the time of writing, a major new epic movie from the Telugu-speaking region of India in the southern state of Andhra Pradesh, titled

RRR, is making waves and projecting the rising Tollywood movie industry into the mainstream global consciousness. As one of India's highest-ever grossing films at the box office, *RRR* is managing to break unusually into wider, non-Indian audiences, with its spectacular and epic tale of two heroic revolutionaries fighting against the British for independence in the 1920s (Rose 2022). Despite its feel-good effect on audiences around the world, *RRR* has not avoided some degree of critical commentary. As the Indian film critic Sowmya Rajendran has said, "cinema as a medium has become extremely politicised" (BBC 2023a). The "saffronization" of the Indian movie industry since the rise to power of the Bharatiya Janata Party (BJP) in 2014 has led many to see the clear promotion of Hindutva (Hindu nationalism) in more recent movies, exacerbating communal tension with Muslims. *RRR*'s Hindu symbolism in places is probably aimed at the British colonialists, if at anyone, but another recent Indian box-office hit, *The Kashmiri Files*, is much more obvious in its use of an "us versus them" characterization of "suffering" Hindu Pandits as opposed to "barbaric" Kashmiri Muslims. This, coupled with enthusiastic promotion of the film by BJP prime minister Narendra Modi, has raised the temperature (Rajendran 2022) and can lead to serious violence on the streets in mixed neighborhoods.

In a South Asia in which routine access to television has not been a feature of daily life for many citizens, the movie theater has always been a critically important element of cultural life. Furthermore, given the similarity between Hindi and Urdu dialects, Indian films have often been as popular in Pakistan as in India itself. As early as 1949, the cultural commentator Muhammad Hasan Askari (2014) was writing about the connection between the making of movies and the formation of the new state of Pakistan's identity. This reveals that some of the more recent controversies about nationalism, communalism, and film have a long tail. Askari noted that many of the early movies in pre-Partition "Hindustan" reflected a paucity of interest in the role of Muslims within the emergent nation, reflecting their political "stagnation." Other than a few epics about the Moghal princes, such as *Noor-e Islam*, Muslims "began to appear in films increasingly as thugs" (Askari 2014, 177).

Akbar Ahmed's (1992, 289) survey of the Mumbai-based Bollywood industry some years later began by suggesting it was "difficult to distinguish between art and life in South Asian society; they no longer imitate each other but appear to have merged." By this, he suggests that political changes in the region have been reflected in movies—and how those are received—on both sides of the India–Pakistan border. Ahmed suggests that the trauma of the 1971 defeat to Indian forces that saw the dismemberment of Pakistan, for example, led to a shift in Indian cinema from focusing on romantic, apolitical love stories to a more assertive and robust approach, reflecting the anointing of Indira Gandhi as the new hegemonic power in the region (292). By the 1980s, movies were starting to reflect the global trend toward more violent and action-filled stories. Movies such as *Khamosh*, *Hukumat*, and *Karma* characterized the trend (298).

By the end of the period of Ahmed's review, there is a sense of moral panic over the way in which movies had lost their former air of romanticism. "The hero reaches for his *battli* (bottle) at every crisis" Ahmed lamented: "No moral restriction is suggested" (304). More importantly, the post-9/11 period that followed this analysis has seen not only a continuation into Hollywood-style action and violence as central themes in South Asian movies but also an increasing element of political and nationalistic symbolism. A suggestion of Hindu revivalism has been creeping into Indian movies since the rise of the BJP in the 1980s (312). This precipitated a generalized ban on the screening of Indian movies in Pakistan during General Zia's increasingly Islamizing regime, a moratorium that continued into the 1990s (Atif and Shafiq 2019, 166), despite being routinely circumvented. Pakistan's own fledgling movie industry, meanwhile, made little impact outside of the country, apart, perhaps, from a very tongue-in-cheek depiction of author Salman Rushdie as a faintly ridiculous, anti-Muslim, Bond-villain character in the movie *International Gorillay* (International Guerrillas 1990).

The increasing politicization of movies in the contemporary era could be said to be a cause for concern and is attracting much commentary across South Asia. A handful of recent movies typify the situation. In India, the 2015 Bollywood blockbuster *Phantom* (not to be confused with a slightly earlier Cold War thriller of the same name) dramatized the Mumbai terrorist attacks of 2008. The premise of the film is an Indian RAW intelligence officer's mission to hunt down and kill all of those responsible for the attacks, including a key ISI agent. (Perhaps unsurprisingly, the film was banned in Pakistan; Atif and Shafiq 2019,

171). Numerous charges that have been leveled against Pakistan about the actual Mumbai attacks, notably that the LeT group responsible were sponsored and directly coordinated by the ISI (which, as we have seen, has been denied by Islamabad), are taken as givens in *Phantom*.

Whatever the intent of the movie, Atif and Shafiq's detailed analysis of its Hindi script assesses that "Bollywood constructs its own version of discourse that brackets terrorism and Pakistan together." As for the ISI, the suggestion is that it is "more powerful than the Government of Pakistan" for the way in which it can freely orchestrate events within and beyond its borders (Atif and Shafiq 2019, 179). Given the increasingly broad spread of these movies, not only across diaspora communities but into other markets also, the fear is that the fundamentally negative portrayal of Pakistan described earlier is promulgated far and wide. While an angry scene at the Karachi airport in which *Phantom*'s director, Kabir Khan, was confronted by "shoe-wielding" protestors a year after the movie's release was dismissed by the movie's director as a minor event orchestrated by a small number of fanatics (*Dawn* 2016c), the tension exacerbated by such productions should not be underestimated and is often felt on the streets in more serious form.

On the Pakistani side of the border, the release of *Waar* (Strike) two years before *Phantom* marks a very interesting juxtaposition. Hussan's (2020, 179) fascinating comparative analysis of the two movies offers some thoughts on "how we can begin to understand how cultural elements such as cinema can be used to understand the enemy." In particular, the ubiquitous theme of terrorism in the modern era, coupled with a sense that the intelligence agencies on both sides of the border are locked in a perpetual operation to use proxy militants covertly against each other, become the core narrative themes. The perceived interplay between these two movies, released very close to each other on either side of the border, tells us something about the "way in which the two states derive parts of their identity from one another" (180). Thus, the process is not just about entertainment but also about continuing national identity and its construction.

Waar is a modern Hollywood- (or indeed Bollywood)-style action movie, with dialogue in a mixture of English and Urdu, in which an army colonel turned ISI agent (Maj. Mujtaba Rizvi) comes reluctantly out of retirement to undertake an against-all-odds operation to thwart a major terrorist attack within Pakistan. The movie is a far cry from the romantic dance-scene epics of early South Asian cinema and is much more akin to gritty and violent blockbusters about the war on terror period, such as *Zero Dark Thirty* or indeed the *Homeland* TV series. The troubled, compromised, egotistical hero of Mujtaba reflects Tom Cruise or Arnold Schwarzenegger at their most cheesily patriotic, donning aviator sunglasses at opportune moments and issuing pithy one-liners about duty. The style is perhaps surprising for a religious society such as Pakistan, reflecting many of Akbar Ahmed's fears about moral degeneration in South Asian cinema. The dialogue is frequently punctuated with profanity, and the violence is often graphic. Alcohol is frequently consumed, and non-hijab-wearing female intelligence officers are depicted as being as tough and robust—if not more so—as many of their male colleagues.

The style and behavior of Mujtaba in *Waar* says many important things about how the establishment in Pakistan would like the ISI to be portrayed. Much as the Pentagon and the House Un-American Activities Committee have an occasional say in how US movie directors should develop their narratives (Power and Crampton 2006, 194), there are yet unsubstantiated rumors that the ISPR funded the production of *Waar* (Sama 2013).

Various elements in the movie stand out as key themes. First, on the behavior of Mujtaba and his colleagues, there is a clear suggestion that the ends justify the means in contemporary counterterrorism. Torture is often deployed by Mujtaba, frequently resulting in gruesome death. But, "at the end of the day," notes Hussan (2020, 183), "all of these actions culminate in a net benefit for the state and its people." Second, the "guardianship myth" that the army and ISI have developed for themselves over the history of Pakistan manifests itself in the film as a "paternalistic" process, protecting the people from terrorist attack. Hussan (2020, 182) notes that a "clear delineation" is established between the military and democratically elected government, with the former acting entirely independently of the latter, and the civilians undertaking a "subservient" role to Mujtaba and his fellow officers in key decision-making.

The third theme is critical in that it marks a key difference between Pakistan's depiction of the relationship between terrorism and the state and that in Indian movies. In *Phantom*, the LeT is depicted as a violent actor subverting Indian civil society, and the ISI as a rogue agency hell-bent on using such Islamist militant proxies for their own ends. In *Waar*, the point is reiterated that there are good and bad militants and that Pakistan is actually battling bad Islamist "terrorists" as much as anyone else. In a sense, the message is that we are all fighting terrorists, if different ones. This clearly connects with the ISPR's messages described earlier, namely, that Pakistan *is* fighting the terrorists as much as anyone else.

Perhaps more importantly, Mujtaba's frequent monologues in *Waar* about what it means to be a good serviceman reflect an important ideological connection between military service for national security and Islamic faith (Hussan 2020, 184). Within this factor, there is an implied differentiation between the "good" Muslims and the "bad" (the latter epitomized by the terrorists). Similarly, when meeting the leaders of political parties, Mujtaba asks them if they are Muslims ("Mir sahab yeh bataiye, kya aap Musalman hain?") Again, the implication is that he, as an ISI officer, is motivated in his actions by being a good Muslim but that the same cannot necessarily be said with certainty of civilian politicians.

Similarly, the ideological connection between military service and faith says much about what it is to be Pakistani rather than Indian, since this is one of the key factors underpinning the notion of Pakistan in the first place and the reason it split from India. Whether *Waar* was directly financed by the ISPR, therefore, it is certainly a fine example of propagandist cultural expression in promotion of the ISI and its military masters.

Conclusions

It is clear that *Waar* carries a nakedly nationalistic message. To ensure that point is beyond any doubt for viewers, at one stage in the film, the Pakistani national anthem accompanies the heroic driving of a truck laden with explosives by Mujtaba, away from a group of innocent civilians. It is also clearly the case that the messages carried in the movie are ones that the military establishment in Pakistan would like to be promulgated, evidenced by the fact that *Waar* was passed by the Islamabad Censor Board, when many others with similar content depicting alcohol and profanity have not been cleared. In this sense, the movie could reasonably be described as "propagandist" (Hussan 2020, 189).

The close juxtaposition of the release of *Waar* and *Phantom* in Pakistan and India, respectively, sheds much light on the manner in which the popular entertainment industry has become part and parcel of political opinion-forming as well as providing mass entertainment. Both also take their respective external intelligence agencies (ISI and RAW) as avenging angels at the center of the narrative. Significantly, the manner in which this happens and the messages being portrayed are different on each side. In terms of cultural history, the process also shows that big-screen productions have defied early predictions of their death following television and, later, the internet. This certainly seems to be the case in South Asia, where the movie industry is evolving in very interesting ways.

In Indian cinema, there is concern that nationalistic Hindutva messages are increasingly permeating cultural representation at the movie theater, as shown by BJP leader Modi's vigorous promotion of the nakedly us-versus-them film *The Kashmiri Files*. Charges of the PM's interest in promoting communal violence have been angrily rebuffed by the Indian government. A 2023 BBC documentary about Modi's involvement in the 2002 Hindu/Muslim communal riots in Gujarat, where he was chief minister at the time, implied he was instrumental in the worsening of the violence, attracting ire from the government in New Delhi, which pointed out that Modi was exonerated in a High Court judgment in 2012 (*Al Jazeera* 2023). While Pakistan is often criticized for wielding the censor's knife too readily—a point to which we will return—Indian authorities decided to arrest a group of students at the Jamia Milia Islamia University in New Delhi for planning to air the BBC documentary (Sen 2023).

The episode highlights how tense communal relations can be in India and how they can be inflamed by broadcast media and entertainment. Numerous examples exist of communal violence accompanying the release of movies thought to carry inflammatory messages. In 2018, for example, the release of *Padmaavat*, a dramatization of the story of a fourteenth-century Hindu queen, caused serious civil disturbance in Uttar Pradesh and Jammu over its controversial (and almost certainly fictional) depiction of a Muslim lover of the queen (*Voice of America* 2018).

For Pakistan, the military establishment provides a different force at the heart of the state than is the case in India. There is no doubt that the ISPR is clear and organized about the narratives it wishes to portray to society, and that it does so in impressively professional and modern ways. These narratives pick up on the guardianship myth that, as we have seen, has frequently been promoted over the years by the ISI and army establishment. In this, the upholding of national security, using all means necessary, trumps the frailties of a corrupt and incompetent political class. Within this narrative is a complex interweaving of the professionalism of military service with Islamic values, in a way that is fundamentally different from the inherently secular and democratic notion of national identity in India (notwithstanding fears of a rising Hindutva). This also allows for a somewhat tortured dance around the notion of which Islamist forces are good and which are bad. The implication is that organizations such as LeT—despite the denials—are clearly feted by the regime in Islamabad and considered to be strategic assets. Others, such as the TTP, which regularly attacks Pakistani officials and citizens with extreme violence, are clearly not "good" Muslims under this narrative. The ISI and the army, in turn, are engaged in the global struggle against terrorism and should be thanked for so doing, even if their conception of who the enemy is may be at odds with that of partners and neighbors.

The downside, of course, is that the ISPR's professionalism in developing and promulgating the narrative can also be seen as highly oppressive. Pakistan has always had a very vibrant media that is unafraid to cast aspersions on the excesses of the military establishment, often valiantly so, in the face of violent oppression and censorship. In the contemporary era, a general fascination with political life has seen a number of excellent YouTube channels emerge in English, Urdu, and other dialects, in which a critical spotlight is frequently shone on the ISI and its army colleagues. The numerous examples include *Talk SHOCK*, a YouTube channel chaired by leading journalists Azaz Syed and Umar Cheema.

At the same time, the price for going against the official establishment narrative can be high. The TV news channel Geo TV, for example, has faced repeated interest from the military establishment for its unflinching analysis. In 2014 the channel aired an allegation that the ISI had attempted to murder one of its journalists, Hamid Mir, leading to efforts to force the Pakistan Electronic Media Regulatory Authority (PEMRA) to revoke the channel's license: an attempt that appeared to fail in the face of disagreements within the PEMRA board (Boone 2014b).

Geo TV's difficult experiences highlight the complexities of delivering critical commentaries on the ISI and the military establishment of which it is a part, whether those are in news or fictional forms. DG ISI Anjum's efforts to come out of the barracks and personally appear before journalists could mark a historic change in direction. An alternative reading, however, could suggest that the ISI is simply becoming more aware of the importance of promulgating the narrative through contemporary mechanisms of PR and digital media. Either way, the heavy hand of the ISI through Pakistan's history on the development of public messages and representations of national identity and society is one of the most significant and problematic of the agency's legacies.

7

Legacy, Impact, and Future

On July 2010, during a visit to an IT company in Bangalore, British prime minister David Cameron commented publicly on his view of Pakistan's position on terrorism. In his robust and critical message, he said, "We cannot tolerate in any sense the idea that this country [Pakistan] is allowed to look both ways and is able, in any way, to promote the export of terror" (Watt 2010). In the diplomatic storm that followed Cameron's comments, Paul Reynolds (2010) observed drily that "Cameron has invented a new diplomacy—go to one country and criticize another." In the South Asia context, the fact that the prime minister had chosen India as the place in which to make a critical comment of Pakistan made it all the worse diplomatically. Senior Pakistani intelligence officials abruptly canceled a visit to London, and the agenda for a visit shortly afterward by Pakistan's president Asif Ali Zardari was largely hijacked by the issue.

Leaving aside the time and location of Cameron's statement, there was nothing particularly new in the notion that the West had grave reservations about Pakistan's position on terrorism and militancy. In 2006 a leaked report from Britain's Defence Academy, which accused Pakistan's army of indirectly supporting the Taliban through the ISI (BBC 2006a), drew an angry rebuttal from the late president Musharraf. He said that the ISI was "a disciplined force, breaking the back of Al Qaeda" (BBC 2006b), and that he was totally satisfied with their performance in the war on terror. In a 2009 television interview US defense secretary Robert Gates had presaged David Cameron's language by saying of Pakistan that "to a certain extent, they play both sides" by considering the Taliban a "strategic hedge" (Bajoria and Kaplan 2011). In July 2010 the Wikileaks release of US diplomatic cables provided further evidence that the ISI may have been working directly in support of insurgents in Afghanistan, particularly with the Haqqani Network. The US Joint Chiefs of Staff chair, Adm. Mike Mullen, has been quite explicit about the connection. In a parliamentary committee hearing in 2011, he noted that the Haqqani Network had "long enjoyed the support and protection of the Pakistani government and is, in many ways, a strategic arm of Pakistan's Inter-Services Intelligence Agency" (Memmott 2011). Pakistan again rebutted the allegations angrily. In a statement to the press, DG ISI Pasha claimed that his organization has "never paid a penny or provided even a single bullet to the Haqqani network" (*Dawn* 2011e). This claim could be said to be as outrageous as it is implausible.

Professor Shaun Gregory of the Pakistan Security Research Institute at Bradford University has publicly said that the British prime minister was right to criticize Pakistan in the way that he did and, indeed, wrote a letter to the *Times* supporting Cameron's statement. In this letter, he added three other "big lies" that Pakistan has peddled toward the West in recent years, including the suggestion that the nuclear proliferator A. Q. Khan did not enjoy the support of the Pakistani state, that the Afghan Taliban and its leader Mullah Omar Khan did not enjoy safe havens in Pakistan, and that bin Laden was not to be found in Pakistan (Chand 2011). Gregory's mention of the latter point in particular was, of course, somewhat prescient. Such an assessment is hard-hitting, but is it fair and accurate?

In this final chapter, we consider the legacy created by the ISI for the country and the region since its creation shortly after the independence of Pakistan in 1948. In practical terms, the growth in the agency's power and capability has been impressive and causes it to be ranked among the most significant and capable intelligence services in the world. This is particularly so in the development of humint networks and tradecraft and the coordination of proxy militants in covert action. In other respects, however, the journey is far from complete, particularly in the context of democratization and transformation to meet the needs of a modern age of accountability and rights. The ISI's practice of using violent Islamist militants for its strategic interests has not only helped to plunge the region into crisis in many respects but caused misery for millions of citizens. Most puzzling for Pakistan in this equation has been the fact that militant groups sometimes turn against their masters to devastating effect, as has been seen with the "Pakistani Taliban," the TTP. This surely casts some doubt on the merits of the ISI's longer-term strategy.

Domestically, as is the case with many comparative cases considered in this analysis, the legacy on questions of oversight and accountability, on the freedom of the press to publish critical accounts without violent reprisal, and on the rights of many families who have lost loved ones in unaccountable "disappearances" all make for a grim scorecard. Looking to the future, these are the questions on which the ISI has to adapt and find more positive pathways, a process that will be to the benefit of the country and entire region in the longer term. The progress may be slow and stuttering, but there are grounds to consider a more positive future.

Speaking Different Languages

Politically, Pakistan and the West tend to speak in very different languages about strategic objectives in the region. This clearly leads to problems in translation. Indeed, across the South Asia region, political affairs have always tended to be discussed in very realist and Machiavellian ways, in which "hidden hands" and intangible dark forces loom large. In discussing the Caucasus region, Thomas de Waal (2018) laments the manner in which that region is often viewed in the context of the Great Game between competing powers in the region, whereby geopolitical developments are depicted using the analogy of a chess game. Studies of Afghanistan, similarly, often begin with reference to the Great Game, which Loyn (2009, 34) defines as "the imperial struggle for influence across Asia." Such an analogy, argues de Waal (2018), is not necessarily helpful in understanding contemporary realities, and "implies that these countries are not agents and actors in themselves, but that they are spoils to be either won or lost."

Certainly, the imperial legacy in the tribal borderlands between Pakistan and Afghanistan was one in which a strategic model of "arm's reach" governance has been largely continued. The Federally Administered Tribal Areas in Pakistan were an administrative continuation of British policy, underscored by the Frontier Crimes Regulations of 1901. Under this system, local tribal leaders were granted a degree of autonomy and the right to administer tribal law in return for general compliance with the wishes of the central state and a gentleman's agreement that the center's political representatives would not be attacked. The central government was represented by a "political agent" in each tribal "agency" who worked with local tribal elders. The ISI increasingly entered this mix, deriving benefit from loose governance and oversight by developing a complex network of tribal informants and agents across the region.

Created as a buffer against restive tribes in Afghanistan in the late nineteenth century, this system of governance feels anathema in the twenty-first century and contributes to the general feeling that the state of Pakistan is a vague and problematic concept in this particular part of the world. The formal incorporation of Federally Administered Tribal Areas into the settled Khyber Pakhtunkhwa Province under a 2018 constitutional amendment is unlikely to change the deeply entrenched dynamics on the ground for some time to come.

On the question of contemporary Afghanistan, it is fair to say that the normative view is that the Taliban were heavily backed—or even created directly—by the ISI in the early 1990s in order to establish strategic depth to the west of the Durand Line, providing a cooperative ally (sharing Islamic fervor and thus suspicion of India) to which Pakistan could turn in the event of a major conflict to the east. This cooperation could extend to the use of territory for counterattack, and feasibly even the temporary situating of tactical nuclear weapons. Additional impetus was provided for the Taliban operation by the way Afghanistan had descended into chaotic civil war between competing warlords after the Soviet Union's departure in 1989. An effective strategic depth would require some degree of peace and stability, allowing forces to be concentrated elsewhere. (Initial backing by Pakistan of Gulbuddin Hekmatyar's Hezb-e-Islami force did not provide sufficient national influence in the post-Soviet chaos.)

The importance of this theory can be seen in the way Pakistan reacted with agitation to the perceived expansion of Indian interests in

Afghanistan after the initial ousting of the Taliban after 2001. There has clearly been a certain amount of jockeying for position in Afghanistan between India and Pakistan in the contemporary period. Brahma Chellaney from the Centre for Policy Research in New Delhi notes that "India and Pakistan have been vying for influence in Kabul for decades." He further notes that India had pledged the highest figure in aid for reconstruction in Afghanistan following the 2001 invasion by any country not actually engaged militarily in the country, at $850 million up to 2008 (cited in Thottam 2008).

Now, Great Game analogies are still widely used when approaching this part of the world. An article in *The Economist* in July 2010, for example, which looked at the diplomatic aftermath of the Wikileaks cables release on politics in the region, was headed by a cartoon picture of the chief of the Pakistan army and former DG of the ISI, Gen. Ashfaq Kayani, looming over a giant chessboard on which the pieces were small soldiers and militants.

With this said, there is no doubt that the Pakistan military has itself seen regional foreign policy in essentially realist terms, in which dynamic interests and requirements trump cross-cutting rights or principles. Indeed, the fact that the military has been firmly in control of national security strategizing and decision-making since independence in Pakistan, even during the infrequent periods of civilian rule, has meant that a perceived need for "perpetual confrontation" with India, as S. S. Pattanaik (2000, 940) describes it, has defined regional foreign policy. In a number of military conflicts with India, and in the belief that the Indian corollary to the ISI, the RAW, is instigating covert destabilization across Pakistan, a national psyche has developed that sees India determined to see the disintegration of Pakistan. Such fears were clearly inflamed in 1971, when Pakistan was indeed dismembered under Indian military intervention.

In terms of tactics in pursuing the perpetual confrontation, it appears that, during the 1980s and General Zia's rule in Pakistan, a policy of direct military conflict with India was slowly supplanted by a policy of working primarily through proxy militant groups in Kashmir. The Kargil confrontation of 1999 aside, there is no doubt that Pakistan's strategic view toward India has been that a low-level insurgency, backed up by a nuclear deterrent, is the best way to mitigate the asymmetry of the two states' respective military capabilities. As we have seen, a former DG ISI in the mid-1990s, Lt. Gen. Javed Nasir (1999), displayed this strategic mindset in his writings on the "bottomless bucket" logic of militant operations against a larger foe. The effects of sustaining an extended low-level counterinsurgency operation are both physical and psychological: "These operations sap energies and resources with such rapidity that even the strongest economies and the best of soldiers start wilting under it very quickly," wrote Nasir.

If local actors in South Asia view politics in essentially Bismarckian terms, therefore, in which friends and allies are supplanted by interests, the West tends to speak in terms of higher values and aspirations. Returning to Cameron's pronouncement in July 2010, the message was an unequivocal one that supporting terrorism is wrong in every circumstance and cannot be viewed in utilitarian or consequentialist terms. Cameron said,

> It is not right to have any relationship with groups that are promoting terror. Democratic states that want to be part of the developed world cannot do that. The message to Pakistan from the US and UK is very clear on that point. (Watt 2010)

In this way, we can see the "with us or against us" message that George Bush delivered following the 9/11 attacks in the United States. D. Tripathi (2010, 25) concludes that Bush was an avowed idealist, "a captive of his own romantic vision of America." This Wilsonian idealism can also be seen in contemporary British politics in the post–Cold War period, starting with Tony Blair's Chicago speech of 1999, in which he articulated how the notion of "national interest" had changed into a "subtle blend of mutual self-interest and moral purpose in defending the values we cherish" (Global Policy Forum 1999). Indeed, the contemporary national security strategy launched under David Cameron's government defined "national interest" as a need to "stand up for the values our country believes in—the rule of law, democracy, free speech, tolerance and human rights" (HM Government 2010, 9). National Security Secretariat officials in the UK are also not averse to speaking of the "moral dimension" of the work in the new National Security Council (Richards 2012a, 119).

It was this values-based framework of foreign policy that underpinned

Cameron's pronouncement on Pakistan in July 2010, reflecting an avowedly idealist worldview against Pakistan's realist outlook. The problem with this clash of political languages and cultures, however, as Farzana Shaikh (2010) of Chatham House argues, is that it could be seen to reflect a profound hypocrisy on the part of the West. During the 1980s, when the Cold War had set a very realist agenda for world politics, and the Soviet Union had invaded Afghanistan, a policy of working through the ISI to fund and manage the proxy Mujahideen factions was considered entirely appropriate. Now, it seems, when such militants are turning to bite the hand that fed them, the calculations are different. It may also be particularly galling to be lectured on such issues by the "Britishers," as Narendra Modi described them when being interviewed for the aforementioned BBC documentary on accusations of communalism (BBC 2023b).

Of course, this may or may not be a reasonable accusation, but it does not necessarily help with an understanding that the political situation and realities do change over time, as do alliances. It is also the case that, while the West can come and go from the Afghanistan region, Pakistan is stuck there and has to find a permanent strategy for survival and strategic effect. This may lead to a different set of calculations for agencies such as the ISI.

Aside from this issue, political leaders in Pakistan have been expressing a growing feeling that the country has been bearing a heavy burden for its participation in the war on terror, which, in their eyes, makes criticism of Pakistan's approach particularly unwarranted. Indeed, at the time of writing, Pakistan has been hit by yet another major terrorist attack believed to be authored by the TTP, a suicide attack on a mosque inside a security compound in Peshawar, which killed more than one hundred people (CBS 2023). The fact that most of the victims were police officers and that it happened within a high-security complex underlines the narrative that the Pakistani security establishment is facing a direct and lethal challenge from militants within its own borders: this, in essence, is Pakistan's own war on terror.

The outgoing PM and leader of Pakistan Tehrik-e Insaf, Imran Khan, gained much support by being vocal about what he described as "America's war" in the region. He pointed out that thirty-five thousand people (military and civilians) had died in the regional conflict within Pakistan since 2001, which is many times higher than International Security Assistance Force casualties in the region, and that figure hardly suggests that Pakistan is in any way half-hearted about the conflict (Jeffries 2011). In this way, Pakistan faces the classic "proactive response dilemma" (Rosendorff and Sandler 2004), whereby support for the West in the regional conflict has to be set against radicalizing the population in the face of a heavy-handed response to militancy. In a 2015 report of the Pakistan Senate Committee on Foreign Affairs, Khan—then in opposition—was noted suggesting that the issue of US drone strikes in Pakistani territory should be taken to the UN Security Council, a position for which the foreign secretary expressed support (Government of Pakistan 2015, 162).

The discussion occurred during a period in which relations between the United States and Pakistan became severely strained. The downward trajectory worsened sharply when the United States conducted the operation to kill bin Laden in Abbottabad in May 2011. The end of the same year was marked by the accidental bombing of a Pakistan army border post by US fighter jets in Salala, which killed twenty-four Pakistani soldiers (BBC 2011). This incident led to the closure of border crossings for International Security Assistance Force supplies, at some disruption to the operation in Afghanistan.

The US ambassador to Pakistan, Cameron Munter, tried to pour oil on troubled waters by suggesting that "those people who threaten Pakistan and those people who threaten America are the same people" (*Dawn* 2012a). The US secretary of state at the time, Hillary Clinton, also said that the United States and Pakistan had "shared interests" and the "same enemies" (*Dawn* 2012b). The problem may be that not everyone agrees that the two countries have entirely convergent interests in the region. The secretary general of the Pakistan Muslim League–Quaid party in Pakistan, Mushahid Hussain, took a different tack by suggesting that the United States treats Pakistan "like a rainy day girlfriend" (Schmitt 2011), with a fluctuating alignment of interests depending on wider strategic interests. Teresita Schaffer and Howard Schaffer noted that the "hope of a common strategy in Afghanistan is completely unrealistic" and that the goals of the United States and Pakistan "diverge in ways that are too important to sweep under the rug" (Schaffer and Schaffer 2012).

The difference was perhaps partly one of timescales. As noted, the United States and its allies were in the region temporarily, ostensibly to pursue a specific counterterrorist goal revolving around the neutralization of Al-Qaeda. Pakistan, on the other hand, needs stability and strategic depth on its doorstep for the future, and preferably a solution in which India does not play a major part. A particular point of detail on which the United States and Pakistan increasingly disagreed was in confidence over the Karzai regime. There was little love lost between the Afghan president, whom the United States generally favored, and Pakistan, with Karzai increasingly and vocally accusing the ISI of directly supporting the Haqqani Network militants, who attempted to assassinate him at least once, in 2008 (Richards 2011, 29). Indeed, the former chief of Afghanistan's intelligence agency, the National Directorate of Security, Amrullah Saleh, indicated that there were welters of evidence of the ISI supporting Islamist militants within Afghanistan. The question must be asked whether this is the right strategy for the future peace and stability of the region.

The Wider Regional Question

There is no doubt that the area in which there is perhaps the largest divergence of interest—or perhaps more accurately, *attention*—between the West and Pakistan is on the question of Kashmir. For Pakistan, the dispute with India over the status of the province, which erupted at the time of Partition in 1947 and has simmered ever since, has been squarely at the hub of most foreign policy, intelligence, and military objectives. As we have seen, the dispute has been at the center of three military conflicts between the countries (1947, 1965, and 1999), with the fourth major conflict in 1971 inevitably developing an aspect in the region despite its epicenter being in East Pakistan. The most recent of these conflicts included an element of nuclear brinkmanship between the two countries, at least in rhetoric if not in actuality.

We have also seen how the ISI's early evolution was very much connected with the military confrontation in Kashmir, and with an early recognition that both tactical battlefield intelligence and strategic use of proxy militant groups to shape the confrontation with Delhi were not performing as well as they should have been, needing much better direction and coordination. The embarrassing realization in the 1947–48 skirmishes in Kashmir was that the intelligence theory about a widespread popular support for the incoming militants proved to be naive if not dangerously misguided. The querulous excuse from the ISI's longest-serving chief to date, Brig. Riaz Hussain, that the mistakes had been caused through being distracted with too much attention on internal counterespionage requirements, fell on dangerously deaf ears for General Ayub Khan. Far from causing a major rethink of the strategy, however, the experience seemed to make the military establishment in Pakistan more determined to become better at covert warfare and to give the ISI increasingly centralized tools and power in so doing. Riaz had already presided over a strengthening of the ISI's capabilities, aided in part by the perceived regional significance of the agency to the United States in the early days of the Cold War with the Soviet Union. His successor, Maj. Gen. Mohammed Akbar Khan, marked a further shift by becoming the first two-star general to serve as DG ISI.

Akbar had personal experience on the ground attempting to organize militants in the ill-fated 1965 Operation Gibraltar in Kashmir (in which some of the miscalculations of 1947–48 were repeated), and subsequently became a key architect of the brutal suppression of opposition in East Pakistan. By then a mindset at the ISI's heart about the value of covert action using proxy militants was becoming an established part of the strategy. This was not least as the experience of direct military confrontation with the much larger Indian military was clearly proving to be a tall order, even if the "martial mindset" within the Pakistani military establishment fundamentally disrespected the commitment and capabilities of "Hindu" Indian troops.

The ISI-led covert action policy in Kashmir has evolved somewhat over the years in terms of the nature of the proxy force favored, with the largely indigenous Kashmir movement the Jammu and Kashmir Liberation Front increasingly being supplanted through the 1980s and 1990s by groups such as Hizb-ul-Mujahideen (HM, Party of Muslim Fighters), Lashkar-e-Taiba, and Jaish-e-Mohammed. These latter groups contain a preponderance of hardened fighters from other parts of Pakistan, notably the Pashtun tribal areas. From the mid-1980s onward, many of these fighters had guerrilla warfare experience through fighting the Soviets in Afghanistan. They also constituted a more extreme and millenarian

Salafi Islamist worldview than did the earlier militants, which led them to forge an ideological affinity with Al-Qaeda when that movement emerged in the late 1980s. In turn, this prompted such groups to widen their attacks into India itself in the pursuit of a more general conflict with the infidel Hindu. Notable examples included the 2001 terrorist attack on Parliament House in Delhi, which killed twelve and in which Jaish-e-Mohammed was implicated, and the 2008 terrorist attacks in Mumbai, which have been closely linked to an LeT allegedly operating under direct ISI coordination. While the intent of these attacks may have been to send a warning to India that violent influence could be projected beyond Pakistan's borders, the effect was to place millions of citizens under the shadow of war and nuclear attack.

The importance of these strategic developments is central to the difference of opinion between the West and Pakistan on regional foreign policy objectives. On the one hand, there is a strong feeling in Pakistan that the West needs to recognize, as Farzana Shaikh (2010) notes, that resolution of the situation in Afghanistan and militancy in the Pashtun tribal lands must be linked to the wider regional question of Kashmir and to the need to apply pressure on India to come to the negotiating table over the province. "There is no reason why we can talk about Gaza," says Shaikh, "but not Kashmir." The link established here between these two places is telling, as much of what the ISI and military establishment may be attempting to achieve is perhaps similar to Iran's "Lebanese model," which uses proxies such as Hezbollah and Hamas in the Middle East to achieve its aims. In this way, the support of asymmetric warfare in Kashmir by Pakistan is not just about leveling the military playing field with India and neutralizing its influence in the wider region but also about keeping the situation on the international agenda such that it does not become forgotten. P. R. Chari (2005, 216) argues, as do many, that resolution of the Kashmir issue is central to the whole question of South Asia stability, not least as many of the specific items in the tentative dialogue between Pakistan and India on regional security involve the Line of Control in Kashmir.

For the West's part, while there has been some recognition of the fact that the rivalry between Pakistan and India over Kashmir almost completely defines Pakistan's security perspectives in the region (President Obama said that diplomatic progress on the issue was one of his "critical tasks" upon election in 2008; Sappenfield and Mufti 2008), there has been a notable lack of progress on the matter, as the central objectives of tackling Al-Qaeda and related militants in the Pashtun tribal areas occupied the center of attention. It is interesting that the United States' National Security Strategy of 2010 mentioned the need to "continue to work to resolve the Arab-Israeli conflict" and to "strengthen Pakistan's capacity to target violent extremists," but there is no mention of Kashmir in any shape or form as a security objective (Office of the President 2010, 21, 22). Subsequent years have seen a similar lack of attention. The problems arising from this situation are twofold. First, while the West is perceived to be ignoring—or failing to understand—the manner in which Kashmir is linked to wider regional stability in South Asia, Pakistan will see little incentive to cease its policy of support for proxy militants in the province in its dispute with India. Second, continuance of such a policy in Pakistan further embeds the realist security mindset among senior decision-makers in the country, which sees support for, and manipulation of, militant groups as an entirely justified and appropriate mechanism for achieving regional foreign policy objectives. This has fed into the very foundation and essence of groups such as the Taliban, and Pakistan's continued promotion of them as legitimate players in the regional political settlement. It is also a major legacy of the ISI, whose expertise in the coordination of proxy militants for covert warfare has become extremely adept over the years.

Democratization

David Cameron's words that opened this chapter made lofty reference to "democratic states that want to be part of the developed world." In this, we see a key factor of specific importance to Pakistan, namely, its attempt to shake off a long history of military rule since independence, underpinned by an increasingly capable ISI, which has placed Pakistan sharply at odds with its democratic Indian cousin to the east. During his own visit to India a few months after David Cameron's, President Obama called on Indian legislators to help support a fledgling Pakistan that is "stable and prosperous and democratic," rather than to undermine it (Rashid 2010). Indeed, Pakistan's parliamentary debate in 2012 on how to reset foreign policy relations with the United States in Pakistan's favor was as much a story about the rise of parliamentary influence in Pakistan, free from interference by the army, as about relations with the United States. The chair of the Parliamentary Committee on National Security, Senator Mian Riaz Rabbani, noted that, if his report was approved by Parliament, it would be the first time that the Pakistani Parliament had been able to frame foreign policy guidelines (Pakistan Institute of Legislative Development and Transparency 2012).

As the fictional Colonel Mujtaba, the hero at the center of the movie *Waar*, demonstrated, the "guardianship myth" (U. Khan et al. 2021, 376) that grew in Pakistan from an early stage, and which has been actively nurtured by the ISI, traditionally sees civilian politicians as questionable, bit-part players in Pakistan's governance. A professional and "martial race" military establishment, led almost exclusively by male Pashtun and Punjabi officers, and following the codes of professionalism and duty engendered in roots deriving from the British colonial army, has developed into a sense that not only do the ISI and its army colleagues have a responsibility to keep Pakistan on the right path but that they are the only people able to do so with any degree of competence. This is similar to the model in countries such as Turkey, for example, where the army has seen itself as the guardians of the political system (U. Khan et al. 2021, 376). In both cases, but arguably more so in Pakistan, an Islamic element of guardianship has been deftly combined with the martial culture to mark a further difference with secular and democratic India and a leaning toward the Muslim world rather than toward greater South Asia.

Historically, the military has shown that it fundamentally distrusts the civilian government's ability to make sensible decisions on matters of national security. During Benazir Bhutto's tenure as prime minister, S. S. Pattanaik (2000, 957) notes, many senior personnel in the military and intelligence, notably Lt. Gen. Hamid Gul (the DG of the ISI who was eventually removed by Bhutto), believed that Bhutto's family had "real or imagined" direct links with the Indian leadership. Such was the distrust that the ISI covertly recorded a private discussion between Bhutto and Indian prime minister Rajiv Gandhi and played it to her political opposition to win their support before helping to ensure she was deposed (Pattanaik 2000).

On the legal front, the ISI and its compatriot agencies continue to appear to operate with little or no formal legal oversight. As former DG of both the ISI and Military Intelligence Lt. Gen. Asad Durrani described, intelligence agencies "have to use unconventional means. And, to neutralize similar methods by the other side, they will be seriously handicapped if they were to strictly operate under the law" (Pakistan Institute of Legislative Development and Transparency 2007, 9). When civilian government returned to power in Pakistan in 2008, the ruling PPP attempted to reopen dialogue about placing the activities of the intelligence agencies under a proper statutory footing. There was an attempt to place the ISI under the Interior Ministry, but this ordinance was publicly reversed within twenty-four hours (Farooq 2011).

Subsequently, there have been few further attempts at serious institutional and legislative reform of PIC activities, other than statements of intent. The intelligence services are still not on a clear statutory footing, and, while there are senate and cabinet committees on national security, experience suggests they have little power or mandate to ask questions and obtain answers on the activities of the ISI or its sister agencies, the IB and MI. The only nuance to this situation is the holding of formal commissions of inquiry, such as the Abbottabad Commission of 2012, examined earlier in this volume. Where there have been legislative developments, they mostly concern the extension of powers of security agencies in the counterterrorism struggle, such as the Protection of Pakistan Act of 2014, which allowed, among other measures, for speedy "special courts" to handle terrorist cases.

The key problem politically could be said to be a combination of a still very weak and undeveloped democratic political culture in Pakistan with a continued position of power and influence of the military establishment, including the ISI. As Abbas (2008) noted, "Pakistani intelligence outfits have so often proved (especially in the 1990s) that they are stronger than the parliament." Thus, while commissions of inquiry may generate embarrassing publicity on occasion, they do not in themselves effect legislative reform and can be waved away with a "rosy picture" of national security guardianship.

Difficult questions of human rights abuses by Pakistani intelligence agencies, such as the findings of the Commission of Enquiry on Missing Persons (Anjum 2011) and evidence of the severe intimidation of journalists (on which more later), merely reflect the degree to which the Pakistani state sometimes feels it can operate with impunity. While these are serious questions in themselves, they also reflect the essential inefficiency and lack of challenge within the senior military and intelligence decision-making circles in Pakistan, which are likely to contribute to faulty assumptions about enemies and targets.

In June 2011 Pakistani journalist Saleem Shahzad was abducted and his dead body dumped by the roadside near Islamabad. Shahzad claimed to have received death threats from the ISI on at least three occasions in recent years after publishing articles about the agency. His last warning had come after a report critical of the military's handling of the siege at the Mehran naval base (*Dawn* 2011d). Around the same time, another journalist, Najam Sethi, reported that he had been abducted, threatened, and beaten on more than one occasion by ISI officers after he published critical articles, and that torture "was an interrogation technique long favored by Pakistan's police and intelligence agencies" (Waraich 2011).

A 2021 report by the NGO Amnesty International makes for grim reading on the question of media suppression in Pakistan. The Asia director at Human Rights Watch declared in the report that "the frequency and audacity with which journalists are being attacked in Pakistan is appalling." Numerous cases were cited: the television journalist Absar Aam, for example, was shot by an "unidentified assailant" outside his house in April 2020 and was then formally charged by the authorities with sedition and "using derogatory language" about the government on social media. In several recent cases, the authorities have also blocked broadcasts by media outlets considered to be critical of the government. In July 2020 the PEMRA regulator took 24NewsTV off the air indefinitely for alleged "illegal transmission of news and current affair content." Meanwhile, Pakistan languishes in ninth-worst position on the Committee to Protect Journalists' Global Impunity Index, by virtue of having fifteen unsolved murders of journalists on its books and overturning previous judgments such as those of four men convicted of the murder of *Wall Street Journal* reporter Daniel Pearl in 2002 (Committee to Protect Journalists 2020).

The ISI is likely not directly responsible in all of these cases, but it does operate at the vanguard of a hybrid military-bureaucratic system in which the police, military, and security agencies routinely and collectively participate in a generalized culture of violence and oppression of dissent. This appears to have not improved at all at the time of writing, despite Pakistan having emerged into civilian democracy after 2008. To the charge of media suppression and intimidation can be added numerous cases of "disappearances" of individuals considered to be seditious, especially (though not exclusively) in the restive Baluchistan Province. A 2022 report by Amnesty International cites the case of Sammi Baloch, a protestor against forcible disappearances. In February 2021 she and her fellow protestors were tear-gassed while marching in protest in Islamabad. Baloch's father, Deen Baloch, had been abducted in 2009 while on duty as a medical officer in the Khuzdar district. During press conferences about his disappearance, Sammi claimed that "people from intelligence agencies" would take photographs and videos of attendees. In 2019, while a student in the city of Karachi, Sammi Baloch was visited by a man who presented himself as a "military officer." He told her that "if you want to continue your studies and supporting your family then stop the struggle" (Amnesty International 2021, 14). Baloch further claims that she received numerous intimidating phone calls from unknown callers, who pressured her to stop her activism, saying, "If you don't stop, we will do the same [to you] as we did to your father" (15).

The work is almost certainly that of the ISI, and it adds up to a lamentable legacy of intimidation, violence, and arbitrary and unaccountable action against those considered to be dangerous to national security. A culture of national guardianship in which the ends are justified by such means can surely not be a legacy of which the ISI should be especially proud. A US Department of State report on human rights in Pakistan in 2021 noted,

> While military and intelligence services officially report to civilian authorities, they operate independently and without effective civilian oversight. Members of the security forces committed numerous abuses according to domestic and international nongovernmental organizations. (US Department of State 2021, 1)

A subsequent list of "significant human rights issues" makes for very grim reading indeed, and includes extrajudicial killings, forced disappearances, and torture "by the government or its agents," among whom we can credibly include the ISI.

As Peter Gill and Lee Wilson (2013, 163–64) noted in the context of security sector reform in Indonesia, we should be mindful that different states and different systems will not always be directly comparable when considering processes of reform and "democratization." Not only are there as many different pathways toward reform as there are states, but political histories and cultures will vary a great deal. It may not always be appropriate, for example, to apply every aspect of the "liberal individualism of Europe" when considering more collective and communitarian societies in Asia. While this may mean lowering the "margin of appreciation" in some contexts, the risk of conflating some notion of community allegiance to a national ideal can clearly lead to the risk of "obligations of loyalty to a predatory state by authoritarian governments and their allied elites" (Gill and Wilson 2013). In this context, legal and institutional notions of national security, sedition, and even "derogatory language" can take on potentially dangerous connotations and can lead to abuse. This risk may be especially high in a country like Pakistan, where agencies such as the ISI are not only extremely powerful but are not subject to any meaningful controls or processes of oversight.

One of the interesting strands of literature in intelligence studies considers the case of various postcolonial and post-military states, who have been attempting to move from repressive and authoritarian military-led systems of national security and intelligence to more accountable, democratic, and civilian-led environments. Cases include a variety of states, from those in former communist eastern European countries, such as Romania; to Latin American states dominated by authoritarian, right-wing military regimes during the Cold War; and to other postcolonial states in Asia and Africa whose independent life has been hitherto dominated by military coups and martial law. In many cases, strides have been made toward a new environment, but progress has not been without complications and will take a long time to reach fruition.

Measuring the appropriate indicators for democratization of post-authoritarian systems involves a complex interweaving of developments in legislative, institutional, and societal structures. Within the broader picture, the building (or indeed rebuilding) of trust in intelligence services requires the development of a range of measures, from new legislation to processes of oversight, accountability, and open communications, both with parliamentarians and with civil society. All of this takes time and is particularly difficult when dealing with an area of policy in which secrecy is central to successful operations. It can also be a very technical business, especially in elements of intelligence that require sophisticated capabilities. This, in turn, can mean that finding the right people for oversight and scrutiny bodies with the right experience and knowledge can be very challenging, certainly when trying to assemble new structures with no history.

Various post-authoritarian states have made progress against these challenges. On the question of introducing appropriate legislation to place intelligence services and their activities on a statutory footing, countries such as Ghana (the 1996 Security and Intelligence Services Act) and Argentina (the 2001 National Intelligence Law) have shown better progress than Pakistan in this area of development. At the same time, the Ghanaian process of parliamentary oversight and scrutiny of the intelligence services can be weak, and the oversight institutions can be driven by partisan political agendas (Aning et al. 2013, 210–11). In Argentina, meanwhile, a series of corruption and political scandals, such as the "ideological surveillance scandal" in 1993, in which academics and journalists were found to have been illegally monitored for seditious thinking, show that post-authoritarian, nominally democratic administrations can be just as flawed on these issues as their military predecessors if the right controls are not in place (Estévez 2013, 230). In short, a range of complexities relating to the particular political and institutional environment in the state in question can act as considerable barriers to progress (Matei and Bruneau 2011, 607).

In the comparative analysis, notice should also perhaps be taken of the Islamic factor in national security culture. Much as the fall of the Berlin Wall allowed for a wave of post-authoritarian rebuilding in eastern European intelligence policy, the Arab Spring uprisings from 2011 onward appeared to open the door for a complex new wave of democratization in Arab states. In asking the question of how states can be both religious and democratic in essence, Alfred Stepan had talked of the "twin tolerations" needed to make things work: that is, the secular government needed to tolerate the religious leaders, and vice versa (Stepan and Linz 2013, 17). As subsequent history has shown, the Arab world transformations have been complex; sometimes very violent, as the case of Syria attests; and largely unresolved.

As noted several times in this volume, both the ISI and the army's cultural narrative in Pakistan has developed into an amalgam of professional duty toward the people, with a strongly expressed Islamic faith. Indeed, Gen. Qamar Javed Bajwa seemed to encapsulate this thinking by claiming that safeguarding the sovereignty and territorial integrity of Pakistan was the army's "sacred duty" (Syed 2022). Similarly, the Iranian Revolution of 1979 ushered in a new Islamic republic in which the combination of secular government and Shia religious mission are central. But here, the ethnic and political complexities of the country are overlaid with a multiplicity of security and intelligence actors and combine to make the internal security situation very parlous (Wege 2013, 147). It is also the case that Iran's development of the "Lebanese model" of using proxy Islamist militants for strategic effect in the region has effectively made Iran a pariah on the international stage, subject to comprehensive sanctions for sponsoring terrorism. The ISI will also need to consider whether a similar approach to using violent Islamist proxies such as the LeT will eventually lead to much more harm than good for Pakistan, especially if it becomes formally listed as a state sponsor of terrorism, as has been mooted in congressional committee hearings in Washington, DC (US Government Printing Office 2016).

Eduardo Estévez (2013, 230) noted that one of the key positive developments in Argentina's progress toward democratization of intelligence was the appointing of civilian rather than military officials to head up the agencies. This seems a very unlikely development at the time of writing for the ISI in Pakistan, but a recent statement by the retiring COAS of the army, General Bajwa, has caused many to sit up. Speaking at the annual Martyr's Day ceremony in Rawalpindi, Bajwa proclaimed that a decision had been taken the previous year that the army would never again interfere in political affairs in Pakistan, as it was "unconstitutional" (Associated Press of Pakistan 2022). The statement was made about a month after the historic news conference at which DG ISI Anjum appeared alongside the chief of the ISPR and made a similar claim. If this new policy of stepping permanently back into the barracks was genuine, it would be one of the most significant moves toward the democratization of the national security decision-making process in Pakistan's history. The NGO Pakistan Institute of Legislative Development and Transparency, however, is not optimistic about the substance of the shift. It notes that the recent testimony from the leader of the PML party, Moonis Elahi, that General Bajwa had urged his party to vote against the ruling PTI party of Imran Khan in the April 2022 no-confidence vote, postdates the supposed decision made by the army and ISI in February 2021 and suggests that nothing has yet changed (Pakistan Institute of Legislative Development and Transparency 2023). The institute's assessment was that, far from being a momentous year for democratization, 2022 proved to be "depressing."

Conclusions

Despite the Pakistan Institute of Legislative Development and Transparency's assessment that 2022 had been a depressing year for democratization in Pakistan, the announcement that the army was sticking to its constitutional role henceforth and stepping aside from political interference is potentially very significant and a measure to which the military establishment should be rigorously held to account. It is also the case that, as many comparative examples have shown, moving into a post-authoritarian era in which newly democratic cultures and institutions take shape is extremely complex and takes a very long time, especially where the previous history has been diametrically opposed to such an environment. Progress will be slow and probably tortuous, but it will be progress nonetheless.

DG ISI Anjum's appearance at a news conference for the first time in history is also a potentially positive development and should be fostered as the harbinger of a wholly new communications environment. There is perhaps a responsibility for such leaders, particularly those holding such an influential position at the heart of the state as does the DG of the ISI, to drive the change agenda forward.

As noted throughout this volume, the ISI and its military colleagues have always considered civilian politicians to be flawed and incompetent. While this is not necessarily a judgment to be made by the military establishment, it is the case that democratic politics in Pakistan has always been a deeply problematic process, in which corruption, partisanship, elitism, and opportunism have all loomed large. Much needs to change not only with the attitude of the military establishment toward the democratic process but also to the proper democratization of politics in the state. While General Bajwa recently pronounced it unconstitutional for the army to be involved henceforth in domestic politics, he did display a standard defensive posture at the same event about criticism of the military in Pakistan. On the 1971 fall of East Pakistan, for example, in which the ISI and the army played an extremely questionable role about which serious questions concerning human rights abuses have to be asked, Bajwa announced that the defeat to India was a "political" rather than military failure and that it was a "grave injustice" that the army's "exemplary sacrifices" were not properly recognized (Singh 2022). In this way, he volleyed an assessment of past mistakes resolutely back into the court of the politicians.

While the general could perhaps be partially excused for shaping his words to be appropriate for a military audience on Martyr's Day, at the same time, a great deal will need to change with the ISI and army's legacy for substantive progress to be made. To appear unable to display any humility about the mistakes and actions of the past would seem to suggest that a fundamental culture shift is needed for progress to be made. Pakistan may need to consider something akin to South Africa's truth and reconciliation process, or to Argentina's post–"dirty war" mantra of *nunca más* (never again). The culture of suppression of critical media commentary, not to mention a culture of torture, disappearance, and extrajudicial execution of those considered to be seditious, is a grave mark on Pakistan's and the ISI's scorecards, and the situation currently appears to be a long way away from where it needs to be. Again, enlightened leadership might help to improve the situation, building on the creditable professionalism and commitment that many in the ISI have shown to their cause over the years.

Appendix: Further Reading

General Sources on the ISI

The two most definitive books hitherto on the history, structure, and operations of the ISI are probably Hein Kiessling's *Faith, Unity, Discipline* (2016) and Owen Sirrs's *Pakistan's Inter-Services Intelligence Directorate* (2017). Other chapters and scholarly articles specifically dealing with the ISI include those by Gregory (2007a), Johnson (2009), and Richards (2015).

The Army and Political Development in Pakistan

It is difficult to consider the history and development of the ISI without simultaneously considering those of the army in Pakistan. To that end, the books by Christine Fair (*Fighting to the End*, 2014) and Aqil Shah (*The Army and Democracy*, 2014) are invaluable. Shuja Nawaz's two immaculately researched volumes (*Crossed Swords*, 2008, and *The Battle for Pakistan*, 2020) are similarly essential readings on the subject. For the earlier period, from pre-independence to the end of the 1980s, Ayesha Jalal's *State of Martial Rule* (1990) is an excellent account.

Memoirs by Key Military and Intelligence Figures

General Ayub Khan's diaries (Baxter 2007) and his own autobiography, *Friends Not Masters* (1967), make for essential reading on Pakistan's early years and on the emergence of the military establishment at the heart of power. The book written in prison by Zulfikar Ali Bhutto while contesting his impeachment, *If I Am Assassinated* (1979), is also a compelling source on the military and intelligence history at this key stage of Pakistan's development. The account of the ISI's Afghan Bureau chief, Mohammad Yousaf (*Afghanistan*, 2001), is probably the most comprehensive and significant account of the Mujahideen operations in the 1980s, albeit a selectively rendered one that inevitably champions the ISI's role. Meanwhile, in the 1990s, the controversial *Spy Chronicles* (Dulat et al. 2018), coauthored by former ISI DG Asad Durrani and former RAW chief, A. S. Dulat, makes for interesting reading on the period, if perhaps revealing rather less of substance than initially promised.

Kashmir

Victoria Schofield's *Kashmir in Conflict* (2003) offers a comprehensive historical analysis of this most important of regions to Pakistan's security history, including the myriad militant groups central to the conflict in the region. For a detailed account of the 1947–48 conflict, Lt. Gen. L. P. Sen's *Slender Was the Thread* (1994) is a compelling read, taking the perspective of the Indian army.

Afghanistan and the War on Terror

The list of the most useful and comprehensive sources on the war on terror period (about which many books have been written) is probably headed by Steve Coll's two epic volumes, *Ghost Wars* (2005), which deals with the conditions in which Al-Qaeda emerged in Afghanistan, and *Directorate S* (2018), which examines the ISI's central role in the coordination of counterterrorism activity in the region subsequently. Among the countless other accounts of the period, Cathy Scott-Clark and Adrian Levy's *The Exile* (2017), which dissects the flight of the Al-Qaeda leadership after 9/11 and the long road to bin Laden's death, is a fascinating and revealing source. On the history of conflict Afghanistan in general, Peter Tomsen's epic *The Wars of Afghanistan* (2011) is highly recommended.

Comparative Intelligence Case Histories

As with the war on terror, intelligence studies has been a burgeoning subject in the contemporary era. Much of the output has concerned the histories of Western and Soviet intelligence agencies, but the edited volumes by Philip Davies and Kristian Gustafson (2013) and Paul Maddrell (2015) offer an excellent set of comparative intelligence case studies dealing with a range of countries outside of the traditional Cold War context.

References

Abbas, Hassan. 2006. "Inside Story of Musharraf-Mahmood Tussle." Belfer Center for Science and International Affairs, September 26, 2006. https://www.belfercen ter.org/publication/inside-story-musharraf-mahmood-tussle.

———. 2008. "Reform of Pakistan's Intelligence Services." *Analysis and Opinions*, March 15, 2008. https://www.belfercenter.org/publication/reform-pakistans-intelli gence-services.

Abbasi, Ansar. 2020. "Ex-DG ISI Zaheerul Islam Says He Never Sought Resignation from Nawaz Sharif." *The News*, October 15, 2020.

Abbottabad Commission. 2013. "Bin Laden Dossier." https://s3.documentcloud.org /documents/724833/aljazeera-bin-laden-dossier.pdf.

Afzal, Madiha. 2020. "Evaluating the Trump Administration's Pakistan Reset." Brookings Institute, February 20, 2020. https://www.brookings.edu/blog/order -from-chaos/2020/10/26/evaluating-the-trump-administrations-pakistan-reset/.

Ahmad, Manzoor, Zahir Shah, and Jehangir Khan. 2014. "Pakistan-Iran Relationship in the Context of Regional and International Challenges (2001–2013)." *International Journal of Academic Research in Business and Social Sciences* 4: 404–19.

Ahmed, Akbar S. 1992. "Bombay Films: The Cinema as Metaphor for Indian Society and Politics." *Modern Asian Studies* 26: 289–320.

Ahmed, Gulzar. 1967. *Pakistan Meets Indian Challenge*. Rawalpindi: Al Mukhtar.

Al Jazeera. 2023. "India Says BBC Film on Modi's Role in Gujarat Riots 'Propa-ganda.'" January 19, 2023. https://www.aljazeera.com/news/2023/1/19/india-slams -bbc-film-on-role-of-indias-modi-in-gujarat-riots.

Ali, C. M. 1967. *The Emergence of Pakistan*. New York: Columbia University Press.

Amnesty International. 2021. "Pakistan: Escalating Attacks on Journalists." Press Re-lease, June 3, 2021. https://www.amnesty.org/en/latest/press-release/2021/06/paki stan-escalating-attacks-on-journalists/.

ANI. 2022. "Pakistan President Meets Imran Khan Hours after PM Shehbaz Picks Army Chief." November 24, 2020. https://www.aninews.in/news/world/asia/pakis

tan-president-meets-imran-khan-hours-after-pm-shehbaz-picks-army-chief20221
124173422/.

Aning, Emmanuel Kwesi, Emma Birikorang, and Ernest Ansah Lartey. 2013. "The Processes and Mechanisms of Developing a Democratic Intelligence Culture in Ghana." In *Intelligence Elsewhere: Spies and Espionage Outside the Anglosphere.* Edited by Philip H. J. Davies and Kristian C. Gustafson. Washington, DC: Georgetown University Press.

Anjum, Shakeel. 2011. "Missing Persons Report Submitted to Govt." *GeoNews*, January 14, 2011.

Arcos, Rubén. 2013. "Academics as Strategic Stakeholders of Intelligence Organizations: A View from Spain." *International Journal of Intelligence and Counterintelligence* 26: 332–46.

Askari, Muhammad Hasan. 2014. "Building Pakistan and Filmmaking." *Bioscope* 5: 175–81.

Associated Press of Pakistan. 2022. "General Bajwa Reaffirms Army's Apolitical Role in Farewell Address at Defence and Martyrs Day Ceremony." November 23, 2022. https://www.app.com.pk/national/general-bajwa-reaffirms-armys-apolitical -role-in-farewell-address-at-defence-martyrs-day-ceremony/.

Atif, Kashan, and Zubair Shafiq. 2019. "Discourse on Terrorism: Image of Pakistan in Bollywood Film *Phantom*." *Pakistan Journal of History and Culture* 40, no. 2: 163–80.

Azeem, Munawar. 2006. "ISI Takes Note of FIA Staff's Malpractice: Illegal Travellers." *Dawn*, September 15, 2006. https://www.dawn.com/news/210479/isi-takes -note-of-fia-staff-s-malpractice-illegal-travellers.

Aziz, Shaikh. 2016. "The Ojhri Camp Disaster: Who's to Blame?" *Dawn*, February 7, 2016. https://www.dawn.com/news/1237794.

Bajoria, J., and E. Kaplan. 2011. "The ISI and Terrorism: Behind the Accusations." Council on Foreign Relations, May 4, 2011. http://www.cfr.org /pakistan/isi-terrorism-behind-accusations/p11644.

Bakhtiar, Idrees, and Zaffar Abbas. 2018. "The Mysterious Case of Operation Midnight Jackal." *Herald*, November 19, 2018.

Ball, Desmond. 1996. *Signals Intelligence (SIGINT) in South Asia: India, Pakistan, Sri Lanka (Ceylon)*. Papers on Strategy and Defence 117. Canberra: Australian National University.

Baloch, Kiyya, and Mark Townsend. 2021. "Dissident Pakistani Exiles in UK 'on Hit List.'" *The Guardian*, August 7, 2021.

Baxter, C. 2007. *Diaries of Field Marshal Mohammad Ayub Khan, 1966–1972*. Karachi: Oxford University Press.

BBC. 2006a. "Newsnight: Key Quotes from the Document, on the War on Terror." September 28, 2006. http://news.bbc.co.uk/1/hi/programmes/newsnight/5388426 .stm.

———. 2006b. "Musharraf Defends His Spy Service." September 28, 2006.

———. 2011. "Pakistan Outrage after 'NATO Attack Kills Soldiers.'" November 26, 2011. https://www.bbc.co.uk/news/world-asia-15901363.

———. 2016. "Sheikh Nimr al-Nimr: Anger at Execution of Top Shia Cleric." January 2, 2016. https://www.bbc.co.uk/news/world-middle-east-35214536.

———. 2020. "Karima Baloch: Pakistani Rights Activist Found Dead in Toronto." December 22, 2020.

———. 2023a. "Oscar Nominee 'RRR': Why the Indian Action Spectacle Is Charming the West." January 24, 2023. https://www.bbc.co.uk/news/world-asia india-64286680.

———. 2023b. "The Modi Question." January 2023. https://www.bbc.co.uk/pro grammes/p0dk9z6x.

Bennett-Jones, Owen. 2013. "Altaf Hussain, the Notorious MQM Leader Who Swapped Pakistan for London." *The Guardian*, July 29, 2013.

Bernays, Edward. 1923. *Crystallizing Public Opinion*. New York: Boni and Liveright.

Bezhan, Faridullah. 2014. "The Pashtunistan Issue and Politics in Afghanistan, 1957–1952." *Middle East Journal* 68, no. 2: 197–209.

Bhutto, Zulfikar Ali. 1965. "Speech Delivered at the UN Security Council on September 22, 1965, on Kashmir Issue." https://bhutto.org/index.php/speeches/speeches -from-1948-1965/speech-delivered-at-the-un-security-council-on-september-22 -1965-on-kashmir-issue/.

———. 1979. *If I Am Assassinated*. New Delhi: Vikas.

Bokhari, Farhan, Katrina Manson, and Kiran Stacey. 2018. "Pakistan Halts Intelligence-Sharing with US after Aid Suspension." *Financial Times*, January 11, 2018. https://www.ft.com/content/59969778-f6b1-11e7-88f7-5465a6ce1a00.

Boone, Jon. 2012. "Former ISI Chief Says Army Money Used to Influence 1990 Pakistan Election." *The Guardian*, March 9, 2012. https://www.theguardian.com /world/2012/mar/09/former-isi-chief-1990-pakistan-election.

———. 2014a. "Pakistan 'Soft Coup' Fears as Army Chief Holds Talks with Protest Leaders." *The Guardian*, August 29, 2014. https://www.theguardian.com/world /2014/aug/29/pakistan-army-chief-talks-khan-qadri.

———. 2014b. "Bid to Take Pakistan's Geo TV Off the Air Fails." *The Guardian*, May 20, 2014.

Brogden, Mike. 2004. "Commentary: Community Policing, a Panacea from the West." *African Affairs* 103, no. 413: 635–49.

Bruneau, T. C., F. C. Matei, and S. Sakoda. 2009. "National Security Councils: Their Potential Functions in Democratic Civil-Military Relations." *Defense and Security Analysis* 25, no. 3: 255–69.

Burke, S. M. 1972. "India's Offer of a No-War Declaration to Pakistan: Its History and Import." *Pakistan Horizon* 25, no. 3: 23–37.

Burki, Shahid Javed. 1988. "Pakistan under Zia, 1977–1988." *Asian Survey* 28, no. 10: 1082–1100.

Business Recorder. 2018. "A Joint Venture of Spooks." June 3, 2018.

Buzan, Barry. 1988. "The Southeast Asian Security Complex." *Contemporary Southeast Asia* 10: 1–16.

———. 2006. "Will the 'Global War on Terrorism' Be the New Cold War?" *International Affairs* 82, no. 6: 1101–18.

CBS. 2023. "Pakistan Bombing: Death Toll in Suicide Attack on Mosque Hits 100 as Officials Blame 'Security Lapse.'" January 31, 2023.

Census of India. 1951. Vol. 1, Part II-A, Table D-IV. New Delhi.

Census of Pakistan. 1961. Vol. 3 (West Pakistan), Table 9, II: 302–5. Karachi.

Chand, K. 2011. "A Battle Won Does Not Mean the War Is Over." *Tribune Magazine*, May 17, 2011. http://www.tribunemagazine.co.uk/2011/05/a-battle-won-does-not -mean-the-war-is-over/.

Chari, P. R. 2005. "Strategic Stability in South Asia: The Role of Confidence-Building and Threat-Reduction Measures." *Contemporary South Asia* 14, no. 2: 211–17.

Chengappa, Bidanda M. 2000. "The ISI Role in Pakistan's Politics." *Strategic Analysis* 23, no. 11: 1857–78.

Clarke, Ryan. 2010. "Lashkar-i-Taiba: The Fallacy of Subservient Proxies and the Future of Islamist Terrorism in India." Strategic Studies Institute, *The Letort Papers*, i–108.

Cobain, Ian. 2009. "Torture at Hands of Pakistan Secret Services." *The Guardian*, February 6, 2009. https://www.theguardian.com/world/2009/feb/06/torture-pakistan-mi5-imran.

Cohen, Stephen Philip. 2002. "The Nation and the State of Pakistan." *Washington Quarterly* 25, no. 3: 109–22.

Coll, Steve. 2005. *Ghost Wars: The Secret History of the CIA, Afghanistan and Bin Laden, from the Soviet Invasion to September 10, 2001.* London: Penguin.

———. 2018. *Directorate S: The C.I.A. and America's Secret Wars in Afghanistan and Pakistan, 2001–2016.* London: Penguin.

Committee to Protect Journalists. 2020. "Getting Away with Murder." October 28, 2020. https://cpj.org/reports/2020/10/global-impunity-index-journalist-murders/.

Cornell, Svante E. 2003. "Regional Politics in Central Asia: The Changing Roles of Iran, Turkey, Pakistan and China." New Delhi: SAPRA Foundation. https://isdp.eu/content/uploads/images/stories/isdp-main-pdf/2004_cornell_regional-politics-in-central-asia.pdf.

Cowasjee, Ardeshir. 2002. "We Never Learn from History." *Arab News*, August 14, 2002. https://www.arabnews.com/node/223354.

Daily Pakistan. 2016. "How Many Radio Stations, Journalists Work for You? Asma Jahangir Asks ISPR." July 20, 2016. https://en.dailypakistan.com.pk/20-Jul-2016/how-many-radio-stations-journalists-work-for-you-asma-jahangir-asks-ispr.

Davies, Philip H. J., and Kristian C. Gustafson, eds. 2013. *Intelligence Elsewhere: Spies and Espionage outside the Anglosphere.* Washington, DC: Georgetown University Press.

Davis, K. 1951. *The Population of India and Pakistan.* Princeton, NJ: Princeton University Press.

Dawn. 2009a. "Proof of India's Involvement in Militancy Found." November 2, 2009. http://www.dawn.com/wps/wcm/connect/dawn-content-library/dawn/news/pakistan/13+proof+of+indian+hand+south+waziristan+army-za-02.

———. 2009b. "India behind Most Terrorist Attacks, Says Malik." October 21, 2009. http://www.dawn.com/wps/wcm/connect/dawn-content-library/dawn/news/pakistan/13+we+are+aware+of+indian+involvement+in+balochistan-za-02.

———. 2011a. "Deactivating ISI's Political Wing." May 24, 2011. http://www.dawn.com/2011/05/24/2008-deactivating-isis-political-wing.html.

———. 2011b. "Counter-Terrorism Authority Dormant." May 25, 2011. http://www.dawn.com/2011/05/25/counter-terrorism-authority-dormant.html.

———. 2011c. "US-Pakistan Intelligence Operations Frozen: Official." April 10, 2011. http://www.dawn.com/2011/04/10/us-pakistan-intelligence-operations-frozen-official.html.

———. 2011d. "APNS President Rejects ISI Charge." June 2, 2011. http://www.dawn.com/2011/06/03/apns-president-rejects-isi-charge.html.

————. 2011e. "Pakistan Never Backed Haqqani Network: ISI Chief." September 30, 2011. http://www.dawn.com/2011/09/30/pakistan-never-backed-haqqani-network-isi-chief.html.

————. 2012a. "Munter to Reply 'Openly and Honestly.'" March 21, 2012. http://www.dawn.com/2012/03/21/munter-to-reply-openly-and-honestly.html.

————. 2012b. "US, Pakistan Have Shared Anti-terror Interest: Clinton." March 22, 2012. http://www.dawn.com/2012/03/21/us-pakistan-have-shared-anti-terror-interest-clinton.html.

————. 2013. "Hafiz Saeed Leads Mass Rally in Islamabad." September 7, 2013.

————. 2016a. "Lt Gen Naveed Mukhtar Appointed as DG ISI." December 11, 2016. https://www.dawn.com/news/1301868.

————. 2016b. "Dossier on Indian Interference Finalised." December 31, 2016.

————. 2016c. "Protestors Surround 'Phantom' Director Kabir Khan at Karachi Airport." April 27, 2016. https://www.dawn.com/news/1254738.

————. 2016d. "Scotland Yard Drops Money Laundering Investigation against Altaf Hussain." October 13, 2016.

————. 2022a. "US Cannot Walk Away from Pakistan: Report." October 5, 2022. https://www.dawn.com/news/1713476.

————. 2022b. "Army, ISI in Unprecedented Presser Question Arshad Sharif's Exit from Pakistan, Point to PTI's Involvement." October 27, 2022. https://www.dawn.com/news/1717163.

de Waal, Thomas. 2018. *The Caucasus: An Introduction.* 2nd ed. Brussels: Carnegie Europe.

Deflem, Mathieu. 1994. "Law Enforcement in British Colonial Africa: A Comparative Analysis of Imperial Policing in Nyasaland, the Gold Coast and Kenya." *Police Studies* 17, no. 1: 45–68.

Denham, Jess. 2014. "Homeland Criticised by Pakistan Officials for Portraying Country as 'Grimy Hellhole.'" *The Independent*, December 30, 2014. https://www.independent.co.uk/arts-entertainment/tv/news/homeland-criticised-by-pakistan-officials-for-portraying-country-as-a-grimy-hellhole-9950501.html.

Department for International Development. 2008. *Elections in Pakistan in 2008.*

Deva, Yashwant. 1999. "Of Tapes and Tapping: Technical Intelligence Scores over Human Intelligence." New Delhi Institute of Peace and Conflict Studies, no. 217.

Dulat, A. S., Asad Durrani, and Aditya Sinha. 2018. *Spy Chronicles: RAW, ISI, and the Illusion of Peace.* Noida: HarperCollins.

Economic Times. 2015. "Pakistan Army Chief General Raheel Sharif Seeks British Help against Baloch Dissidents in UK." January 15, 2015.

Economist. 2010. "Kayani's Gambit." July 29, 2010. https://www.economist.com/asia/2010/07/29/kayanis-gambit.

————. 2021. "Democracy Index 2021: The China Challenge." London: Economist Intelligence Unit.

Edwards, Brian T. 2017. "Moving Target: Is 'Homeland' Still Racist?" *Los Angeles Review of Books*, March 31, 2017. https://lareviewofbooks.org/article/moving-target-is-homeland-still-racist/.

Estévez, Eduardo E. 2013. "Intelligence Community Reforms: The Case of Argentina." In *Intelligence Elsewhere: Spies and Espionage outside the Anglosphere.* Edited by Philip H. J. Davies and Kristian C. Gustafson. Washington, DC: Georgetown University Press.

Express Tribune. 2017. "Lt Gen Rizwan Akhtar, Ex-ISI Chief, Takes Premature Retirement." October 7, 2017. https://tribune.com.pk/story/1525846/lt-gen-rizwan-akhtar-ex-isi-chief-decides-retire-early.

————. 2020. "PML-N Warns Army ISI to Stop Supporting PTI." November 29, 2020.

Fair, Christine. 2009. "Pakistan's Own War on Terror: What the Pakistani Public Thinks." *Journal of International Affairs* 63, no. 1: 39–55.

————. 2011. "Why the Pakistan Army Is Here to Stay: Prospects for Civilian Governance." *RUSI Journal* 87, no. 3: 571–88.

————. 2014. *Fighting to the End: The Pakistani Army's Way of War*. New Delhi: Oxford University Press.

————. 2015. "Democracy on the Leash in Pakistan." In *Pakistan's Enduring Challenges*. Edited by Christine C. Fair and Sarah J. Watson. Philadelphia: University of Pennsylvania Press.

Farooq, U. 2011. "Herald Exclusive: Revealing the Secret." *Herald*, January 24, 2011. http://www.dawn.com/2011/01/24/revealing-the-secret.html.

Fayaz, Shabana. 2019. "Pakistan and the SCO: Aspirations and Challenges." *Journal of Political Studies* 26, no. 1: 95–102.

Fukuyama, Francis. 1992. *The End of History and the Last Man*. New York: Free Press.

Gauhar, A. 1997. "How Intelligence Agencies Run Our Politics." *The Nation*, August 17, 1997.

Gill, Peter, and Lee Wilson. 2013. "Intelligence and Security-Sector Reform in India." In *Intelligence Elsewhere: Spies and Espionage outside the Anglosphere*. Edited by Philip H. J. Davies and Kristian C. Gustafson. Washington, DC: Georgetown University Press.

Global Policy Forum. 1999. "The Blair Doctrine." April 22, 1999. https://archive.globalpolicy.org/empire/humanint/1999/0422blair.htm.

Goodman, Michael S, 2008. "Learning to Walk: The Origins of the UK's Joint Intelligence Committee." *International Journal of Intelligence and Counterintelligence* 21, no. 1: 40–56.

Government of Pakistan. 1979. *The Offence of Zina (Enforcement of Hudood) Ordinance*. https://pakistani.org/pakistan/legislation/zia_po_1979/ord7_1979.

————. 2015. *Report of the Standing Committee on Foreign Affairs, Senate of Pakistan*.

————. 1972. *The Hamood-ur Commission Report*. https://ia904602.us.archive.org/10/items/hamood_ur_rehman_commission/hamood_ur_rehman_commission.pdf.

Grare, Fréderic. 2015. *The Challenges of Civilian Control over Intelligence Agencies in Pakistan*. Washington, DC: Carnegie Endowment for International Peace.

Gregory, Shaun. 2007a. "The ISI and the War on Terrorism." *Studies in Conflict and Terrorism* 30, no. 12: 1013–31.

————. 2007b. "Nuclear Command and Control in Pakistan." *Defense and Security Analysis* 23, no. 3: 315–30.

Haider, Syed Zeeshan. 2017. "The General Jahnagir Karamat Formula." *Pakistan Today*, December 9, 2017.

Hamid, Syed Ali. 2021. "Early Years of the ISI." *Friday Times*, May 7, 2021. https://www.thefridaytimes.com/2021/05/07/early-years-of-the-isi/.

Haqqani, Husain, and Lisa Curtis. 2017. "A New U.S. Approach to Pakistan: Enforcing Aid Conditions without Cutting Ties." Heritage Foundation, Briefing Paper.

Hardy, P. 1972. *The Muslims of British India.* Cambridge: Cambridge University Press.

Hasan, K. Sarwar. 1951. "The Foreign Policy of Mr. Liaquat Ali Khan." *Pakistan Horizon* 4: 181–99.

Hashim, Asad. 2013. "Leaked Report Shows bin Laden's 'Hidden Life.'" *Al Jazeera*, July 8. https://www.aljazeera.com/news/2013/7/8/leaked-report-shows-bin-ladens-hidden-life.

Hasnain, Syed Ata. 2015. "Hamid Gul: Villain of the Peace." *Swarajya*, August 17, 2015. https://swarajyamag.com/politics/hamid-gul-villian-of-the-peace.

Heath-Kelly, C. 2012. "Reinventing Prevention or Exposing the Gap? False Positives in UK Terrorism Governance and the Quest for Pre-Emption." *Critical Studies on Terrorism* 5, no. 1: 69–87.

Hillyard, P. 1993. *Suspect Community: People's Experience of the Prevention of Terrorism Acts in Britain.* London: Pluto Press.

Hindustan Times. 2018. "Review: 'The Spy Chronicles,' by AS Dulat, Asad Durrani and Aditya Sinha." June 8, 2018.

Hirshberg, M. S. 1993. "Consistency and Change in American Perceptions of China." *Political Behavior* 15, no. 3: 247–63.

HM Government, 2010. *A Strong Britain in an Age of Uncertainty: The National Security Strategy.* London: TSO.

Hudson, Valerie M., and Christopher S. Vore. 1995. "Foreign Policy Analysis Yesterday, Today and Tomorrow." *Mershon International Studies Review* 39, no. 2: 209–38.

Hulnick, Arthur S. 2006. "What's Wrong with the Intelligence Cycle." *Intelligence and National Security* 21, no. 6: 959–79.

Human Rights Watch. 2009. *Cruel Britannia: British Complicity in the Torture and Ill-Treatment of Terror Suspects in Pakistan.* New York: Human Rights Watch.

Huntington, Samuel P. 1993. "The Clash of Civilizations?" *Foreign Affairs* 72: 22–49.

Hussain, Zahid. 2007. *Frontline Pakistan: The Struggle with Militant Islam.* New York: Columbia University Press.

Hussan, Kanza. 2020. "Nationhood and the Representation of Military Elements in Cinemas of the Subcontinent." *Reel Pakistan: A Screen Studies Forum* 1: 179–91.

Hutchison, Peter. 2010. "Binyam Mohamed: A Timeline." *The Telegraph*, November 15, 2010. https://www.telegraph.co.uk/news/uknews/terrorism-in-the-uk/8135812/Binyam-Mohamed-a-timeline.html.

Intelligence and Security Committee. 2018. *Detainee Mistreatment and Rendition.* London: House of Commons, HC1113.

Intelligence Online. 2022. "ISI Chief Najeem Anjum Spearheads Quiet Intelligence Revolution in Pakistan." September 2, 2022.

International Movie Database. n.d. "Aasar Khan." https://homeland.fandom.com/wiki/Aasar_Khan.

Jackson, Richard. 2005. *Writing the War on Terrorism: Language, Politics and Counter-terrorism.* Manchester: Manchester University Press.

Jalal, Ayesha. 1990. *The State of Martial Rule: The Origins of Pakistan's Political Economy of Defence.* Cambridge: Cambridge University Press.

Janes. 2002. "Pakistan to Reorganize Intelligence Services." *Defence Weekly*, April 3, 2002.

———. 2008. "Spy Games: Pakistan's Elusive ISI." *Intelligence Digest*, August 12, 2008.

Jayaram, Rajiv. 2011. "The Other Face of Pakistan's ISI." *Economic Times*, June 23, 2011.

Jeffries, S. 2011. "Imran Khan: 'America Is Destroying Pakistan. We're Using Our Army to Kill Our Own People with Their Money.'" *The Guardian*, September 18, 2011. http://www.guardian.co.uk/global/2011/sep/18/imran-khan-america-destroying-pakistan.

Jillani, Shahzeb. 2014. "Pakistan Protest Cleric Tahirul Qadri Rejects Army Links." BBC, August 18, 2014. https://www.bbc.co.uk/news/world-asia-28832476.

Johnson, Robert. 2009. "Uncertain Loyalties: Pakistan's Inter-Services Intelligence (ISI) and Its Relationship with Western Intelligence Agencies." In *Spooked: Britain, Empire and Intelligence since 1945*. Edited by Patrick Major and Christopher R. Moran. Newcastle upon Tyne: Cambridge Scholars.

Khan, Ayub. 1967. *Friends Not Masters: A Political Autobiography*. London: Oxford University Press.

Khan, Gulawar, Jalal Faiz, and Jan Amir. 2021. "The Dynamics of Baloch Ethno-nationalist Conflicts within the Federation of Pakistan (1948–2012)." *The Dialogue* 16: 75–84.

Khan, Iftikhar A. 2016. "Iran Responds to Letter about Indian Spy." *Dawn*, June 16, 2016.

———. 2021. "NACTA Drafts First-Ever Policy to Counter Violent Extremism." *Dawn*, December 15, 2021. https://www.dawn.com/news/1663850.

Khan, Khurram Ali. n.d. "Zarb-e-Azb: A Tale of Valiant Army against Terrorism." *Hilal (English): The Pakistan Armed Forces' Magazine*. https://www.hilal.gov.pk/eng-article/detail/MTEwNQ==.html.

———. 2015. "Zarb-e Azb: A Tale of Valiant Army Against Terrorism." *Hilal: The Pakistan Armed Forces Magazine*. https://hilal.gov.pk/view-article.php?i=1105.

Khan, Mariam. 2020. "From Mute to Menacing: Why TV's Portrayal of Muslims Still Falls Short." *The Guardian*, October 15, 2020. https://www.theguardian.com/tv-and-radio/2020/oct/15/why-tvs-portrayal-of-muslims-still-falls-short-ramy-bodyguard.

Khan, Sanaullah. 2018. "Saudi Arabia Agrees to Provide Pakistan $3 Billion to Address Balance-of-Payments Crisis." *Dawn*, October 23, 2018. https://www.dawn.com/news/1440860.

Khan, Usman, Jalal Shah, and Bakhtiar Khan. 2021. "Analyzing Civil-Military Relations in Pakistan and Turkey (2002–2018)." *Pakistan Journal of International Affairs* 4, no. 2: 367–82.

Kiessling, Hein G. 2016. *Faith, Unity, Discipline: The ISI of Pakistan*. Gurugram: HarperCollins.

Knowles, Emily, and Abigail Watson. 2018. *Remote Warfare: Lessons Learned from Contemporary Theatres*. London: Oxford Research Group.

Kundi, Mansoor Akber. 2003. "Militarism in Politics: A Case Study of Pakistan." *Pakistan Horizon* 56, no. 1: 19–34.

Kuszewska, Agnieszka, and Agnieszka Nitza-Makowska. 2021. "Multifaceted Aspects of Economic Corridors in the Context of Regional Security: The China-

Pakistan Economic Corridor as a Stabilising and Destabilising Factor." *Journal of Asian Security and International Affairs* 8, no. 2: 218–48.

Lifschultz, Lawrence. 1983. "Independent Baluchistan? Ataullah Mengal's 'Declaration of Independence.'" *Economic and Political Weekly* 18: 735–52.

Loyn, D. 2009. *Butcher and Bolt: Two Hundred Years of Foreign Engagement in Afghanistan.* London: Windmill.

Los Angeles Times. 2009. "Iran: Bin Laden Family Said to Be Held Captive in Tehran." December 24, 2009. https://www.latimes.com/archives/blogs/babylon-beyond/story/2009-12-24/iran-bin-laden-family-said-to-be-held-captive-in-tehran.

Lurie, Devin. 2020. "The Haqqani Network: The Shadow Group Supporting the Taliban's Operations." *American Security Project.* https://www.americansecurityproject.org/wp-content/uploads/2020/08/Ref-0241-The-Haqqani-Network.pdf.

Mackenzie Institute. 2015. "Gulbuddin Hekmatyr's Faction of the Hezb-Islami, Hezb-e Islami Gulbuddin (HIG)." *Terrorism Profiles*, December 16, 2015.

Maddrell, Paul, ed. *The Image of the Enemy: Intelligence Analysis of Adversaries since 1945.* Washington, DC: Georgetown University Press, 2015.

Marshall, Tim. 2021. *The Power of Geography: Ten Maps That Reveal the Future of Our World.* London: Elliot and Thompson.

Matei, Florina Cristiana, and Thomas Bruneau. 2011. "Intelligence Reform in New Democracies Factors Supporting or Arresting Progress." *Democratization* 18, no. 3: 602–30.

Matthews, Owen. 2022. *Overreach: The Inside Story of Putin's War against Ukraine.* Dublin: HarperCollins.

Mbembe, Achille. 1992. "Provisional Notes on the Postcolony." *Africa* 62: 3–37.

McCalman, Molly. 2016. "A. Q. Khan Nuclear Smuggling Network." *Journal of Strategic Security* 9: 104–18.

McKew, Molly K. 2017. "The Gerasimov Doctrine." *Politico.* https://www.politico.com/magazine/story/2017/09/05/gerasimov-doctrine-russia-foreign-policy-215538.

Memmott, Mark. 2011. "Pakistan's Proxies Are Attacking Afghans and Americans, Mullen Says." *NPR*, September 22, 2011. https://www.npr.org/sections/thetwo-way/2011/09/22/140710972/pakistans-proxies-are-attacking-afghans-and-americans-mullen-says.

Ministry of Foreign Affairs. 2017. "Pakistan's Membership of the Shanghai Cooperation Organization (SCO)." Press release, June 9, 2017.

Narasaki, Rosie. 2014. "What's the Deal with ISI on 'Homeland'?" *Bustle*, October 20, 2014. https://www.bustle.com/articles/44864-what-is-isi-on-homeland-farhad-ghazis-organization-seems-connected-to-everything.

Naseer, Hassan, and Abdul Wajid Khan. 2020. "Portrayal of Pakistan in USA Print Media." *Pakistan Social Sciences Review* 4: 221–33.

Nasir, J. 1999. "Calling the Indian Army Chief's Bluff." *Defence Notes*, February–March 1999.

Nawaz, Shuja. 2008. *Crossed Swords: Pakistan, Its Army, and the Wars Within.* Oxford: Oxford University Press.

———. 2020. *The Battle for Pakistan: The Bitter US Friendship and a Tough Neighborhood.* Lanham, MD: Rowman and Littlefield.

Office of the President of the United States. 2010. *National Security Strategy,*

May 2010. https://obamawhitehouse.archives.gov/sites/default/files/rss_viewer /national_security_strategy.pdf.

Oldenburg, Philip. 1985. "'A Place Insufficiently Imagined': Language, Belief, and the Pakistan Crisis of 1971." *Journal of Asian Studies* 44, no. 4: 711–33.

O'Loughlin, Ben. 2011. "Distancing the Extraordinary: Audience Understandings of Discourses of 'Radicalization.'" *Continuum* 25, no. 2: 153–64.

Orissa Post. 2021. "Pakistan Refuses to Hand Over Ex-ISI Chief Javed Nasir to Bosnia Tribunal." July 18, 2021. https://www.orissapost.com/pakistan-refuses-to -hand-over-ex-isi-chief-javed-nasir-to-bosnia-tribunal/.

Pakistan Institute of Legislative Development and Transparency. 2007. "Peace and Conflict in Pakistan: The Structure and Role of Intelligence Agencies." Islamabad, Dialogue Group on Civil-Military Relations, Background Paper.

———. 2012. "Democratic and Parliamentary Oversight of Defence Has Begun, but a Long Way to Go." March 21, 2012. https://pildat.org/parliamentary-development1 /democratic-and-parliamentary-oversight-of-defence-has-begun-but-a-long-way -to-go.

———. 2023. "State of Democracy in Pakistan, 2022: A Depressing Year for Democracy." January 1, 2023. https://pildat.org/assessment-of-democracy1/state-of -democracy-in-pakistan-2022-a-depressing-year-for-democracy.

Panda, Ankit. 2019. "Pakistan's Approach to Navigating the Saudi-Iranian Split." *United States Institute of Peace, Special Report* no. 439.

Pande, Aparna. 2011. *Explaining Pakistan's Foreign Policy: Escaping India*. Abingdon: Routledge.

Pattanaik, S. S. 2000. "Civil-Military Coordination and Defence Decision-Making in Pakistan." *Strategic Analysis* 24, no. 5.

Pears, Louise. 2016. "Ask the Audience: Television, Security and Homeland." *Critical Studies on Terrorism* 9: 76–96.

Peter, T. A. 2010. "Blair Iraq War Enquiry: Calculus of Risk on WMD Changed after 9/11." *Christian Science Monitor*. http://www.csmonitor.com/World/terrorism-se curity/2010/0129/Blair-Iraq-war-inquiry-Calculus-of-risk-on-WMD-changed-af ter-9-11.

Petkus, Donald A. 2010. "Ethics of Human Intelligence Operations: Of MICE and Men." *International Journal of Intelligence Ethics* 1: 97–121.

Power, Marcus, and Andrew Crampton. 2006. "Reel Geopolitics: Cinemato-Graphing Political Space." *Geopolitics* 10, no. 2: 193–203.

Raghavan, Pallavi. 2016. "The Making of the India-Pakistan Dynamic: Nehru, Liaquat, and the No War Correspondence of 1950." *Modern Asian Studies* 50, no. 5: 1645–78.

Rahman, Maseeh. 2013. "Sanjay Dutt Ordered to Finish Jail Sentence over 1993 Mumbai Bombings." *The Guardian*, March 21, 2013. https://www.theguardian .com/world/2013/mar/21/sanjay-dutt-jail-mumbai-bombings.

Rajendran, Sowmya. 2022. "How Blockbuster Films Are Aiding the Hindutva Nationalism Project." *News Minute*, April 6, 2022. https://www.thenewsminute.com/artic le/how-blockbuster-films-are-aiding-hindutva-nationalism-project-162635.

Rashid, Ahmed. 1993. "Obituary: Maj-Gen. Syed Shahid Hamid." *The Independent*, March 15, 1993. https://www.independent.co.uk/news/people/obituary-majgen -syed-shahid-hamid-1497723.html.

———. 2010. "The Road to Kabul Runs Through Kashmir." *Foreign Policy*,

November 10, 2010. https://foreignpolicy.com/2010/11/11/the-road-to-kabul-runs -through-kashmir/.

Raza, Syed Irfan. 2018. "17 Years On, NAB Reopens Case against Three Ex-Army Generals." *Dawn*, February 21, 2018. https://www.dawn.com/news/1390710.

Reynolds, Paul. 2010. "Cameron's New Diplomacy Brings Problems with Pakistan." *BBC News*, August 1, 2010. http://www.bbc.co.uk/news/uk-10831580.

Richards, Julian. 2010. *The Art and Science of Intelligence Analysis*. Oxford: Oxford University Press.

———. 2011. "Intelligence Burden: Afghanistan Grapples with Security Reforms." *Janes Intelligence Review*.

———. 2012a. *A Guide to National Security, Threats, Responses and Strategies*. Oxford: Oxford University Press.

———. 2012b. "Intelligence Dilemma? Contemporary Counter-terrorism in a Liberal Democracy." *Intelligence and National Security* 27, no. 5: 761–80.

———. 2015. "Pakistani Intelligence and India." In *The Image of the Enemy: Intelligence Analysis of Adversaries since 1945*, edited by Paul Maddrell, 219–47. Washington, DC: Georgetown University Press.

———. 2018. "Defining Remote Warfare: Intelligence Sharing after 9/11." Oxford Research Group briefing no. 5.

Richards, Julian, and Chaudhry Miraj. 2015. "No Easy Walk to Democracy: Politics, Security and the State in Pakistan." Pakistan Security Research Unit, Briefing Papers, no. 72.

Rose, Steve. 2022. "Wrestling Tigers and Hurling Motorcycles: How SS Rajamouli's 'RRR' Cast a Spell over the World." *The Guardian*, December 30, 2022. https:// www.theguardian.com/film/2022/dec/30/wrestling-tigers-and-hurling-motor cycles-how-ss-rajamoulis-rrr-cast-a-spell-over-the-world.

Rosendorff, B. P., and T. Sandler. 2004. "Too Much of a Good Thing: The Proactive Response Dilemma." *Journal of Conflict Resolution* 48: 657–71.

Sadaqat, Muhammad. 2022. "Two Get Death over Chinese Bus Attack in Kohistan." *Dawn*, November 11, 2022. https://www.dawn.com/news/1720205.

Saikia, Jaideep. 2011. "The ISI Reaches East: Anatomy of a Conspiracy." *Studies in Conflict and Terrorism* 25, no. 3: 185–97.

Salik, Siddiq. 1977. *Witness to Surrender*. Karachi: Oxford University Press.

Sama, F. 2013. "Film Review: 'Waar.'" *Newsline*. https://newslinemagazine.com/ma gazine/film-review-waar/.

Sappenfield, Mark, and Shahan Mufti. 2008. "Is Kashmir Key to Afghan Peace?" *Christian Science Monitor*, November 21, 2008. https://www.csmonitor.com /World/Asia-South-Central/2008/1121/p01s01-wosc.html.

Sareen, Sushant. 2014. *ZARB-e-AZB: An Evaluation of Pakistan Army's Anti-Taliban Operations in North Waziristan*. New Delhi: Vivekananda International Foundation.

Schaffer, Teresita C., and Howard B. Schaffer. 2012. "Resetting the U.S.-Pakistan Relationship." *Foreign Policy*, March 19, 2012. https://foreignpolicy.com/2012/03 /19/resetting-the-u-s-pakistan-relationship/.

Schmidle, Nicholas. 2018. "The C.I.A.'s Maddening Relationship with Pakistan." *New Yorker*, January 12, 2018. https://www.newyorker.com/news/news-desk/the -cias-maddening-relationship-with-pakistan.

Schmitt, Eric. 2011. "US Prepares for a Curtailed Relationship with Pakistan." *New York Times*, December 26, 2011. http://www.nytimes.com/2011/12/26/world/asia/us-preparing-for-pakistan-to-restrict-support-for-afghan-war.html.

Schofield, Victoria. 2003. *Kashmir in Conflict: India, Pakistan and the Unending War*. London: I.B. Taurus.

Scott-Clark, Cathy, and Adrian Levy. 2017. *The Exile: The Flight of Osama bin Laden*. London: Bloomsbury.

Sen, L. P. 1994. *Slender Was the Thread: Kashmir Confrontation, 1947–48*. New Delhi: Orient Longmans.

Sen, Sudhi Ranjan. 2023. "India Detains Students Planning to Screen BBC Film on Modi." Bloomberg UK, January 26, 2023. https://www.bloomberg.com/news/articles/2023-01-26/india-detains-students-planning-to-screen-bbc-film-on-modi.

Shah, Aqil. *The Army and Democracy: Military Politics in Pakistan*. Cambridge, MA: Harvard University Press, 2014.

Shah, Sabir. 2018. "Average Tenure of 22 ISI Chiefs in 70 Years Has Been 3.18 Years." *The News*, October 12, 2018. https://www.thenews.com.pk/print/379832-average-tenure-of-22-isi-chiefs-in-70-years-has-been-3-18-years.

Shah, Saeed. 2012. "'Memogate' Scandal Deepens as US Accuser Threatens to Tell All." *The Guardian*, January 12, 2012. https://www.theguardian.com/world/2012/jan/12/memogate-scandal-pakistan-isi-haqqani.

Shaikh, Farzana. 2010. "Pakistan Is Guilty of Supporting Terrorism and David Cameron Was Right to Point It Out." Chatham House, Intelligence Squared debate, London, August 4, 2010.

Shams, Shamil. 2016. "Mumbai Attacks and Pakistan's Spy Agency." *Deutsche Welle*, October 2, 2016.

Sharma, Shubham. 2020. "Understanding Turkey's Tryst for Kashmir, but Not for Kurdistan." *Modern Diplomacy*, March 4, 2020. https://moderndiplomacy.eu/2020/03/04/understanding-turkeys-tryst-for-kashmir-but-not-for-kurdistan/.

Siddiqui, Naveed. 2022. "Imprudent Comments by Politicians about Lt Gen Faiz Hameed 'Very Inappropriate': ISPR." *Dawn*, May 12, 2022. https://www.dawn.com/news/1689311/imprudent-comments-by-politicians-about-lt-gen-faiz-hameed-very-inappropriate-ispr.

Singh, Sudeshna. 2022. "Pak's General Bajwa Extricates Army from Defeat against India in 1971." *RepublicWorld.com*, November 23, 2022.

Sirrs, Owen L. 2017. *Pakistan's Inter-Services Intelligence Directorate: Covert Action and Internal Operations*. Abingdon: Routledge.

South Asia Tribune. 2002. "Ex-ISI Chief Reveals Secret Missile Shipments to Bosnia Defying UN Embargo." December 23–29, 2002.

Stepan, Alfred, and Juan J. Linz. 2013. "Democratization Theory and the 'Arab Spring.'" *Journal of Democracy* 24, no. 2: 15–30.

Stolworthy, Jacob. 2017. "Riz Ahmed Warns Parliament That a Lack of Diversity in TV Is Leading People to ISIS." *The Independent*, March 4, 2017. https://www.independent.co.uk/arts-entertainment/tv/news/riz-ahmed-warns-parliament-that-lack-of-diversity-in-tv-leads-people-to-isis-a7610861.html.

Syed, Baqir Sajjad. 2022. "Safeguarding Sovereignty Army's 'Sacred Duty.'" *Dawn*, June 9, 2022. https://www.dawn.com/news/1693894.

Taqi, Mohammad. 2021. "Pakistan: Trouble in Hybrid Regime's 'Paradise' over Appointment of ISI Chief." *The Wire*, October 15, 2021.

Tayyeb, A. 1966. *Pakistan: A Political Geography*. London: Oxford University Press.

Tellis, Ashley J. 2008. *Pakistan and the War on Terror: Conflicted Goals, Compromised Performance*. Washington, DC: Carnegie Endowment for International Peace.

Tharoor, Ishaan. 2011. "Why Did Pakistan's Spy Chief Make a Secret Trip to China?" *Time*, August 3, 2011. https://world.time.com/2011/08/03/why-did-pakistan%E2%80%99s-spy-chief-make-a-secret-trip-to-china-this-week/.

ThePrint. 2022. "Pak MQM Leader Altaf Hussain Acquitted in 'Encouraging Terrorism' Case in London." February 16, 2022.

Thottam, Jyoti. 2008. "Afghan Bombing Fuels Regional Furor." *Time*, July 7, 2008. https://content.time.com/time/world/article/0,8599,1820716,00.html.

Times of India. 2015. "Hamid Gul, Who Bled India as ISI Chief, Dead." August 17, 2015. https://timesofindia.indiatimes.com/world/pakistan/hamid-gul-who-bled-india-as-isi-chief-dead/articleshow/48506550.cms.

Tomsen, Peter. 2011. *The Wars of Afghanistan: Messianic Terrorism, Tribal Conflicts, and the Failures of Great Powers*. New York: PublicAffairs.

Traynor, Ian. 2003. "Pakistan Admits It May Be Source of Iran's Nuclear Expertise." *The Guardian*, December 24, 2003. https://www.theguardian.com/world/2003/dec/24/iran.pakistan.

Tribune. 2022. "Intelligence Report: Turkey Hub of Anti-India Operations." January 31, 2022. https://www.tribuneindia.com/news/nation/intel-report-turkey-hub-of-anti-india-operations-365670.

Tripathi, D. 2010. *Overcoming the Bush Legacy in Iraq and Afghanistan*. Washington, DC: Potomac.

TRT World. 2019. "Is Pakistan Shifting from Its Neutral Stance on the Yemen Conflict?" March 11, 2019. https://www.trtworld.com/middle-east/is-pakistan-shifting-from-its-neutral-stance-in-the-yemen-conflict-24846.

UN Security Council. 2017. *Resolution 2396*. December 21. https://digitallibrary.un.org/record/1327675/files/S_RES_2396%282017%29-EN.pdf.

US Department of State. 2021. "2021 Country Reports on Human Rights Practices: Pakistan." https://www.state.gov/reports/2021-country-reports-on-human-rights-practices/pakistan/.

US Government Publishing Office. 2016. "Pakistan: Friend or Foe in the Fight against Terrorism?" Committee of Foreign Affairs, House of Representatives, Joint Hearing, July 12, 2016. Serial number 114-173. https://www.govinfo.gov/content/pkg/CHRG-114hhrg20742/html/CHRG-114hhrg20742.htm.

Verghese, B. G. 1996. *India's Northeast Resurgent*. New Delhi: Konark.

Vinayak, Ramesh. 1998. "Wireless Wars." *The Nation*, September 14, 1998. http://www.india-today.com/itoday/14091998/war.html.

Voice of America. 2018. "Riots Roil India ahead of Controversial Movie Release." January 24, 2018. https://www.voanews.com/a/riots-roil-india-ahead-controversial-movie-release/4222535.html.

———. 2022. "Taliban's Most Wanted Mostly in Plain Sight." May 18, 2022. https://www.voanews.com/a/taliban-s-most-wanted-mostly-in-plain-sight/6579407.html.

Walsh, Declan. 2011. "Pakistan's Spymaster Hamid Gul: Angel of Jihad or Windbag Provocateur?" *The Guardian*, May 31, 2011. https://www.theguardian.com/world/2011/may/31/hamid-gul-pakistan-spymaster-taliban.

Waraich, O. 2011. "Risky Business: When Pakistani Journalists Take on the ISI." *Time*, July 5, 2011. https://content.time.com/time/world/article/0,8599,2081413,00.html.

Watt, Nicholas. 2010. "Pakistan Must Not Be Allowed to Promote Export of Terror, Says David Cameron." *The Guardian*, July 28, 2010. http://www.guardian.co.uk/world/2010/jul/28/pakistan-promote-terror-david-cameron.

Wege, Carl Anthony. 2013. "Iranian Intelligence Organizations." In *Intelligence Elsewhere: Spies and Espionage outside the Anglosphere*. Edited by Philip H. J. Davies and Kristian C. Gustafson. Washington, DC: Georgetown University Press.

Wilson, John. 1999. " ISI Fangs." *The Pioneer*, June 30, 1999.

Wintour, Patrick. 2018. "'All-Weather Friendship': But Is Pakistan Relying Too Heavily on China?" *The Guardian*, August 3, 2018. https://www.theguardian.com/cities/2018/aug/03/all-weather-friendship-but-is-pakistan-relying-too-heavily-on-china.

Yadav, V., and C. Barwa. 2011. "Relational Control: India's Grand Strategy in Afghanistan and Pakistan." *India Review* 10, no. 2: 93–125.

Yousaf, Kamran. 2021. "FM, ISI Chief in Beijing on Crucial Visit." *Express Tribune*, July 24, 2021. https://tribune.com.pk/story/2311869/fm-isi-chief-in-beijing-on-crucial-visit.

Yousaf, Mohammad, and Mark Adkin. 2001. *Afghanistan: The Bear Trap, the Defeat of a Superpower.* Barnsley: Pen and Sword.

Zahid, Farhan. 2022. "Origins of Al-Qaeda: Revisiting Maktab Ul Khidmat Al Mujahedeen (Services Bureau for the Holy Warriors)." Cf2R, *Foreign Analysis*, no. 22. https://cf2r.org/foreign/origins-of-al-qaeda-revisiting-maktab-ul-khidmat-al-mujahedeen-services-bureau-for-the-holy-warriors-2/.

Ziring, Lawrence. 1974. "Militarism in Pakistan: The Yahya Khan Interregnum." *Asian Affairs: An American Review* 1, no. 6: 402–20.

Index

About the Author

Julian Richards is the director of the Centre for Security and Intelligence Studies (BUCSIS) at the University of Buckingham. He gained a PhD on the subject of political violence in Pakistan from Cambridge University in 1993. He then worked for nearly twenty years for the UK government in intelligence and security before moving into academia in 2008 to jointly found BUCSIS at the University of Buckingham. He is the author of five books in addition to numerous book chapters and articles on a range of contemporary intelligence and security issues. He is a regular commentator in national and international media, including Sky News, France24, the BBC, and *Al Jazeera.*